The
ABCs
of
Environmental
Regulation

Joel B. Goldsteen

PhD, AICP, NCARB

Government Institutes
Rockville, Maryland

#39868212

Government Institutes, Inc., 4 Research Place, Rockville, Maryland 20850, USA.

03 02   01   00   5   4   3   2

The reader should not rely on this publication to address specific questions that apply to a particular set of facts. The author and publisher make no representation or warranty, express or implied, as to the completeness, correctness, or utility of the information in this publication. In addition, the author and publisher assume no liability of any kind whatsoever resulting from the use of or reliance upon the contents of this book.

Library of Congress Cataloging-in-Publication Data

Goldsteen, Joel B.
     ABCs of environmental regulation / by Joel B. Goldsteen.
        p.   cm.
     Includes bibliographical references and index.
     ISBN: 0-86587-629-0
     1. Environmental law--United States.   I. Title.
  KF3775.G65   1998
  344.73'046--dc21
                               98-44128
                                 CIP

Printed in the United States of America

CONTENTS

Chapter 15: Storage Tanks

Chapter 16: Federal Compliance

Section Five: Safety 153

Chapter 17: Workplace

Chapter 18: Chemicals

CHAPTER 19: PESTICIDES

CHAPTER 20: LAND

CHAPTER 21: NUCLEAR SAFETY

Section Six: Responding to Contaminant Releases 189

CHAPTER 22: PUBLIC NOTICE AND SPILL PLANNING

CHAPTER 23: HAZARDOUS WASTE SPILL CLEANUP

CHAPTER 24: ASBESTOS IN BUILDINGS

Section Seven: Nature and Natural Resources 215

CHAPTER 25: EXTINCTION

CHAPTER 26: SEACOASTS

How
to Use
this Book

The first two chapters of this book provide a quick overview of the federal environmental framework and the regulations. The reader who needs a comprehensive view should read them first. Other readers can easily turn to the chapter of choice. Each chapter is an edited version of a federal act. The chapter explains the act's contents, concepts, and essence. A condensation of each chapter is provided in a short overview at the beginning of the chapter. A reader may obtain the essence of the information that follows from those overviews. Finally, at the end of most chapters, a brief chronology outlines the history of the act.

In editing and compiling the information for this book, I had many decisions to make. I selected sections of the federal environmental regulations based upon my own perspectives and experiences gained from consulting, conducting research, and teaching. I have taught courses in federal and state environmental regulations to graduate students in civil engineering, environmental science, city and regional planning, and the hazardous materials management programs—the four university environmental programs with which I am affiliated. During my first attempts at teaching courses, students in the environmental professions—city and regional planning, public administration, engineering, geology, and law—did not understand the comprehensive structure of the regulations and agencies until after almost an entire semester of study. It took that long for them to put the pieces together. Even then, I was not certain that a comprehensive picture was conveyed, because a satisfactory written compilation did not exist. Because of the materials that were available, we had to study and discuss one area of an environmental regulation at a time. In order to fulfill my need to have the federal laws and regulations in a form that would allow my students to obtain that comprehensive understanding more quickly, I wrote this book.

It should be noted that this book cannot be considered a complete compilation of the regulations, nor a volume guaranteed to contain a reader's specific need for information about a law or regulation. Only a direct reading of an entire regulation can fulfill that kind of need.

In gathering the information for this book, I set out to be as thorough as possible. I reviewed my selected federal environmental regulations word for word, along with related library sources, agency handouts, Internet sites, and mailings. In addition, I made visits and phone calls to agencies and researched particular issues. I solicited, collected, and reviewed photographs, and when necessary, I took some of my own photos. When no source is noted in a photograph caption, the photo was obtained from the U.S. Environmental Protection Agency site files under the Freedom of Information Act. Sites shown in the photographs are not identified intentionally; they have been selected to illustrate the subject only. The captions are explanations of this author's intent only and deliberately tell a different story from the text. Readers should not expect to understand the content of the book from the text of the captions only.

No personal opinions or criticisms are intended in *ABCs of Environmental Regulation*. The book is simply my attempt to more clearly and succinctly explain the laws and agency interrelationships (when relevant), as well as those subjects necessary to supplement that information. Parts of the book are compiled and edited—but not authored—by me, especially the lists of requirements under the various regulatory provisions.

Legal terms, scientific language, and acronyms appear throughout the environmental regulations. Most of these terms and acronyms are familiar to environmental professionals and government employees responsible for monitoring compliance. When these terms are introduced to the reader, they are printed in italic type. When needed, definitions are provided in the paragraphs that contain the related information about the regulation. All applicable acronyms are defined in each chapter the first time they are used. By using acronyms, the text avoids repeating long sets of identifier names of acts, tests, conditions, and agencies. For example, the Environmental Protection Agency is the EPA throughout the book. This method of abbreviation through acronyms has drastically shortened the book and made it more readable. Any time one becomes lost in the acronyms, a look at the glossary at the end of this book will refresh the memory.

Section headings cluster the environmental regulations into broad subject areas. Within the sections, each chapter is devoted to a detailed explanation of a single regulation. The endnotes provided at the back of the book are not complete, but are intended to be used as a reference. There is no need to refer to the endnotes when reading. For the reader who wishes more detail, the section of the law or regulation cited is listed here.

There are differences between regulations and programs. Each regulation may be viewed as a separate set of instructions that must be followed when dealing with a specific topic, such as underground storage tanks. The federal environmental regulations for air include thousands of separate instructions. Together, these regulations or instructions can be viewed as "the air program." But portions of the total set of regulations for air—let us say 124 separately published regulations—may be considered as "the hazardous substance release program for industrial facilities."

To date, there is no general agreement about the precise names, titles, divisions, or separate programs within the federal environmental framework. Most officials and professionals give names to programs at will, according to their need in communicating with others. For example, some lump together all storage tank programs into a category that they call "tank programs." Others divide storage tank programs into aboveground and underground storage tank programs. Still others place storage tanks under the overall program name of the Resource Conservation and Recovery Act (RCRA) or even the Solid Waste Disposal Act (SWDA). The SWDA, with its RCRA amendments, is the name of the federal act containing the sets of regulations about storage tanks. For these confusing reasons, this book does not clearly divide the federal environmental regulatory framework into separate programs. If the reader wishes to do so, she or he may use the generic chapter subtitles that precede the names of the acts that serve as chapter titles in this book. [For example, Chapter 6: *Air Pollution*—Clean Air Act (CAA)]

Environmental laws and regulations (and their programs) may be viewed as the outcomes of the legislation originally passed by the federal government. Many federal, state, and local environmental agency personnel worked with legislators in the House of Representatives, Senate, and Office of the President to develop this "protective blanket" of environmental legislation. However, the laws and the framework are quite dynamic. As field personnel from the Coast Guard, Department of the Interior, Environmental Protection Agency, and others are confronted with threats to our environmental future, they respond as guardians of the public interest. Thus, new provisions are added to the laws and regulations almost daily.

A word of caution. Currently, there is a such a great interest and passion for using the Internet to find information that a warning is necessary. This author is quite concerned about the quality of information available and worries about Internet site maintenance, quality reviews of the information placed there, and the potential to be sidetracked by the barrage of advertising messages for products and services connected to the information. Moreover, when one is searching for government information, reports, laws, *Federal Register* postings, or the *Code of Federal Regulations*, it is easy to reach an official-looking site that presents itself as an authoritative source of information. But many of these sites have no official sanction, and the quality of the information they provide varies considerably. Therefore, please treat any Internet information as potentially incomplete, out of date, or even incorrect. You may reach the wrong site for your needs and not know it. Your chance of this misfire increases with every Internet search, as more and more information is added daily. Any information that is important must be verified with written, published records—especially the federal regulations themselves. Be careful!

Maneuvering around the Internet sites containing the CFRs is difficult. Their search engines are slow and almost unusable on both of my computers, even on the one that is networked directly through our university's computers (and not a telephone line). Consider using the CD-ROM versions of the *Code of Federal Regulations*. To date, I have not seen a better way to get this information than from the CD-ROMs available from the publisher of this book. They are easy to navigate and allow you to reach the updates or additions to the CFRs quickly and easily.

SECTION ONE

The Framework

CHAPTER 1

Introduction

Understanding Programs and Agencies

Overview

♦ The scope of environmental protection is explained.

♦ Public environmental policy is created by legislation, regulations, rules, administrative orders, memoranda, acts, and programs.

♦ Many departments of the federal government, in addition to the U.S. Environmental Protection Agency (EPA), have environmental program responsibilities.

♦ Regional federal offices are scattered throughout the United States.

♦ Because environmental threats cannot be predicted, our current programs cannot anticipate all of our future needs.

Scope of protection

The federal government enacts laws about the environment and implements them through regulations, rules, administrative orders, memoranda, acts, and programs.[1] Although not all of these restrictions are precisely defined, they remain the major methods used to implement public environmental policy as developed by the three branches of government (executive, legislative, and judicial). In order to make certain that people follow these laws about the environment, enforcement methods are devised to compel citizens to willingly comply with their intent.

Exhibit 1: Sky, air, ocean, eroded rocks, and seacoast vegetation are just a few elements of this California coast that compose the natural environment. The federal environmental framework of regulations protects these esthetic and wilderness assets. (Photo: author)

At times, the threat of police action or legal suits may be all that is necessary; but some programs may require field enforcement and policing.

A number of federal agencies are responsible for regulating the environment, even though the best known one is the U.S. Environmental Protection Agency. For example, the U.S. Department of Labor regulates for workplace environmental safety, the U.S. Coast Guard enforces protection of the seas from contamination, and the U.S. Department of Agriculture protects food and animals.[2] Besides the major federal agencies, there are many other agencies and departments at all levels of government (city, county, and state) that regulate the environment; however, in this book, these other levels of government are discussed only in relation to their responsibilities for federal programs. In addition to the federal agencies, many federal environmental regulations are passed down to the states for their implementation.

Most of the federal agencies, such as the U.S. Environmental Protection Agency, have regional offices outside of the Washington DC area. These offices may be considered field offices because they are closer to the sites and problems needing federal environmental protection.[3] Commonly, each office contains community liaison contact persons who serve as conduits for complaints, inquiries, and other matters. Also, they contain information officers, small libraries, and enforcement officers for each of the EPA's programs. Regional office duties and responsibilities include working with the appropriate agencies of their region's state and local governments (cities and counties, etc.).

The environmental framework has been developed piecemeal by enacting laws that responded to contamination events or that anticipate potential spills and accidents. As a result, the framework cannot be considered comprehensive. Many activities with potential environmental consequences have been neither regulated nor ignored, but rather, overlooked.[4] A patchwork structure contains many programs and areas that are well regulated and many that are not. Consider the federal framework of environmental protection as a protective wall containing many solid areas, some holes, and other structurally unsound portions. For some areas of concern, the solid areas function well, while, in many, the number of holes is alarming. Many future environmental threats have been anticipated; yet many cannot be predicted. Restricting vehicle emissions can help clean the air, but the methods used may lead to unanticipated contamination. Likewise, chlorine or other chemicals used in water purification may well be identified as problems in the future.

Programs, laws, acts, and regulations

It is difficult to separate the enacted laws or acts from the program and regulatory functions. The targets of the regulations—or *what* is regulated—can be confusing. Certainly, the media carrying pollution is approached or addressed in most of the regulations. Air, water, soils, food, animal, and human paths to pollution are both *hard* and *soft*. *Hard paths* are industrially produced contamination. *Soft paths* are people produced contamination. Each path may well produce half of the total, but the precise amount cannot be pinpointed. Since the federal environmental regulations address both paths even in the same act, it would be difficult to divide any discussion about environmental controls into two distinct categories.

Controls on people and industries are intertwined, and either path affects the other. For example, strict controls are placed on the processing of sewage liquids so that they can meet safe standards and be returned to the streams and lakes. Also, pesticides are highly controlled in their packaging and labeling to avoid dangerous human contact. Are these requirements for industry or people? The architects of the regulations have attempted to develop the most effective sets of environmental protection. Most of the time, environmental protection must alternate between controls on people and controls on industry.

Air programs

As mandated by the Clean Air Act, air programs control or regulate releases or transmission of contaminants in the air. They also control noises transmitted through the air, which are covered by the Noise Control Act or the Airport Noise Abatement Act. Some programs that were intended for other purposes could also be considered air programs. These latter categories are radioactive releases to the air, which are covered by the Atomic Energy Act, and contaminants emanating from waste storage areas, which are covered by the Solid Waste Disposal Act; the Comprehensive Environmental Response, Compensation, and Liability Act; the Surface Mining Control and Reclamation Act, the Federal Insecticide, Fungicide, and Rodenticide Act; or the Toxic Substances Control Act.

Water programs

These programs control or regulate releases or transmission of contaminants in the water, as explained in the Clean Water, Safe Drinking Water, or Oil Pollution Acts. Also, they may regulate the containment of wastes, covered by the Solid Waste Disposal and CERCLA Acts; the Federal Land Policy and Management Act; the Surface Mining Control and Reclamation Act; the Forest and Rangeland Renewable Resources Planning Act; the Coastal Zone Management Act; or the Marine Mammal Protection Act.

Waste programs

Waste programs control or regulate the release or transmission of contaminants contained in wastes of all kinds, such as those wastes covered by CERCLA and the Resource Conservation and Recovery Acts,[5] and through any media, such as those covered by the Noise Control or Airport Noise Abatement Acts. Some programs that were intended for other purposes could be considered waste programs, such as chemical inventories, which are covered by the Emergency Planning and Community Right-To-Know Act (EPCRA); the Toxic Substances Control Act; the Federal Insecticide, Fungicide, and Rodenticide Act; the Atomic Energy act; the Pollution Prevention Act; or the Surface Mining Control and Reclamation Act.

Other programs

Other programs have been enacted into law to regulate a variety of potential environmental, health, and safety hazards.

- Controlling leaks in underground storage tanks (Underground Storage Tank program in RCRA)
- Reporting chemical releases (EPCRA)
- Maintaining radiation safety or containing atomic energy (Atomic Energy Act)
- Securing federal facilities and construction (National Environmental Policy Act)
- Optimizing workplace safety (Occupational Safety and Health Act)
- Regulating pesticide programs (Federal Insecticide, Fungicide, and Rodenticide Act)
- Controlling potentially dangerous chemicals (Toxic Substances Control Act).

In summary, the federal environmental regulation framework controls both the industrial and people paths to pollution (hard and soft paths). It controls a number of programs through acts that cross boundaries of media and subjects of concern. The major programs divided into sections of this book are air, water, wastes and tanks, safety, responding to contaminant releases nature, and natural resources.

Abstracts of each environmental program and act are presented in the front of most of the chapters in this book to provide the scope and basic structure of the regulations. Methods of enforcement vary, and change regularly. Additionally, the roles or emphases of each regulatory agency can vary depending on public policy changes.

CHAPTER 2

Summary Perspectives

Overview of Programs

Overview

- The Clean Air Act (CAA) is the primary air regulation. Under the CAA, no one is allowed to contaminate the air in any way. A contaminant list is developed and published by the EPA providing ranges of allowable toxicity for certain chemical substances—the National Ambient Air Quality Standards (NAAQs).

- The Clean Water Act (CWA) and the Safe Drinking Water Act (SDWA) are the major federal regulations controlling water purity. Surface and groundwater are protected under those acts.

- The Oil Pollution Act (OPA) regulates vessels and facilities to prevent oil spills into the ocean and waters and promote prompt cleanups.

- Waste programs are directed at household, industrial solid (nonhazardous), hazardous, and hazardous medical wastes.

- Readiness programs to respond to spills are promoted in the Emergency Planning and Community Right-to-Know Act (EPCRA) and the Comprehensive Environmental Response, Compensation, and Liability Act (CERCLA)—Superfund.

Air programs

The primary regulatory device controlling air pollution is the Clean Air Act (CAA). Individuals, business, industry, and state and local governments are restricted and prohibited from contaminating the air. Since it was enacted in 1967, the CAA has been amended to become even stricter. Most of those additions require state government involvement. The EPA has directed its Health Effects Laboratory to work with the

Centers for Disease Control and Prevention (CDC)[6] to regularly develop sound information for guiding state and local governments in protecting their air. As new scientific information has been discovered, regulations have increased and the amendments reflect these findings.

Penalties are assessed for violators of the CAA, and fines, prison sentences, and special operating requirements are mandated. A list of contaminants and their ranges of safety are developed and published by the EPA. This list is called the "national ambient air quality standards," or NAAQS. Not only is toxicity a concern, but also visibility, acid rain, lower atmospheric ozone chemical content, and changes in air quality from mobile pollution sources (vehicles) and facilities. From time to time the NAAQS list is modified, ranges changed, and chemical and biological agents added and deleted. Each state must develop a state implementation plan (SIP) to ensure that their methods for keeping their air clean meet EPA requirements.

Water programs

The federal government regulates water by developing partnerships with different agencies. As the major regulatory agency for water programs, the Environmental Protection Agency (EPA) devises, develops, and enforces the environmental water laws passed by Congress. At times, EPA delegates specific duties to other agencies.[7] Even though the EPA reviews, inspects, and approves the programs and actions of its partner agencies, it also maintains field staff in its regional offices to administer many of the water rules and regulations. In some areas of water protection, other federal agencies like the U.S. Army Corps of Engineers, the U.S. Coast Guard, or the U.S. Department of Transportation have responsibilities for protecting water; and the EPA allows states to administer many of its water programs under close supervision. States can further delegate water responsibilities to their local governments.

The major statutes are the Safe Drinking Water Act (SDWA) and the Clean Water Act (CWA). In order to prevent or contain water pollution, the Clean Water Act lists the following requirements:[8]

- ◆ No discharges of chemicals, biological agents, or waste materials are allowed into surface waters, groundwater, or soils.

- ◆ Prior to any releases of potential contaminants, individuals or companies must apply for a permit and be approved.

- ◆ The states can become the regulatory agency for the federal programs, if approved by the EPA.

* All limitations devised by the EPA must follow a prescribed method.

* The prescribed process must be followed for reporting, responding, and preventing spills.

* Any placing or discharging of dredge wastes (from scraping the bottom of water bodies) must adhere to approved permit provisions.

* Established enforcement methods must be used for violations.

As can be seen from these provisions, the Clean Water Act attempts to eliminate any discharge of contaminants into water, and tries to protect human life, fish, and wildlife.

The EPA has established offensively dirty-substance-in-water standards for specific industries. These national effluent standards are based on the technical ability of an industry to comply, considering its ability to continue to operate as an economically sound industry. To properly administer the effluent standards a permit system is used, called the "National Pollution Discharge Elimination System (NPDES)." States may administer the permits or allow the EPA to do so. Dredging and filling of waters are regulated. Ocean discharges are regulated, also. Pretreatment of water is required prior to any discharges, and permits required. Spills must be reported, and special requirements are established for safe drinking water.

EPA regulates public drinking water under the Safe Drinking Water Act (SDWA). SDWA protects people from contaminated or poisoned water by setting national standards for contaminant levels. Acceptable levels of contaminants are set for public drinking water systems, groundwater, and underground injection wells. Standards for drinking water near Superfund sites must meet the SDWA requirements; thus, Superfund is tied to the SDWA. The number of contaminants regulated may well become an ongoing issue. Some tests for some chemicals are quite costly. Regular testing requirements are always questioned by public health experts as to costs and benefits.

Purity of surface waters (rivers, lakes, bays, inlets, and oceans) are controlled by the Oil Pollution Act (OPA). This act is much more comprehensive than any other national or international oil pollution act. OPA attempts to prevent water pollution from oil spills from vessels and facilities by requiring clean up and removal and corporate and personal liability for costs. To prevent spills, there are stringent operational requirements. A list of damages are specified that can be imposed on violators. As a result of this act, there have been major changes in the oil production, transportation, and distribution industry.

OPA defines the responsible parties, establishes a standard for measuring natural resource damages, defines financial responsibilities, requires that a fund be established from the five cents per barrel federal tax on oil received at U.S. refineries or petroleum products, and establishes penalties for not complying with the act.

Waste programs

Household and industrial (nonhazardous) wastes are solid wastes. Typically, cities or counties arrange for weekly or twice weekly household waste collection. They may use private companies or create their own waste collection departments of government. Industrial facilities usually contract directly with a private waste handling company to collect their industrial wastes. Both are regulated by programs developed in the Solid Waste Disposal Act (SWDA). There is more to solid waste environmental protection than meets the eye. Under the SWDA, state and regional solid waste plans must be developed that promote materials and energy recovery and conservation. Each state must consider its different geological, hydrogeological, and climatic circumstances to protect ground and surface waters from landfill contamination. All open dumps must be closed or converted to sanitary landfills. A sanitary landfill is one that is lined according to detailed engineering standards, has leaching pipes for methane collection and disbursement, and that covers its wastes daily with earth cover. Sanitary landfills are required for all land disposal, and most household wastes in the United States are deposited in them. Waste to energy (burning of household and industrial solid wastes to create electricity or gas) is promoted in the SWDA.[9]

Hazardous wastes, as expected, require much more careful handling. Those companies or persons that generate and transport hazardous waste, and owners and operators of treatment, storage, and disposal (tsd) facilities are regulated under the Resource Conservation and Recovery Act of 1976 (RCRA) and its 1984 Amendments.[10] The act contains a number of provisions that prohibit the thoughtless handling and careless permanent storage of hazardous wastes. RCRA only applies to companies or individuals generating over 275 tons (550,000 pounds) of hazardous waste per year.

Hazardous wastes must be reduced in quantity at their sources, neutralized with high technology equipment, or securely contained in land disposal areas to minimize present and future risks. In order to meet the act's expectations the following requirements must be met:

* Hazardous wastes must be properly stored and managed.
* State and regional solid waste plans must be developed.
* Resource and recovery must be provided.
* Federal responsibilities must be defined.
* A medical waste tracking program must be implemented.
* Requirements must be imposed on research, development, demonstration, and information dissemination regulating underground storage tanks.

Federal facility compliance programs

Federally owned facilities, such as military bases, airports, buildings, and munitions storage areas, can be fined by the U.S. EPA for violations of any environmental regulations. Prior to the Federal Facility Compliance Act (FFCA), facilities owned by the federal government were exempt from the same penalties for polluting as the private sector. This act was created to ensure that the federal government complies with all waste regulations imposed on residents, private landowners, and operators. One federal agency can fine another for wrongdoing.[11] FFCA was an amendment to the Resource Conservation and Recovery Act (RCRA), or a part of the Solid Waste Disposal Act (SWDA). Unlike the RCRA controls for individuals and private companies in transporting, treating, storing, and disposing solid and hazardous wastes, the FFCA regulations relate to federally owned facilities only. The facilities regulated are the realm of landfills, radioactive mixed waste, public vessels, waste munitions, wastewater treatment works, and so on.

Toxic substance programs

The Toxic Substances Control Act (TSCA) was enacted and amended later to increase the number of toxic substances controlled. A major objective of this act is to identify and control toxic substances before they can be introduced in the marketplace and affect the environment. By contrast, other federal regulations, such as RCRA, control toxic chemicals after they have been released. Within TSCA, there are four major sections:

1. Control of toxic substances
2. Response to asbestos hazard emergencies

3. Abatement of indoor radon

4. Reduction of exposures to lead.

TSCA creates several enforcement tools for use by EPA. First, suspected dangerous chemicals can be identified and tested. Next, EPA can require the review and testing of any new chemical substances before their introduction. Last, EPA can limit or prohibit the manufacture, use, distribution, or disposal of any existing chemical substances. Finally, EPA can require recordkeeping and reporting on any new chemical substances, and require export notices and import certification.

Responding to contaminant release programs

Two acts are summarized in this section that develop environmental programs to respond to contaminant releases. Each requires public notice of risk and taking action before an accident happens. The first Act is the Emergency Planning and Community Right-to-Know Act (EPCRA), which requires states to establish and develop local chemical emergency preparedness programs and disseminate information about the hazardous chemicals located within their communities.[12] This first act had been devised to disclose to the public their potential risks from accidental chemical spills.[13]

There are four major components to the EPCRA:

1. Emergency response planning

2. Emergency chemical release notices

3. Community right-to-know reports

4. Toxic chemical release inventory reports

Each of these four components has special reporting requirements. The requirements for disseminating this information enable states, towns, and cities to understand the potential chemical hazards around them.

EPCRA requires the governor of each state to designate a State Emergency Response Commission (SERC) and appoint a local emergency planning committee (LEPC). The SERC must designate emergency planning districts within each state to prepare and implement emergency plans. The owner or operator of a facility that produces, uses, or stores a hazardous chemical must notify the SERC and the LEPC immediately when a listed hazardous substance is released and exceeds the reportable quantity (RQ).

Material safety data sheets (MSDSs) must be prepared and be available from each owner or operator of a facility storing a listed hazardous material. The MSDSs are required under the Occupational Safety and Health Administration's (OSHA) hazard communication standard regulations. They must be submitted to the SERC, the LEPC, and the local fire department (LFD) having jurisdiction over the facility. Minimum threshold quantities are established by EPA for reporting hazardous chemicals at a facility.

Under EPCRA, owners or operators of certain manufacturing facilities must submit annual reports on the amounts of listed toxic chemicals that are released from their facilities. These reports must be submitted regardless of whether the chemical or biological release is an accident or intentional and routine. All releases to the air, water, or soils must be reported. Discharges from publicly owned treatment works (POTWs) and transfers to offsite locations for treatment, storage, or disposal are also required. In order to avoid violations, any facility subject to reporting requirements under EPCRA must develop and implement written complaint procedures, response plans, and information management programs to avoid enforcement actions.

The second act is the Comprehensive Environmental Response, Compensation, and Liability Act (CERCLA) and is known as both CERCLA and *Superfund*.[14] As a primary feature of this act, the EPA receives combined taxes from the petroleum and chemical industries, general tax revenues, and a specially levied environmental tax on corporations. CERCLA, or Superfund, regulates the releases of hazardous substances, provides for compensation for cleanups of hazardous waste spills until responsible parties are identified, and addresses abandoned hazardous waste disposal sites not controlled under existing laws.

This Superfund is used by EPA to clean up sites before parties responsible for a spill or release can be identified. Even though most EPA actions under CERCLA relate to hazardous substance dangers, the act requires that EPA develop nationwide criteria for priority assignments for releases or threats of releases. EPA develops the criteria based on risks to public health, welfare, and the environment. In applying these risk criteria, EPA scores and ranks different sites for possible listing on the National Priorities List (NPL). The NPL is part of the National Contingency Plan (NCP), and the NCP is the major guide for CERCLA decisions about responses and actions.

EPA can remove or remediate. *Removal* means that wastes are taken away. *Remediate* means that dangerous waste sites are modified, treated, or redesigned to safely contain the wastes. Environmental emergencies often result in removal of contaminants. Remedial actions are usually long term, permanent cleanups. After a cleanup, the EPA recovers its costs from potentially responsible parties (PRPs), or compels PRPs to perform the cleanup themselves—after administrative or judicial proceedings.

Summary

The chapters that follow describe these programs and many others in greater detail, and their reading is necessary to fully understand the federal environmental framework and programs. Each act is discussed within its proper setting, characteristics, program concepts, and with a view to providing a first step toward a comprehensive grasp of the scope of each important regulation. As stated earlier in the chapter, the framework is set for federal environmental regulation. By now the reader has some very basic knowledge. The rest of these *ABCs* may well become a first or a last stop for readers needing this information.

CHAPTER 3

National Policy

National Environmental Policy Act (NEPA)

Overview

* The National Environmental Policy Act (NEPA) states the comprehensive environmental policies and goals for the United States.

* NEPA creates a national environmental oversight committee, a science advisory board, and an environmental health task force.

* NEPA specifies research and development requirements and budgets.

* NEPA establishes programs, grants, funds, assistance programs, and demonstration projects.

* NEPA creates an environmental data base.

* NEPA requires reporting by the Environmental Protection Agency (EPA) to Congress, state, and local governments.

Structure and public policies

NEPA declares that there is a need for a national policy to promote environmental safety and protect public health. The act encourages research and new findings leading to new knowledge of natural resources and ecological systems. By creating a committee—the Council on Environmental Quality (CEQ)—the act established an advocate for this policy, giving this committee special powers.[15] These presidential appointees are responsible for providing a safe and healthful environmental future for all citizens.

Pollution emergencies are to be handled by the U.S. Environmental Protection Agency (EPA), and any violations of laws or regulations, contamination events, or related environmental problems are to be prosecuted and pursued by that agency's Office of Criminal Investigation. A National Enforcement Training Institute was created under NEPA to train environmental lawyers, inspectors, civil and criminal investigators, and technical experts.

Concepts, ideas, and policies promoted by NEPA are quite focused. Nature and man are to live in harmony with regard to influences such as population growth, urbanization, industrialization, resource exploitation, and technological advances. The federal government must work closely with the state and local governments as stated therein. Financial and technical assistance is to be provided to relevant groups, companies, and public agencies in order to achieve these goals.

All means must be used to improve and coordinate federal plans, functions, programs, and resources and meet these goals:

- Responsibilities of one generation are not passed on to the next.
- Healthy, safe, and esthetically pleasing surroundings are maintained.
- The environment is not degraded by unintended consequences.
- Historical, cultural, and natural features are preserved, thus providing diversity and variety of choice.
- Population and resource use are balanced in the interest of high standards of living and perceived quality of life.
- Recycling of vanishing resources is encouraged, and the quality of renewable resources is improved.[16]

In order for our society to reach these goals, each citizen must accept the responsibility to preserve and enhance the environment. All policies, regulations, and laws must respect NEPA, and all agencies of government must follow agreed-upon practices:

- Interdisciplinary approaches from the natural sciences and social sciences, as well as city and regional planning for deciding about the man-built environment.
- Methods and procedures that are appropriate for environmental decision making (not only economic and technical considerations).
- Statements on the environmental impact of adverse environmental effects that cannot be avoided, along with possible

alternatives, the relationship between short- and long-term impacts of an action, and any irreversible or irretrievable commitments of resources that would be involved in the proposed action should it be implemented.

(Statements can be developed by the states or the federal government. Every major federal action must contain an environmental impact statement. Alternative courses of action must be suggested if there are unresolved conflicts).

Agencies must comply

Under NEPA, the worldwide and long-range character of environmental problems must be recognized and federal foreign policy and national policy must be consistent. Information about restoring, maintaining, or enhancing the quality of the environment must be made available to the states, counties, municipalities, institutions, and individuals. When resource projects are planned or developed, ecological information must be used and developed. All the agencies of the federal government are required to conform to the provisions of NEPA.[17] Each year, the President must transmit to Congress an Environmental Quality Report that explains the condition of major natural, man-made, or altered environmental media (air, water, and land). It must include trends in the quality, management, and use of these media and the effects of those trends on the social, economic, and physical characteristics of the United States in view of increased population. The report to Congress must contain a review of programs and activities at all levels of government with regard to their effect on the environment and natural resources. Finally, the report has to contain a program to solve the problems of existing programs and activities and enact needed legislation.[18]

The duties and functions of the Council on Environmental Quality (CEQ) are as follows:

- ◆ Assist and advise the president.
- ◆ Prepare the annual report (Environmental Quality Report).
- ◆ Review and appraise federal programs and activities.
- ◆ Recommend and develop new national policies about the environment and conduct studies, research, and analyses.
- ◆ Document and define changes in the natural environment and report to the President if requested.[19]

Under NEPA, a Citizens Advisory Committee on Environmental Quality is established. This committee has a membership composed of business and industry, science, agriculture, labor, conservation organizations, state and local governments, and other groups as considered advisable. The role of the Citizens Advisory Committee on Environmental Quality is to consult with the presidential CEQ.

Good science and innovative technology promoted

Full scale pollution control technology demonstrations are developed, arranged, and implemented by the EPA administrator. Funds from the EPA budget must be assigned to research and development as needed by the various program offices for air, water, hazardous materials, pesticides, solid waste, toxic substances, radiation, and noise. A science advisory board is established to give advice, as needed, to the EPA and other agencies and departments. The science advisory board can use any criteria documents, standards, or regulations of the EPA, and use all of the technical and scientific capabilities of the federal agencies and national environmental laboratories to determine the adequacy of the scientific and technical basis of the proposed criteria document. NEPA's science advisory board works closely with the EPA's Scientific Advisory Panel.

The EPA must identify and coordinate environmental research, and perform research, develop, and demonstrate activities that may need to be more effectively coordinated to avoid duplication. The agency must determine the steps to be taken under existing law and promote coordination between other public agencies. Additionally, the EPA must develop any new legislation needed to ensure such coordination between agencies.[20] In providing this new science knowledge, as mandated by NEPA, the CEQ consults with the Office of Science and Technology Policy to coordinate research activities, and report to the President and Congress. The EPA is required to review journals or scientific proceedings in order to develop a data base of environmental research articles. This data base must be indexed according to geographic location.[21] Reports must be made promptly available to the House and Senate, particularly two committees—Science, Space, and Technology (House of Representatives) and Environment and Public Works (Senate)—whenever requested.[22]

Chronology of NEPA

1969:	The National Environmental Policy Act, 42 U.S.C. 4321-4370e
January 1, 1970:	NEPA, Pub. L. 91-190, 42 U.S.C. 4321-4347,
July 3, 1975:	NEPA Amendment, Pub. L. 94-52,
August 9, 1975:	NEPA Amendment, Pub. L. 94-83, and
Sept. 13, 1982:	NEPA Amendment, Pub. L. 97-258, 4(b)

CHAPTER 4

Federal Agency Requirements

Environmental Quality Improvement Act (EQIA)

Overview

- Every federal agency involved with public works follows all environmental laws.
- The President's office provides professional and administrative staff for the Office of Environmental Quality.

Agency compliance is mandated

In this act, Congress declared that people have caused changes in the environment; many of these changes have been negative; and population increases, combined with urban concentrations, contribute directly to pollution and degrading of the environment.[23] The purpose of EQIA is to assure that each federal agency involved with public works (water and sewer supply, treatment, disposal, etc.) follows all environmental laws. An Office of Environmental Quality, whose role is to provide professional and administrative staff for the Council on Environmental Quality (CEQ), is established within the Executive Office of the President.[24]

Chronology of EQIA

1970:	Environmental Quality Improvement Act, 42 U.S.C. 4371 to 4375
1970:	Federal Water Pollution Control Act Amendments, Title II of Pub.L. 224
May 24, 1977:	Executive Order 11991 42 FR 26967, 3 CFR, 1977 Comp.
Sept. 13, 1982:	EQIA Amendments, Pub.L. 97-258 4(b) 96 Stat. 1067 established by NEPA (42 U.S.C. 4343)

CHAPTER 5

Preventing Pollution

Pollution
Prevention
Act
(PPA)

Overview

* Prevention is the best way to decrease the potential for pollution.

* Pollution must be reduced at its source as much as possible.

* Wastes that cannot be recycled must be safely treated.

* Incentives to industry are provided by the EPA.

* States may receive 50 percent matching grants for technical assistance programs promoting source reduction by business.

* The Common Sense Initiative (CSI) involves community participation in helping to create ideas to improve source reduction.

* The Excellence in Leadership (XL) program allows industries to meet regulation requirements through innovative pilot projects.

* A National Environmental Performance Partnership System (NEPPS) transfers some of the responsibilities for pollution prevention to the states.

Preventing pollution

This act promotes a somewhat new approach for the federal government in protecting health and the environment.[25] Prevention is seen as part of the cure, and preventing pollution is considered to be easier than dealing with it later. A national objective is promoted to prevent pollution first. Industry is accused of having missed the opportunity to reduce or prevent pollution through changing the production, operations, and use of less harmful raw materials. If changes to this prevention approach were initiated, then great cost savings, greater environmental protection, and reduced risks would occur. Under this program, strategies are developed by the EPA to encourage industry, public agencies, and citizens groups to innovate. Methods to promote the reduction of pollution at its source must be developed and implemented.[26]

Requirements

Owners and operators, under the PPA must prevent and reduce pollution at its source whenever feasible. Pollution that cannot be prevented, or wastes that cannot be recycled, must be safely treated. Premeditated disposal or release into the environment may be used only as a last resort. The EPA has supported this approach so seriously that it maintains a separate office to review and advise its single-medium program offices about how to promote this multimedia approach. Strategies to be used to prevent pollution include these:

- Establishing standard methods of measuring source reduction
- Considering changes to existing environmental regulations
- Coordinating source reduction efforts at the EPA and other federal offices
- Helping businesses to adopt source reduction methods
- Identifying measurable pollution prevention goals
- Establishing technical advisory panels
- Developing training programs
- Appointing inspection officials
- Reducing barriers to adopting source reduction methods
- Developing waste auditing procedures
- Establishing a Source Reduction Clearinghouse (to serve as an information center for different approaches)
- Establishing an annual award program recognizing companies that are successful and innovative in source reduction.[27]

EPA support to owners, operators, and states

States may be awarded 50 percent matching fund grants from the EPA for their technical assistance programs that promote the use of source reduction programs by business.[28] Owners or operators of facilities that are required to file an annual toxic chemical release form must include a source reduction and recycling report. The Environmental Leadership Program (ELP) of the EPA encourages companies to adopt source reduction efforts. National risk reduction goals are stated in the ELP materials; and corporations are asked to voluntarily develop their own Corporate Statement of Environmental Principles.

Public recognition of source reduction is promoted by the ELP's Model Facility Program. This program is open to all facilities that develop Corporate Statements of Environmental Principles and submit data confirming their reduction of sources as listed in the toxic release inventory (TRI).

CSI, XL, and NEPPS Programs

There are other ways that EPA supports pollution prevention. One is the Common Sense Initiative (CSI). This CSI differs from the pollutant-by-pollutant approach. It protects the environment by focusing on industries rather than the pollutants themselves. The first phase of the CSI is targeted to six industries:

1. Automobiles
2. Electronics
3. Iron and steel
4. Metals (plating and finishing)
5. Oil
6. Printing.

This approach assembles community residents, industry executives, and state and local officials to work together to improve source reduction. The EPA has yet another program called "regulatory reinvention." As a part of the effort to reinvent government, the Excellence in Leadership (XL) program was created. This XL program grants industries the ability to meet regulatory requirements through pilot projects, source reduction, and otherwise technologically innovative approaches. For example, a Permits Improvement Team (PIT) spearheads a process for obtaining public opinion, using performance-based standards, submitting data, and streamlining permitting methods by issuing group permits and granting minor (de minimis) exemptions.

In transferring some of the responsibilities for pollution prevention to the states, a National Environmental Performance Partnership System (NEPPS) has been established. Annual agreements are negotiated between a state and the EPA regional office to establish the state's goals and indicators for environmental protection.

Chronology of PPA

1990:	Pollution Prevention Act, 42 U.S.C. 13101 to 13109

SECTION TWO

Air

CHAPTER 6

Air Pollution

Clean
Air
Act
(CAA)

Overview

* The CAA is the major air regulation.

* Under this Act, no one is allowed to pollute the air. Any building or facility requires a permit to release contaminants into the air.

* Many duties are delegated to the states, such as creating regional air quality plans called "state implementation plans," and issuing facility permits.

* The Act divides the potential sources of pollution into two categories: mobile and stationary.

* A list of contaminants is developed, called the national ambient air quality standards (NAAQS).

* Permits are required for all existing and new stationary sources of potential pollution.

* A nonattainment area is one that does not meet the NAAQS for a particular contaminant.

* Industrial facilities usually must monitor the air around their sites, using scientific measurement instruments.

* There is a national goal to eliminate any cause of impaired visibility.

* Upper stratospheric ozone is protected by phaseouts of certain chemical substances (a global issue).

* Motor vehicle requirements are strict, promoting lower emissions.

* Industrial facilities may buy and sell, or trade, portions of their emissions as a method to stimulate overall air emission reductions.

Regulating air

The major regulation protecting air quality in the United States is the Clean Air Act (CAA); its goal is to prohibit any kind of air contamination. It controls air emissions by requiring individuals, business, industry, and government to eliminate or reduce air contamination. It also regulates against hazardous (poisonous) air and poor visibility. Since the CAA was first enacted, each state's responsibilities under the federal clean air requirements have increased.[1] Typical of many environmental regulations, as new scientific information about the air has been discovered, the regulations have been improved and expanded in different areas. Changes, additions, amendments, and new provisions have been made over the three decades that the CAA has been in effect.

Regardless of the source of the air contaminant—from government, industry, or an individual—strict penalties are assessed for violators. Sources are divided into stationary and mobile classifications, and both are subject to the requirements of the CAA. A stationary source is one that has buildings, structures, equipment, installations, or substance-emitting activities belonging to a single industrial classification. It operates on one or more contiguous properties under the control of one owner or operator. A mobile source is any other source related to transportation, including a stationary source used for storage.[2] Naturally occurring hydrocarbon reservoirs are not included.[3] Violators are pros-

Exhibit 2: Smoke stacks from industrial facilities, process lines, and buildings spew visible and invisible emissions. The visible smoke from the left stack may be harmful or harmless; however, air regulations require that any emission must be approved by the government.

ecuted with fines, prison sentences, or their facilities are given special operating restrictions. Clean air is considered to be a right of all individuals, and is so protected by the act.

Existing and new sources of possible air contamination are regulated through a number of devices. A list of contaminants, with their ranges of safety is published by the EPA. This list is called the "national ambient air quality standards (NAAQS)." From time to time the list is modified, ranges changed, and chemical and biological agents added and deleted. For this reason, interested persons must keep informed about the NAAQS.[4] For example, in 1998, explosives were deleted from the list of regulated substances, along with gasoline used as fuel and in naturally occurring hydrocarbon mixtures prior to industrial processing.[5] If an agent or compound is removed from the list and has not been identified for a source, there is considered to be a chance for such a contaminant to be released and to become a hazard. Thus, the source is subject to federal regulation. Specific emission limits for the NAAQS are controlled by the federal government by requiring state implementation plans (SIPs). Each state must develop and enact a comprehensive statewide plan to keep its air clean.

Air permits for sources

Existing and new source owners or operators are required to apply for, and receive, operating permits. The source can be an industrial building that makes cast metal products, a blast furnace, an electrical generating station, a paint shop, a commercial bakery, or anything that emits gases or other airborne contaminants. Any facility that has the potential for air pollution may not operate without a permit. During the permit application process, applicants develop appropriate methods of air pollution control for their own buildings, processes, facilities, or operations. As architects of their own operating permits, owners or operators are involved in deciding about the provisions of their own permits. Review and comment are then made by the EPA or the state agency responsible for air pollution control. In this way, the potential for accidental air emissions is minimized.

New sources are more tightly regulated than existing sources. Facilities that are new sources may not begin operating without first receiving a permit describing all operating stipulations.

Generally, the comprehensive operating permit program is the major method that enforces the Act. Permits usually specify that owners and operators monitor the source periodically or continuously. Any changes in operations or equipment must be documented and materials submitted to the appropriate governmental agency for review and approval, then included as an amendment of new condition of the specific operating permit.

State implementation plans (SIPs)

Under the CAA, each state must formally adopt its own plan after public hearings and notices. There are minimum criteria for the state's SIP to become the major means for the federal government to control pollution. The SIP must include these elements:

1. Emission limitations, with controls, economic incentives, and timetables

2. Air quality data classifying areas of attainment or nonattainment

3. Programs enforcing emission limitations

4. A prohibition on emissions that interfere with attaining and maintaining the NAAQS

5. Compliance with interstate and international pollution abatement requirements

6. Assurance of the financial capability of permit applicants, maintenance of adequate state environmental personnel, and enforcement authority for the designated control program

7. Emission monitoring with periodic reports from stationary sources

8. Adequate contingency plans to restrict emissions after the fact

9. Methods for changing the plan in response to any changes in NAAQS

10. Ways to meet EPA's requirements for new sources of air pollution (and operating existing sources that do not attain the NAAQS)

11. Programs of preconstruction review and notice to prevent significant deterioration (PSD) of major new sources and to operate existing sources in areas that do not attain the NAAQS

12. Models for air quality containing supportable data

13. Methods for owners or operators of major stationary sources to pay fees covering permit review

14. Local government consultation and participation in developing the SIP

The SIP contents may vary from state to state. No model needs to be followed by a state, as long as the above 14 requirements are included. After the EPA approves the SIP, both that state and the EPA are responsible for enforcing it. In order for the EPA to approve a SIP, it must completely meet specific guidelines.[6] If the EPA does not act within 6 months, the SIP is automatically considered complete. Once complete, the EPA has 12 months to approve it. If only part of the SIP is approved, then revisions to other parts may be recommended and later approved. The SIP is considered a dynamic plan, to be updated as local conditions and federal requirements change.

Exhibit 3: Careful thought and engineering are required prior to constructing a chemical (or other) manufacturing facility. Provisions of the Clean Air Act require that a permit application include details of backup systems, methods of scrubbing gases prior to venting to the air, design and as-built drawings of mechanical equipment, valves, connections, and process flow.

Revisions must be submitted to EPA within three years of EPA's adoption of any new NAAQSs. If the EPA believes that a SIP is not adequate for maintaining a NAAQS, then the state may be given a deadline to submit a revision.[7] According to the CAA, the EPA must also notify the public about any SIP inadequacies. A finding of SIP inadequacy is a "SIP call."

If a state receives disapproval for its SIP, the EPA is required to enact a Federal Implementation Plan (FIP) for that state. Any SIP deficiencies can result in federal sanctions. The sanctions include freezing highway funds, eliminating additional emission offsets for new or modified sources seeking new source permits, or other measures. Sanctions can be assessed at the time of a SIP finding of deficiency or any time after.

Nonattainment areas and SIPs

Any area that does not meet NAAQS for a pollutant is a nonattainment area for that pollutant. For example, many urban areas are becoming "ozone nonattainment areas." Atmospheric ozone levels are influenced by automobile emissions in stagnant air, air inversions, or releases of contaminants from major industrial facilities. For any kind of nonattainment area, there are specific requirements that must be met:

- All reasonable available control measures for stationary sources must be adopted (with a minimum of reasonably available control technology (RACT) for existing sources).[8]
- Annual incremental reductions in the emissions of the nonattainment pollutants must be achieved.
- An inventory of current emissions in the area must be developed.
- Permits for new and other major stationary sources must be modified.
- Any new emissions must be quantified to help create an emissions budget for each nonattainment area.
- Automatic implementation measures must be indicated in the SIPs.
- Contingency actions must be specified in case the area fails to make reasonable progress to attain NAAQS by the stated date.
- Other techniques like modeling, inventorying, and planning may be allowed by EPA.[9]

While the EPA has been lenient and considerate of many metropolitan areas that have been nonattainment areas in the past, there is good reason to believe that the EPA will begin to apply even greater compliance pressures on state and local governments.

National ambient air quality standards (NAAQS)

The national ambient air quality standard program is very important to business and industry. Ambient air is the composition of specific pollutants measured at one location and time.[10] It affects business costs.

Exhibit 4: There are exposed stacks, pipes, equipment, and vents in every city, suburb, and small town in the United States. Owners and operators must bear extra costs to comply with environmental regulations.

Six pollutants are established: sulfur dioxide (SO_2), nitrogen oxides (NOx), particulate matter (PM-10)[11], carbon monoxide (CO), ozone, and lead (P6). The primary NAAQS have a range of safety intended to protect public health, and the secondary NAAQS are intended to protect the public welfare. There are difficulties in establishing these factors of safety, because people, animals, birds, fish, and plant life differ so much within each species. A small amount of an air contaminant can greatly affect one person but not another.

Pollutants that must meet national standards (NAAQS) are ozone, carbon monoxide, and particulate matter. *Ozone nonattainment areas* can be marginal, moderate, serious, severe, or extreme. Marginal areas were required to meet ozone NAAQS by 1993; moderate areas had to meet them by 1996; serious areas by 1999, severe areas by 2005; and extreme areas; i.e., California, by 2010. *Carbon monoxide nonattainment areas* are moderate or serious. Moderate areas had to meet the NAAQS by 1995, and serious areas by 2000. *Particulate Matter (PM-10) nonattainment areas* are moderate only. These areas had to meet NAAQS by 1994.

Some releases are exempt from the notification requirements of reportable quantities. For example, releases of radionuclides that are found naturally in the soil on large tracts of land, like golf courses or parks, are exempt. Releases from land disturbances caused by farming, construction, or mining extraction are not reportable.[12] There are some exceptions; reports to EPA must be made for uranium, phosphate, tin, zircon, hafnium, vanadium, monazite, and rare earth mines. Dumping and transporting coal and fly ash, bottom ash, boiler slags and coal ash also are excluded.

Federal conformity to SIP provisions

No federal department can support or provide financial assistance or approve any activity that does not conform to a SIP. Also, all state and federal actions must conform to a state's SIP. For example, highway and transportation plans, programs, and projects, and U.S. Army Corps of Engineers' actions are actions that must conform. Vehicles (mobile sources of air contamination) must also conform with the SIP, and all SIPs need to provide for expected increases in the number of motor vehicles.

Monitoring the air

Monitoring, or watching and measuring a potential contaminant or pollutant, is required for industrial emissions. "Enhanced monitoring" is a monitoring method that is different from, but can provide similar data to, EPA's recommended methods. Enhanced, or increased, emissions monitoring is required only to determine if a facility meets government-specified emission limits. Monitoring plans are required to identify those industrial emission levels that are below acceptable limits in order to provide information for timing improvements to reduce emissions. For example, when 85 percent of the allowable emissions are reached for particulate matter, an industrial process must engage additional air scrubber equipment. A common method of air monitoring is the continuous air monitoring system (CAMS) where electronic data is collected regularly or periodically and later reviewed by owners, operators, or public agencies.

New source performance standards (NSPS)

The federal government controls air emissions from new sources differently than it controls those from old sources. Accepting the principle that the cost of retrofitting old sources of emissions could be prohibitive, it regulates new sources more stringently.[13] However, if an old source is reconstructed or modified, then it must meet the new source performance standards. Categories of new sources are given sets of standards for their emissions to meet. EPA has listed about 60 different source categories.[14] For these categories, the best technology is used to develop the amount of emission reduction to be required. NSPS can be promoted as equipment, design, or work standards, or operating standards when specific emission limits are not feasible. A NSPS only applies to a facility where construction begins after the date of the proposal of the NSPS.

Under the CAA, a large new facility (or source of air pollution) is subject to *preconstruction review* prior to award of a permit. If the location of the new source is in a nonattainment area for a pollutant, the new source may be rejected for a permit outright. If the new source is located in an attainment area, then it is subject to a permit considering the *prevention of significant deterioration* (PSD) of air quality. If a potential source could emit at least 250 tons per year or at least 100 tons per year, of one of 28 designated source categories of pollutants, the source is subject to the nonattainment permit program. If a source can emit at least 10 to 100 tpy of the nonattainment pollutant, the nonattainment program applies. The pollutant in question and the seriousness of the nonattainment problem where the source is located are considerations in awarding the permit.[15] The maximum capacity of a source, or facility, to emit a pollutant according to its design is based on federal emissions limits (such as those limits established in a state implementation plan).

Prevention of significant deterioration (PSD) program

Before a major new source of potential air contamination can be constructed in an attainment area, a permit must be obtained.[16] This PSD program requires that the owner or operator explain the following:

- How the source will comply with national ambient air quality levels
- How it will use the *best available control technology* (BACT) for each pollutant that it will emit
- How it will not create adverse impacts on federal areas, such as national wilderness areas or national parks greater than 5,000 acres.[17]

BACT is the maximum amount of emission reductions possible considering economics, energy needed to be expended to reduce the emissions, and the facility location. In most instances, the BACT is as strict as an applicable new source performance standard (NSPS) for that source.

In most instances, the amount of allowable deterioration (PSD) that a new source can consume and the allowable BACT are state responsibilities. BACT review is applied to any regulated pollutant from a source that could be emitted in a significant amount under the PSD rules.[18] The EPA allows states that have developed PSD permitting programs as part of their SIPs to determine the BACT with broad discretion. For this reason and many others, BACT is often quite controversial. If the source is located near a national park or other classified area, the BACT must address how it will adversely impact the *air quality related values* (AQRVs) for that area. Federal land managers must receive pre-application notices for any source proposed within 60 miles of such classified areas.

Areas not attaining NAAQS, or nonattainment areas

Before new major stationary sources (or major modifications) are constructed, a nonattainment permit must be granted. Both PSD and nonattainment permits may be required for areas that are considered attainment for some regulated pollutants and nonattainment for others.[19] States must administer the nonattainment permit program. Major new or modified existing sources must commit to achieving the *lowest achievable emission rate* (LAER). This rate is the most stringent emission limit contained in a state implementation plan, or one that is achieved in practice by the same or similar source category. A state's permit program must require that offsets of potential nonattainment pollutants be secured from nearby facilities. EPA can determine baseline emission levels against which any offset credits are issued.[20] Offset ratios are set for ozone, carbon monoxide, and particulate material nonattainment areas.

Exhibit 5: A new addition to a facility may include new storage tanks, pipes, valves, and other connectors. Each addition has the potential to modify a process that had been previously approved in a permit.

Rules for reconstructed and modified buildings or facilities

When rebuilding or replacing parts of an existing facility or when expenditures for a project are 50 percent or more of their cost for a comparable new facility, a *reconstruction rule* is triggered. If triggered, the reconstruction rule does not necessarily require that a new source performance standard (NSPS) be used. If an NSPS is considered not feasible for the reconstructed or modified facility, EPA may determine that it is not appropriate.[21] When reconstruction does exceed the 50-percent limits, the NSPS rules apply.

Rules for changes or modifications that increase emissions

Nonattainment permit programs and the NSPS are triggered if there is a physical or operational change resulting in increases in emissions of the regulated pollutant. Activities, such as repair, replacement, or maintenance are not considered to be a facility modification. When a facility initiates operations, EPA will not calculate an emissions increase for the modification, but will calculate a past-to-future-actual comparison. EPA excludes all pollution control projects from the new source permitting rules. If there is equipment failure, the rules for modification of facilities are not triggered. The EPA determines whether a specific project causes increased emissions as a test for new source review. If a facility meets BACT or LAER levels of emission reductions, it may be excluded from the modification rule by EPA.

Rules for minor new source review

In order to comply with the NAAQS, states must include in their SIPs that a preconstruction review of minor new or modified sources is required. Minor new sources are defined, and this minor identification can become a way for owners or operators to comply with federal and state air controls. By applying the minor new-source-review rules to facilities, operating limits on industrial facilities are lowered. States develop their own minor new source review programs in coordination with their SIP.

Air toxics program

The CAA has changed from focusing on health to emphasizing technology as a way of improving air quality. A single stationary source that could emit more than ten tpy of any combination of substances from a facility is considered a *major source*. The major source must have single ownership and it must demonstrate that it intends to use technical methods to reduce its pollution potential. An initial list of 174 major source categories of hazardous air pollutants are scheduled and regularly updated.

Maximum achievable emissions limitations

Standards are promoted by EPA for the maximum degree of technical reductions that can be achieved according to economic situations, energy consumption, and environmental factors. The limitations are called the *maximum achievable control technology* (MACT). Standards are based on the best technology currently available for the particular source category or for the best performing group of sources. There is a minimum level for existing source MACT in terms of the arithmetic mean of the best performing 12 percent of sources in the same category when there are more than 29 sources in that category, or the best performing 5 sources if there are fewer than 30 sources in that category. There are MACT standards for these industrial source categories:

- Aerospace manufacturing
- Agricultural chemicals production
- Aluminum production
- Coke ovens
- Ferroalloys production
- Gasoline terminals and pipeline breakout stations
- Halogenated solvent cleaning
- Industrial cooling towers
- Magnetic tape manufacturing operations
- Oil and natural gas production
- Petroleum refinery sources
- Pharmaceutical production
- Polymer and resin production
- Printing and publishing

- Resin, polymer, and inorganic chemical production
- Steel foundries
- Wood furniture manufacturing.

If a source has voluntarily reduced emissions by 90 percent or more before the MACT standard was implemented, that source may be eligible for an extension of the compliance deadline. Case-specific MACT standards may be established for a source category if the EPA fails to establish a federal standard.[22]

Risk identification program

Since the MACT standards are based on technology, public health is protected by identifying the risks of the technology to be used. A risk identification program sets priorities for regulating hazardous air pollutants in different source categories and geographic areas.[23]

Accidental release controls

Regulated hazardous pollutants and extremely hazardous substances are a major concern. Owners and operators must prepare risk management plans for each substance that could accidentally be emitted from a facility into the air. Annual audits and safety inspections to help prevent leaks and accidents may be required by EPA.[24]

Acid rain controls

Sulfur dioxide (SO_2) and nitrogen oxides (NOx) are regulated to decrease the potential for creating acid rain. Emission allowances and trading programs for SO_2 are established with tracking, trading, monitoring, excess emissions penalties, offset plans, and an administrative appeals process. An allowance may be granted to emit one ton of SO_2, but any facility may not emit more than the allocated, purchased, or traded allowances for a given calendar year. If a facility exceeds this amount, the unit's owners or operators will be subject to penalties. An allowance auction is held yearly.[25] Eligible parties can purchase, trade, or receive a pro rata share of the moneys collected. In the past, average prices have ranged from $70 to $150 per allowance. For NOx emissions, emission rates are tied to categories of coal-fired electric utility boilers, with a second set of NOx emission standards applied to the remaining categories of boilers.

The acid rain program uses a new system, giving market allowances to electric utilities. EPA holds yearly auctions of allowances for a small part of the annually allocated allowances. Private parties also can offer their allowances and prices for sale in the EPA auctions.

Visibility protection and air quality

As a national goal, the CAA attempts to eliminate any man-made visibility impairment. To accomplish this goal, the states must develop their own requirements to apply the *best available retrofit technology* (BART) and other strategies as part of the state implementation plan process. There are federal SIP criteria for improving visibility and eliminating visible plumes.[26]

Visibility is also one of the criteria applied under the prevention of significant deterioration (PSD) permit program.[27] The U.S. Forest Service and the National Park Service guide local Federal Land Managers in deciding whether proposed new sources would have an adverse impact on the air quality-related values (AQRVs) of Class I areas.

Stratospheric ozone protection

No person can manufacture, produce, or sell any Class I substance in annual quantities greater than specified by EPA. In Title VI of the CAA, global warming and ozone depletion are handled through a program that phases out ozone-depleting substances. Initial lists of Class I substances (CFCs, halons, carbon tetrachloride, methyl chloroform) and Class II substances (hydrochlorofluorocarbons) have been developed. Exceptions are made for producing medical substances and aviation substances used for aircraft safety. Beginning in 2000 (and 2002 for methyl chloroform), all Class I substance production is banned.

In addition, there are strict regulations about the safe use, disposal, release, and recycling of Class I and II substances from appliances, industrial refrigeration, motor vehicle servicing, nonessential products, and the labeling of products made with Class I and II substances. A trading system is allowed for substitutions of these materials.

Fuels, additives, and mobile sources of emissions

Certainly, poor air quality has been unequivocally connected to motor vehicles—automobiles, buses, and trucks. These sources and others are mobile sources of air contamination. Automobile manufacturers are required to reduce by 50 percent the amount of tailpipe emissions beginning in 2003 (from 1993).

One new program aimed at reducing air pollution from new motor vehicle engines is the National Low Emission Vehicle Program (called "National LEV"). In a voluntary program to reduce air emissions, motor vehicle manufacturers and the northeastern states can sign up to commit to meet tailpipe standards that are more stringent than EPA mandates.[28]

A reformulated fuel program requires using blended gasoline in certain carbon monoxide and ozone nonattainment areas to reduce VOCs and toxic exhaust emissions.[29] Another clean fuel vehicle program uses alternative fuels such as methanol, ethanol, natural gas, and reformulated gasoline. This program has a California pilot program to produce and sell 300,000 clean fuel vehicles, along with a program that requires the use of clean fuel vehicles by any operator of ten or more vehicles in CO and ozone nonattainment areas. Both a registration system and extensive testing of fuels and additives are required to determine health risks. The clean fuels program seems to support conventional emission control technology in vehicles to obtain the required emission reductions.

Operating permit program

There is a *preconstruction permit program* for new and modified sources, a *state implementation plan operating permit program*, and a *comprehensive operating permit program* for most sources of air pollution. The comprehensive operating permit program is developed and administered by the states and based on EPA's minimum requirements.[30] Sources subject to permits must prepare and submit applications for approval or be in violation of federal law. The sources that require a permit are a major source (one emitting or having the potential for emitting 100 tpy or more of any air pollutant (including fugitive emissions), a designated source category (classification of industrial operation, etc.), or any other source defined by a state or the EPA. States can develop permit exceptions for certain small types of facility with low levels of emission or low production rates.

A permit application must contain information about how source plans can comply with all applicable requirements if there is noncompliance. If a state does not implement an air pollution permit program of their own, the EPA imposes a federal operating permit program. Within

60 days, the state or EPA permit review authority must determine whether the application is complete. During the time that a permit applicant is being reviewed, there is an "application shield," where operating without a permit is considered allowable. The application must contain the following information:

- Air pollution control equipment
- Certification of truth, accuracy, and completeness of the application
- Compliance status statement
- Emission rates listed in tons per year
- Emissions of all pollutants for which the source contains major emissions of regulated air pollutants
- Monitoring and measurement methods
- Identification of points of emissions

Within 18 months after receiving the application, the permitting authority must take action on the permit. Fixed terms of the permits cannot exceed five years. Each permit must include the following information:

- Compliance monitoring, testing, reporting, and recordkeeping
- Compliance schedule and regular progress reports
- Compliance certification
- Emission limitations and standards
- Fees (according to an approved state permit fee schedule)
- Inspection and entry requirements for the permit authority
- Monitoring, measuring, and recordkeeping requirements
- Opportunity to request a public hearing on the draft permit
- Procedures for public notice and comment
- State-only requirements must be clearly noted
- Statement that permit can be modified, revoked, reopened, reissued, or terminated
- Sulfur dioxide emission prohibitions exceeding any allowances.

State and EPA reviews of permit applications

The state permitting agency provides the EPA with copies of each air permit application, draft permit, and final permit. EPA may comment on any of these phases of the submittal. Notice of each draft permit must be given to any affected state before public notice is given.[31] If the EPA objects to a proposed final permit within 45 days of receipt, the state permit agency cannot issue the permit. If the state agency fails to revise and resubmit the proposed permit to EPA within 90 days of receiving the objection notice from EPA, then EPA must issue or deny the permit. If EPA does not object, any person may petition the EPA to object within 60 days after expiration of the 45-day EPA review period.[32]

A *permit shield* is a concept that means compliance with the permit is considered to be compliance with the CAA. This shield is optional with each state, and the permitting agency can expressly require that a permit shield apply. If the permit does not state it, then no shield is assumed.

Permit revisions

Revisions to a permit may be approved by a state agency or the EPA only if the change could not be performed without violating the existing permit. There are a few categories of permit revisions—the administrative permit amendment and the minor or significant permit revision categories are the most common.

An *Administrative Permit Amendment* is a simple revision to correct typographic errors, make changes in names, require more frequent monitoring, or specify new requirements for a preconstruction review permit. No public notice is required for these administrative permit amendments. No permit shield is allowed.

A *Minor Permit Revision* is allowed with only limited review requirements. No public review is required for this kind of revision, but EPA and affected states must be notified. This revision cannot violate any of the permit term requirements. It cannot violate source requirements, and the change may be made immediately.[33]

A *Significant Permit Revision* is one that cannot qualify as an administrative or minor permit revision. The same procedures must be followed that are used for applying or renewing a permit. States are required by EPA to allow sources to trade emissions according to the source's cap as stated in the permit. This requirement provides *operational flexibility through the trading of emissions.*

Alternative operating scenarios

To ensure freedom in operations, a permit can specify a number of anticipated facility operating scenarios. An owner or operator would then give notice to the state agency or EPA that it had changed its operating scenario, but no permit revision would be required. The EPA prefers that permit revisions be avoided, if possible, through such a method.[34] States must create a fee schedule that provides sufficient revenue to cover permit program costs.[35] State fee schedules can include service fees, application fees, emission fees, and others. EPA expects a state to collect at least $25 per year multiplied by the total tons of actual emissions of each regulated pollutant emitted.

Emissions trading

Some states have developed programs where industrial facilities, including public utility facilities, may accumulate credits for not producing their expected amounts of air pollution. These credits refer to a hypothetical area of effect around their facility, like an imaginary bubble around it. Within the area of effect, facilities that do not emit the expected tons per year of contaminants may sell those credits to another facility that exceeded their own allocated amounts of air pollution. Buy-

Exhibit 6: Equipment at some facilities can rust or deteriorate faster if it is exposed to certain chemical substances or gases. These discards provide evidence of the importance of regular replacement and repair to assure continued compliance with the terms of a permit.

ing and selling of credits becomes an incentive for any facility to reduce its emissions.[36]

Enforcing the Clean Air Act

The *operating permit program* allows the government to identify a source's clean air requirements—its methods of operation, industrial processes, if any, monitoring procedures, recordkeeping requirements, limits for pollutants, etc. The permit conditions provide a basis for enforcing the CAA without going to the courts. It should be noted that the CAA administrative enforcement provisions are modeled after the CWA. This model provides for administrative penalties that can be levied up to $200,000 or more.

Violators of the permit process (either those who violate their permits or who avoid applying for a permit) are given notice, after which the violator has 30 days to request a hearing. Agreements are much more quickly reached when the DOJ can be bypassed. A field citation program is used for minor violations. *Field citations* allow inspectors to issue small fines of up to $5,000 per day per violation. Violators can pay or request a hearing. Civil penalties can be sought by private citizens, and the EPA can pay up to $10,000 to anyone providing information leading to criminal or civil convictions.

Criminal penalties can be given for violating the CAA. If one knowingly violates the CAA, he or she is a felon. Enforcement actions can be made against individuals, corporations, and partnerships. Crimes connected to recordkeeping are subject to fines and jail terms. If persons make misstatements, they can be criminally prosecuted. Failure to pay any fees owed the government under the CAA is a criminal act and subject to fines and imprisonment.

Knowing or negligent releases of air toxins that place others in danger of death or serious bodily injury are subject to criminal penalties. Penalties could be assessed as high as $250,000 per day with 15 years imprisonment. Corporations could be fined as much as $1,000,000 per day. Even if an individual honestly lacks knowledge about a release, he or she may be subject to a fine of up to $100,000, and up to a year in prison. By contrast, corporations may be fined as much as $200,000.

Compliance audits are regular inspections of the premises and their operating procedures as developed by the applicant and agencies and stated in the permit(s) for a facility. Companies or facilities desiring to adhere to federal environmental regulations, typically initiate an internal compliance program. A practice of regular audits ensures detection and correction of problems, and is considered by the courts to be a mitigating action against any assessed penalties. For example, any permitted facility should report any departure from a permit requirement.[37]

National priority sectors are designated by the EPA for enforcement attention. For example, one year may be petroleum refining, dry cleaning establishments, and strip mining. The next year may be another set of targets.

Chronology of CAA

1955:	Air Pollution Control Act, ch. 360, 69 Stat. 322.
1963:	Clean Air Act, Pub. L. 88-206, 77 Stat. 392
1967:	Air Quality Act, Pub. L. 90-148, 81 Stat. 465
1970:	Clean Air Act Amendments, Pub. L. 91-604, 84 Stat. 1676
1977:	Clean Air Act Amendments, Pub. L. 95-95, 91 Stat. 685
1981:	Clean Air Act Amendments, Pub. L. 97-23, 95 Stat. 139
1990:	Clean Air Act Amendments, Pub. L. 101-549, 104 Stat. 2399

CHAPTER 7

Sound

Noise
Control
Act
(NCA)

Overview

* Noise travels through the air and is increasingly becoming a danger to the citizens of the nation.

* Sources of noise are machinery, vehicles and equipment, appliances, and other commercial products.

* National uniformity of treatment is promoted in the NCA.

* Noise emission standards are provided by EPA for manufactured products.

* Aircraft and military equipment are not covered under this Act.

* Records, product labeling, and warranties of products are required of manufacturers.

* Noise control education projects are promoted under the NCA.

Policy statements and products regulated

Uncontrolled noise is a growing danger to the health, safety, and welfare of the national population, especially in urban areas, but also in national parks and other special areas. The major sources of noise are motor vehicles and equipment, machinery, appliances, and other commercial products. Primary responsibility for controlling noise lies with state and local governments, but in order to provide uniformity of treatment, federal controls are required under the NCA. All manufactured products are regulated, except aircraft (their engines, propellers, and equipment), military weapons and equipment designed for combat, and research rockets.[38]

Control methods

The EPA consults with other federal agencies to develop and maintain scientifically based criteria for noise. The effect of noise on public health is the major focus for the research used in developing the noise criteria. Studies are done on noise sources and the technology to control them.[39]

Noise emission standards have been developed for commercial products such as construction equipment, transportation equipment, including recreational vehicles (snow mobiles, water vehicles, and motorcycles, etc.), motors or engines, and electrical and electronic equipment. The limits that are established for each product must be standard and consider the amount of use of such product (alone or in combination with other noise sources), the degree of noise reduction achievable through the best available technology (BAT), and the cost of complying with those standards.

Manufacturers' warranties

Each manufacturer of a noisy product must warrant to the final purchaser that the product has been designed, built, and equipped to operate at, or below, the sound level required by the EPA at the time of its manufacture. Any costs that the manufacturer incurs from adding sound-deadening devices or changes to the product cannot be transferred to any dealer. No advertisements for the product can contain the costs or dollar values of the noise emission control devices unless substantiated by the Bureau of Labor Statistics of the U.S. Department of Labor (DOL). This provision of the Act deters the manufacturer from making exaggerated advertising claims.

Manufacturers must maintain records, submit reports to the EPA, and develop information about their products. Testing may be required by the EPA to verify any claims made in reports or records. Penalties and violations may be assessed if records, reports, and information about the product are not provided.

State and local agency limitations

State and local governments cannot change the federal noise limits. Noise limits for a product may not be changed even if a component is added to a product. State and local governments cannot license, regulate, or restrict the use, operation, or movement of any product regulated for noise beyond those limitations set in the NCA. However, a state or local government can petition the EPA to change a noise requirement at any time. The state and local governments are able to require product labeling and information about products in any way, as long they conform to EPA requirements.[40]

Prohibited actions

No one is allowed to remove sound-deadening devices, modify products, or change their operating characteristics to increase their sound. Even if their performance is increased, products can only have their devices or elements of design removed for maintenance purposes.[41] There are criminal penalties for violating the NCA that cannot exceed $25,000 per day of violation, imprisonment, or both the monetary penalty and the imprisonment.

Research, public information, and quiet communities

The EPA, in coordination with other federal agencies, uses grants, contracts, and federal actions to help state and local governments develop their own noise control programs. Educational programs are promoted through school curricula, volunteer organizations, radio and television programs, publications to develop and disseminate information about noise and public health. EPA also sponsors and conducts research about noise and its psychological and physiological effects on people, animals, wildlife, and property. The determination of dose-response relationships suitable for decision making is emphasized. Noise abatement technology is promoted through demonstration projects. State and local noise control programs are encouraged to use monitoring equipment. The economic impact of noise on property and human activities is another research topic. Economic incentives, including noise emission charges, are to be researched to help control noise.

State and local governments can apply for grants to help them carry out these noise controls:

- Determine the extent of the noise problem in a jurisdiction.
- Plan and establish a noise control capability (including the purchase of equipment).
- Develop noise abatement plans around airports, highways, and rail yards.
- Evaluate methods to control noise and demonstrate the best available technologies for each jurisdiction.

A national noise environmental assessment program has been developed and implemented to identify trends in noise exposure and response, ambient levels of noise, and compliance data to determine the effectiveness of noise abatement actions. Regional technical assistance centers are established with universities and private organizations.[42]

Low noise emission products

The EPA must determine which products, according to the NCA, qualify as low-noise emission products, and are thus suitable for use by the public. Then a certificate may be issued for such products. Federal government agencies are required to purchase low-noise emission products in lieu of other products as long as the low-noise products do not exceed 125 percent of the retail price of competing products.

Emission standards

Both motor carrier and railroad noise emission standards are promoted. The DOT must require railroad carriers to limit their equipment noise through BAT, taking into account the cost of compliance. Motor carriers must meet the EPA standards in the same way as railroads.

Chronology of NCA

1972:	Noise Control Act, 42 U.S.C. § 4901 to 4918
1994:	NCA Amendments, Pub. L. 103-272, 108 Stat. 1379

CHAPTER 8

Airplane Sound

Airport
Noise Abatement
Act
(ANAA)

Overview

* The EPA works with the DOT to regulate noise from airports and aircraft.

* A single system of measuring noise is uniformly applied to airports and their surroundings.

* Land uses are identified that are compatible with airport noise.

* Noise exposure maps are required for airports related to runways and operations.

* Noise compatibility programs are required, along with soundproofing and acquisition of certain residential buildings and properties.

* Limits are placed on the amount of damages that can be assessed due to noise.

Airport noise

In the ANAA, land use is recognized as a major factor. The activities that people perform in certain locations have a strong connection to the amount of noise that can be tolerated. Residential land use has the least tolerance for noise for many reasons. Not only do people sit in their backyards, but many dwelling units are constructed of less dense building materials which have a greater tendency to transmit sound to their interiors.

Airports are regulated according to a group of assumptions. The DOT must consult with the EPA to establish a single system of measuring noise at airports. The system must be applied uniformly on and off the airport property. Land uses that are compatible with varying exposures of individuals to noise must be identified. In most cases, industrial and recreational land uses are deemed compatible with airport use. The industrial uses are those industries, such as warehousing, that employ the fewest numbers of people. Labor intensive industries are not compatible.

Noise exposure maps are to be prepared and submitted to the DOT. They must be prepared in consultation with public planning agencies in the areas surrounding the airports, and must comply with the criteria stated in the ANAA. For any changes in airport operations or runways, maps should be revised to indicate any changes in land use compatibility. Noise compatibility programs should be indicated on the airport map, and be implemented at the airport. The noise program may include the following actions:

- Preferential siting of runways
- Restricting the use of the airport to a type or class of aircraft based on the noise characteristics of the aircraft
- Constructing barriers and acoustical shielding
- Soundproofing public buildings
- Changing flight procedures for landings and takeoffs; or
- Acquiring land, air rights, easements, development rights, and other interests to ensure land use compatibility.[43]

The noise program will not be approved by the DOT unless it reduces incompatible uses and prevents the introduction of additional incompatible uses.

Soundproofing and property acquisition

The DOT may make grants available to help soundproof or acquire residential buildings if the noise exposure contours so indicate. Updated noise maps may qualify an airport for these acquisition grants. A number of restrictions apply to these grants, and funds are always limited. For these reasons, airport owners (such as local governments) may need to apply their own revenues to conform to the intent and requirements of the ANAA.[44] Airport noise compatibility planning grants may be made to a sponsor of an airport to develop information necessary to prepare and submit a noise exposure map and related information, or a noise compatibility program.

One legal note from the ANAA should be understood. Noise exposure maps and related information that are submitted to DOT—not a partial list of land uses—may be admitted into evidence or used in a civil action asking for relief for noise resulting from airport operations. Additionally, the aircraft (subsonic, not supersonic) of all foreign air carriers must comply with noise standards of the United States.

Research

Quiet aircraft technology is promoted through the Act's research program for both propeller- and rotor-driven aircraft. The design of the blades is a concern. Certain pitches and curves in the blades can reduce noise, but promote inefficiencies in power and fuel consumption. The goals of the research program are to apply high technology that is cost beneficial and to determine if more research is necessary to supplement existing research activities. If NASA determines that additional research development is necessary and can contribute to developing quiet aircraft technology, then the DOT and NASA shall do so.

Chronology of ANAA

1979:	Aviation Safety and Noise Abatement Act, 49 U.S.C.A. 2101 et seq.
1980:	Airport Noise Abatement Act, 49 U.S.C. 47501–47510
1982:	Airport and Airway Improvement Act, 49 U.S.C.A. 2202
1994:	Airport Noise Abatement Act Amendments, Pub. L. 103-272; 108 Stat. 1284

Water

CHAPTER 9

Water Pollution

Clean
Water
Act
(CWA)

Overview

- The CWA protects people, fish, and wildlife from contaminated water.

- Many federal, state, and local agencies have responsibilities under the CWA.

- Prior to any release of potential contaminants into soils or surface or ground waters, individuals or companies must apply for a permit and be approved for that release.

- Reporting spills is required by law.

- Dredge wastes from the bottoms of water bodies cannot be deposited without a permit.

- Wastewater from industry or public water treatment plants must meet purity standards.

- If a pollutant is discarded from a single place, it is a point source.

- Water discharge permits—National Pollution Discharge Elimination System (NPDES) permits—must be obtained prior to releasing contaminants into surface or ground waters.

- Limits on chemical or biological discharges, called "national effluent guidelines," are established.

- States can establish their own standards of water quality as long as they meet EPA's standards.

- Pollution credits can be traded between watersheds through sale or barter. In this system, one area can have higher measurements than another.

- Storm water discharges require permits.

- Ocean discharges are prohibited.

(Overview continued on next page)

- ◆ Pretreatment of wastewater is required for industrial wastes discharged into a public sanitary sewer system.

- ◆ Bays and estuaries are protected under the National Estuary Program (NEP).

- ◆ Dredge and fill permits are required for surface waters and are managed by the U.S. Army Corps of Engineers.

- ◆ Spill prevention plans are required under the CWA.

- ◆ Oil spills are covered under both the CWA and the Oil Pollution Act (OPA).

Responsibilities are delegated

The federal government regulates water by developing partnerships with different agencies. The Environmental Protection Agency (EPA) is the major agency implementing water-related environmental laws passed by Congress.[1] At times, the EPA delegates specific duties to other agencies. Even though the EPA reviews, inspects, and approves the programs and actions of these partner agencies, it also maintains field staff in its regional offices to administer many of its water-related rules and regulations. In some areas of water protection, the U.S. Army Corps

Exhibit 7: Surface and ground waters can easily receive contaminants from different sources. Concern for purity demands that no one discharge a liquid or solid without first obtaining a permit. (Photo: author)

of Engineers, U.S. Coast Guard, or the U.S. Department of Transportation have responsibilities for protecting water.

Regretfully, there is no clear pattern of responsibilities, nor is there any particular logic that can lead the reader toward intuitively selecting the appropriate agency responsible for her or his water area of interest. For example, while the EPA allows states to administer many water programs under EPA's close supervision, it also allows the states to further delegate water responsibilities to their own local governments.

Water pollution is regulated by the EPA and its designated state agencies by applying these restrictions:[2]

- No discharges of chemicals, biological agents, or waste materials are allowed into surface waters, groundwater, or soils.[3]

- Prior to any release of potential contaminants, individuals or companies must apply for a permit and be approved for that release.[4]

- States can become the regulatory agency for the federal programs, if approved by the EPA.[5]

- All environmental controls and limitations devised by the EPA must follow a prescribed method.[6]

- There is a prescribed process for reporting, responding to, and preventing spills.[7]

- Any deposit or discharging of dredge wastes (from scraping the bottoms of water bodies) must adhere to approved permit provisions.[8]

- Enforcement methods are established for violations.[9]

As can be seen from these provisions, the Clean Water Act attempts to eliminate the delivery of pollutants into water and tries to protect human life, fish, and wildlife.

Water protection and the structure of regulations

The many provisions of the Clean Water Act (CWA) are administered by the EPA and other federal, state, and local agencies. Particularly, the EPA and the U.S. Army Corps of Engineers have major responsibilities for protecting surface water quality. Both agencies work closely with state and local governments to protect all water (surface, ground, and ocean waters) from contamination.

The CWA was preceded by the Federal Water Pollution Control Act (FWPCA). In that act, the EPA established national effluent (offensively dirty substance) standards for specific industries. Effluent standards are the acceptable amounts, given in ranges of measurement of chemicals or substances, that can be safely released into the environment. The standards are based on the technical ability of a particular industry to comply with that standard, compared to its ability to continue its operation as an economically sound industry.

The FWPCA developed a permit system that has been continued in the CWA. This permit system is named the National Pollution Discharge Elimination System (NPDES).

Kinds of Waters

Surface waters are streams, rivers, lakes, rivulets, and creeks.

Ground waters are waters embedded under the surface of the earth within rock formations. Some ground waters move, like underground rivers, and others are fairly still, but contain enough pressure to allow occasional springs to bubble up to the surface.

Ocean waters, or seas, are vast salt water bodies, as well as bays and estuaries that form a transition between ocean water and the land. The Great Lakes may be considered either ocean or surface waters—due to their vast expanses in comparison to other lakes.

Ground waters can mix with surface waters and vice versa. Similarly, ocean waters can invade fresh surface and ground waters, and contaminate them for use as drinking water. Ocean or sea waters can enter bodies of fresh water through inlets or travel through underground rock formations into aquifers (rock bearing water) as a result of tides. Tides are created by gravitational pulls on the earth by the moon, and they occur at regular intervals.

Each state may choose to administer the permit system, but if a state declines or delays taking charge, the EPA regional office will process the permits. Under the NPDES, limits are placed on the composition of effluents, and water quality, or purity, requirements are imposed. Under the CWA, the NPDES permit program is the primary vehicle through which the government attempts to prevent water pollution.[10] Any discharge of a pollutant by any person (or company) is prohibited under the CWA unless a permit is issued and the release or discharge is allowed according to provisions of that permit. The CWA continues to control the amounts of toxic chemicals and biological agents that can be released into waters by using guidelines, performance, and pretreatment standards. Hot spots of contamination in waterways are identified and permanently designated and those waters that can be cleaner are noted.

The CWA Amendments regulate storm water and water quality, and establish a revolving loan fund to construct sewage treatment plants.[11]

Important definitions within the CWA

If a pollutant is introduced (or discharged) into a body of water, it is an *addition*. Discharges of water from dams are not considered additions of pollutants. A *pollutant* may be any of the matter listed on the next page.[12]

If a pollutant is discarded from an observable single place as a single route of contaminants, that place is defined as a *point source*. A place, spot, industrial machine, or storage or manufacturing area can be a point source. This term can be applied to industrial waste streams, process water, cooling water, or storm water runoff in channels, pipes, ditches, or drainage ways. A point source can also be a vehicle, such as a tanker (ship, train, or truck). *Sheet runoff* is a term that implies runoff of rain mixed with chemicals or other agents that originates on large land areas, such as paved areas. Sheet runoff is not classified as a point source.

Waters in the United States include tidal waters, interstate commerce waters, lakes, rivers, streams, or wetlands that are used for recreation, commercial fishing, or industrial purposes. Also, *waters* are tributaries of all of those waters mentioned and the impoundments and wetlands associated with them.[13] EPA does not have jurisdiction over groundwater with regard to point source discharges, but many states have declared that ground waters are part of their regulated bodies of water and so regulate them.[14] *Wetlands* are saturated or flooded land areas that support vegetation common to swamps, marshes, bogs, and similar areas.[15]

Pollutants

- Dredged debris and material
- Solid waste
- Incinerator residue
- Sewage
- Garbage
- Sewage sludge
- Munitions
- Chemical wastes
- Biological materials
- Radioactive materials
- Heat
- Wrecked or discarded equipment
- Rock
- Sand
- Cellar dirt
- Industrial, municipal, and agricultural waste discharged into water

National Pollution Discharge Elimination System (NPDES)

No discharges are allowed without a permit. This program requires that anyone wishing to discharge contaminants from any point source into any waters must apply for a permit and have it reviewed and approved. If a permit application is approved, the applicant (owner or operator) has the right to discharge for as long as five years. Typically, the permit establishes limits on the discharge quantities and composition as a condition of approval. The owner or operator must adhere to all provisions approved in the permit.[16]

States may be authorized by the EPA to issue NPDES permits.[17] By 1997, 41 states and territories had received this authority. For the remaining unauthorized states, the EPA regional office issues the NPDES permits.[18] After issuing state authorization, the EPA issues a Memorandum of Understanding (MOU) that specifies pertinent guidelines and provisions of the state's authorization.[19] Every state program is required to be as strict as the EPA's; it must include requirements for methods of calculating contaminants from the sources, and must set standard procedures for issuing the permits. Appeal procedures and other individual state requirements may vary as long as the state program adheres to the NPDES concepts.[20] Any state that is issued a NPDES permit is subject to EPA review. If EPA does not approve, it may object and issue its own permit for the discharge, setting its own requirements. At any time, EPA can withdraw approval of a state's NPDES permit program and take over its operation.

When a state does not have the authority to grant an NPDES permit and the EPA does, the EPA defers to the state anyway to certify that the discharge to be authorized in the permit complies with the state's standards.[21] A state has a designated period of time in which to respond to the EPA. If the state does not meet that time deadline, the EPA assumes that the state has waived its certification veto.

The NPDES permit requires that an applicant develop and submit information about the facility, place, point source, composition of the discharge, and other pertinent details. When a permit application contains unusual conditions or features, informal meetings may be requested to develop terms and conditions. At times, the EPA or the responsible state agency will issue a *predraft permit*, sometimes with a *14-day letter*. A draft permit may be issued and accompanied by a *fact sheet* or *statement of basis* explaining its calculations and any special

Exhibit 8: Liquid, solid, or hazardous waste treatment plants may need to discharge their clean water from wastes elsewhere. Standards are imposed on all such fluids that must be monitored, measured, recorded, and reported.

considerations. The government agency publishes a notice of intent to issue the draft permit and accepts comments from the public. There may be a public hearing on the permit.

Applicants can appeal a negative decision on the permit or its provisions within 30 days of its issue. Usually, an administrative law judge (from the EPA Environmental Appeals Board or a state agency) decides about the appeal. When the state issues or denies a permit, the state procedures for appeal are observed. Otherwise, the EPA Environmental Appeals Board hears and decides the appeal.

Water discharge permits have the major purpose of limiting offensively dirty substances from contaminating surface and groundwater. Typically, the permits have discharge chemical ranges (or limits), monitoring requirements, reporting requirements, operating and maintenance procedures and requirements, spill procedures, and methods for bypassing the discharge if an emergency occurs. Often a permit may require an owner or operator to perform the best management practices (BMPs). These BMPs assure that the amount of contaminant released is minimized.[22] Monitoring is a self-policing activity, but reports on discharges must be submitted to the state or the EPA on monitoring report forms.[23]

All discharges must be chemically or biologically treated to meet levels that are prescribed by EPA for each specific industry or specific discharge conditions. This limitation ensuring the quality of effluent is based on available technology. The discharge must meet the level of quality required by the body of water receiving it. The permits set maximum limits on both the time period and the average monthly amount of the discharge.

Another set of limit is placed on discharges under the NPDES is technology-based for over 50 industrial facilities according to their category (such as process and cooling water, and wastewater). These limits are called *national effluent guidelines*, which are part of NPDES permits and are enforced under them. If the category is not covered by an applicable effluent guideline, a permit may be issued with provisions established using a *best professional judgment* (BPJ).[24] A BPJ is a somewhat intuitive decision by the permit reviewer.

One program for reducing water pollution by industrial dischargers is to meet the *best practical control technology* (BPT). The BPT hinges on the permit reviewer's relating the economics or costs of the technology to the discharge requested for approval. It is the average of the best conditions achieved by an industry. Another level of pollution control is the *best available technology* (BAT). A BAT is a standard applied to any but BOD, TSP, fecal coliform, pH, or oil and grease. BATs are "maximum feasible pollution reduction for an industry."[25]

A more lenient method and level of pollution control that can be applied to an NPDES permit is the *best conventional pollutant control technology* (BCT). BCT is a reasonableness of cost test for permit applicants. For even more leniency, reasonable costs to the industry are balanced against environmental protection. This consideration dilutes the permit conditions by connecting the costs and availability of a different, potential, control technology to a conventional method of pollution control. The BCT makes the assumption that more conventional methods will be less costly to an applicant, and therefore, more likely to be administered.

New source performance standards (NSPS)

A new source is somewhat difficult to define. According to the CWA, a *new source* is one that began after the publication by the EPA of proposed regulations about standards of performance or after the publication of final NSPS for an industry.[26] NSPSs try to express the highest amount of reduction of effluents that may be achieved by applying the BAT standard. EPA can require the installation of advanced treatment technology in new facilities, but shy away from this requirement in older facilities where it may be economically unreasonable.

Standards of water quality

States establish water quality standards according to uses and criteria for protection. The CWA requires classifying all waters in the state according to use: drinking water supply, fish and wildlife needs, recreation, industrial use, agricultural use, or others.[27] According to EPA, state standards must maintain water as fishable and swimmable wherever possible and not allow water degradation. State criteria for water quality must be based on EPA water quality criteria (50 pollutants, currently). But a state may examine the unique local water body's characteristics and develop its own numerical criteria. Narrative standards for toxic pollutants are not allowed. A *water quality standard* is an assigned number representing a pollutant's contaminant level that cannot be exceeded. For example, arsenic in a stream for trout cannot exceed 0.2 milligrams per liter. Some chemical-specific standards are listed in permits. Each owner or operator obtaining a permit is limited to the amount of contaminated discharge allowed, and cannot exceed the standard set in its permit.

States are required to develop a listing of their "impaired" water bodies under the *toxic hot spots* program.[28] An impaired water body is one where applied technology cannot improve it and water quality standards cannot be met. Point sources of toxic contaminants are identified and *individual control technologies* are applied.

Trading of pollutants in effluents for watersheds

Any facility that can lower its amount of pollution by meeting water quality standards at lower cost can accumulate credits by doing so. These credits can be traded between companies through sale or barter within the same watershed. Traders must meet the technology requirements for their own facility. The trading may be point-to-point source trading, intra-plant trading, pretreatment trading, point-nonpoint source trading, or nonpoint-nonpoint source trading.

Limitations on toxicity

Whole effluent toxicity (WET) limitations require toxicity testing on a permitted facility's effluent. Aquatic species are exposed to one or more concentrations of an effluent in a laboratory to determine the short- and long-term effects of their exposure. Monthly or quarterly toxicity tests may be required after a permit is issued. Any change in the death rate of the tested aquatic species could result in violating the permit. In some WET limitations, *toxicity identification evaluation* (TIE) or *toxicity reduction evaluations* (TRE) may be required. The EPA requires that states coordinate biological assessments with chemical limitation and toxicity tests.

Changing the NPDES permits (variances)

There are only a few ways possible to change the conditions of a permit. Changes are called *variances*. One kind of variance is the *fundamentally different factors* (FDF) variance. The FDF allows a difference from limitations normally set by the new source performance standards (NSPS). This kind of variance cannot be issued to allow changes in water quality limitations.

Factors that could be fundamentally different are:

- The kinds of pollutants in the discharge
- The volume of the discharge
- Non-water-quality environmental impacts of control and treatment of the discharge
- Energy requirements of the treatment technology
- The age, size, land availability, and configuration of the discharger's equipment, facilities, and processes.

Storm water discharges and permits

Storm water runoff (rain water surface runoff, snow melt runoff, or the drainage of either of these) is considered to be a multiple point source discharge of contaminants. Permits are required for this kind of discharge. Storm water discharge from industrial processes and discharges from separate municipal storm sewer systems are controlled by the EPA. Industrial processes can contaminate storm water runoff. Discharges from any point source are connected to industrial activity based on the standard industrial classification system (SIC codes).[29] Processes and activities are places where pollutants can be released into the environment, such as plant yards, material handling sites, refuse sites, shipping and receiving areas, manufacturing buildings, raw material storage areas, and other areas.

There are two kinds of storm water discharge permits—general and individual. An applicant can apply for a NPDES permit by filing a notice of intent to be covered by a *general permit*. Both EPA and some states issue their own versions of general permits. For example, the EPA issued a multi-sector general storm water permit that applied to 11,000 facilities in 29 industrial segments in the unauthorized states and territories.[30] Under this multi-sector permit, programs and facilities that fall within one of the 29 industrial sectors can qualify for a 5-year permit. Approval of the general permit under the multi-sector permit program is based upon an applicant developing and submitting an acceptable, site-specific pollution prevention plan.[31] A facility owner or operator must submit an *individual storm water permit* application if the facility cannot qualify for a general permit. Detailed facility information and quantitative data on discharge sampling during storm events are required.[32]

Storm water management plans and the pollution prevention approach

In order to control the discharge of pollutants from industrial facilities into storm water, careful planning and design decisions are required. A facility operator is expected to develop a storm water management plan that contains *best management practices* (BMPs) in order to avoid pollution. BMPs may be general, industry specific, or site specific. Managing the runoff at industrial facilities is promoted by the EPA and many state environmental agencies.

Heat or thermal discharges

Heat can kill marine life and vegetation. Under the CWA, heat is a pollutant and is regulated according to the limitations of current technology. Some industrial facilities and processes cannot avoid depositing heat into water. Those dischargers are required to develop scientific data that can prove that their discharge of heat will not harm the aquatic system.[33]

Ocean discharges

The National Pollution Discharge Elimination System (NPDES), and the Marine Protection Research and Sanctuaries Act (MPRSA)

NPDES permits are not issued for discharges into the seas, contiguous zones of the seas, or the oceans, unless the applicant complies with special criteria. The marine environment and habitats are a major concern, must be protected, and cannot be degraded by a release of a contaminant or a thermal discharge. There cannot be any changes in ecosystem diversity, productivity, or ecological stability in the discharge area. No threat can be made to human health either from direct exposure to pollutants or from consumption of exposed aquatic organisms. Also, no loss of esthetic, recreational, scientific, or economic value can occur as a result of a discharge. Dumping in the oceans is protected by the Marine Protection Research and Sanctuaries Act (MPRSA). Only the dumping of material dredged off surface water bottoms is allowed, but this activity requires a permit. Under MPRSA, the U.S. Army Corps of Engineers (Corps) can issue permits to transport dredge materials for ocean disposal. More than 140 disposal sites for dredge material are already designated by EPA.[34] Besides the Corps, the Coast Guard regulates ocean dumping and the discharge of sewage from ships.[35]

CWA pretreatment program

This program covers industrial wastes not directly discharged into waters, but into a public sanitary sewer system. None of these kinds of wastes can be discharged into a public sewer without government approval. Industrial users of a *publicly owned treatment works* (POTWs) must obtain permits, orders, or executed contracts from the POTW or the municipality, not the state or EPA. There are general and specific prohibitions; standards, depending on the category of waste; and locally imposed quantity limits on contaminants deposited into POTWs. The general pretreatment program limits do not allow industrial users to introduce any pollutant that might leave the POTW in any condition that could violate any requirement of the NPDES permit. Industrial users cannot discharge a contaminant into a POTW that could cause the POTW to violate its NPDES permit. For example, an industrial user cannot release an excess of any substance that could affect the chemical composition of the POTW's by-product of sewage sludge. There are specific prohibitions against adding any of these pollutants to the POTW:

- explosive or incendiary matter
- matter that is corrosive or damaging to the POTW
- solid or viscous contaminants that could obstruct the flow
- heated matter that could harm an ecosystem
- any contaminant that could cause worker health and safety problems.

Removal credits are given to industrial facilities that discharge wastes into POTWs with contaminant levels lower than levels required if discharged directly into waters. To get the removal credits, an owner or operator of an industrial facility must demonstrate that the best available technology (BAT) is used or achieve the same level of removal of a pollutant as that consistently achieved by the POTW.

Also, local governments can endorse or enact more stringent requirements than the EPA, especially to prevent toxic fumes and to reduce other kinds of air emissions. A pretreatment enforcement program is the responsibility of the local government operating the POTW, but the EPA and the states retain enforcement authority. At any time, a POTW having an approved pretreatment program may make modifications to reflect changing conditions at the POTW.[36]

Nonpoint source discharges

This kind of source is any source that is not a point source discharge.[37] Agricultural runoff is the largest nonpoint source discharge. Nutrients, salts, pesticides, and silt are the more typical nonpoint source pollutants and comprise the largest quantities of pollutants entering our waters. The Nonpoint Source Discharge program depends on state administration. States are required to submit state management programs and timetables to EPA to reduce the amounts of nonpoint source discharges.

CWA and the Coastal Zone Management Program (CZMAP)

Land and water along the coastal shorelines are protected from nonpoint sources of pollution through the CWA and the Coastal Zone Management Program. The CZMAP is explained in Chapter 26. The program is administered by EPA and the National Oceanic and Atmospheric Administration (NOAA).[38] There are 29 coastal states, and each must submit coastal nonpoint pollution control plans to EPA and NOAA. Penalties are awarded and federal grants can be lost if a state does not comply. The EPA provides information and materials to help states manage their shores. Some of this information contains ways to control nonpoint pollution from agriculture, silviculture, urban runoff, marinas, and other sources.

National Estuary Program (NEP)

The National Estuary Program, under the CWA, was created to protect and promote nationally significant bays and estuaries. As one of the major ways to control nonpoint pollution, the NEP requires a Comprehensive Conservation and Management Plan (CCMP). In this plan, industrial facilities' standards, transportation standards, waste management requirements, and enforcement provisions are required. Such a plan (CCMP) usually recommends approaches to correct and prevent problems for estuaries. Currently, there are 28 estuaries included in the NEP.

Dredge and fill permits and the 404 Permit Program

Disposing of dredged or fill material into water is not covered under the NPDES permit program of the CWA. If a point source, such as a bulldozer, plans to push waste material into surface waters, a permit must be obtained from the Corps.[39] The Corps can designate areas for this kind of disposal as a condition for award of the "404 permit." Any land area that may be a wetland requires a 404 permit prior to any discharge of waste materials. This permit must be obtained prior to discharging or placing dredge and fill material; but the permit is not required for dredging operations. Even if dredged materials are redeposited into the wetlands, a 404 permit is required. Violations of the Section 404 permit requirement can result in monetary and criminal penalties.

Input from the community is required by the Corps prior to their award of such a 404 permit. A *Public Interest Review* may be required to help evaluators decide in favor of maintaining a balance between conservation, esthetics, economic benefits to the applicant, historic values, protection of fish or wildlife, flood prevention, water supply and quality, or other factors. EPA guidelines are followed in each Corps review. If any alternative to the release is possible, then no discharge can be approved.[40] Also, no deterioration in the aquatic ecosystem can result from the discharge into the water. In addition, the Corps must obtain certification from the state and consult with EPA and the Fish and Wildlife Service prior to granting the 404 permit.

An applicant desiring to obtain a 404 permit must attempt to do all that is possible to lessen adverse effects from the proposed fill. After wetlands' damage has been reduced to a minimum, even the remaining damage must be minimized. The Corps has tried to avoid the loss of wetlands resulting from its approvals of 404 permits—and subsequent discharges. They have initiated a *no-net-loss policy*: if there is degradation or disappearance of a wetland, that wetland must be restored or new wetlands created.

For any discharge determined by the Corps to have minimal environmental impact, a *nationwide permit* or a *general permit* may be issued. A list of about 36 activities has been devised for nationwide permits. They include backfilling utility lines, bank stabilization, oil and gas structures, hydropower projects, survey activities, minor road crossings, outfall structures, and maintenance. About 13 activities of the nationwide permit are "technically self-executing," but a first contact with the Corps is very important for anyone planning an activity within a wetland area.[41]

Preventing, reporting, and responding to spills into waters

Spills must be prevented under the CWA. No discharges are allowed into any waters. A facility may be required to develop plans and keep records about preventing and responding to spills of oil and hazardous substances. These plans are *Spill Prevention Control and Countermeasure* (SPCC) plans. Some facilities are required to have a *Facility Response Plan*. This plan is quite detailed, must consider a worst case oil spill, and must be approved.[42] The SPCC plan is required if the facility drills, produces, gathers, stores, processes, refines, transfers, distributes, or consumes oil, or might release oil in harmful quantities into water.[43] While it does not have to be submitted to the relevant state or federal agency, the SPCC plan must be filed and available to regulators at all times at the facility, and it must be evaluated once every three years. In the SPCC plan, details are required, such as reports of recent spills and predictions of the direction, flow rate, and the total quantities of oil that might result from a spill. Responsible parties and owner or operator contact persons for the facility must be identified in the SPCC plan.

Oil Pollution Act and Facility Response Plans

Under the Oil Pollution Act (OPA), onshore facilities that are not involved in transportation matters must prepare a Facility Response Plan if they handle, transport, or store oil—or could cause substantial harm to the environment. *Substantial harm* is defined as any discharge into the water, shorelines, or the economic zone around the facility. If a facility does not meet EPA's substantial harm criteria, it must maintain certification that the substantial harm criteria do not apply. This substantial harm is defined for transferring oil over water to or from vessels storing more than 42,000 gallons, or storing oil of at least one million gallons. In the latter case, Facility Response Plans for worst case scenarios must be prepared when any of the following conditions exist:

- If there is no secondary containment for aboveground storage
- If fish and wildlife or other sensitive environmental settings could be harmed
- If a discharge could shut down water purification at a public drinking water intake
- If there had been a reportable spill greater than 10,000 gallons within the past 5 years.

Facility Response Plans must contain these elements:

- Person having authority to implement the plan
- Description of the actions to be taken for spills
- Spill containment plans
- Plans for evacuating the facility
- Methods for immediate communication to federal officials
- Available equipment and personnel to respond to a discharge
- Personnel training plans
- Equipment testing procedures and frequencies.

EPA can require facilities other than substantial harm facilities to prepare and submit a Facility Response Plan. During review of a facility, the EPA considers these factors:

- Method of oil transfer from facility to vehicle or process line
- Site-specific characteristics
- Proximity to water purification plants
- Spill histories
- Oil storage capacities
- Proximity to fish and wildlife environments
- Any other factors.

Under OPA, if a substantial harm facility does not submit a Facility Response Plan, it cannot operate.

Spill notices and responding to spills

The National Response Center must be notified of any harmful quantities of spills under OPA.[44] A harmful quantity is defined as that amount producing a film or sheen on the water, sludge, or emulsion under the surface or shorelines, or a quantity violating the water quality standard. Under the reporting requirements, EPA has designated about 300 hazardous substances with the required reportable quantities. If a spill occurs in a facility holding a NPDES permit, notification may not be required.

Owners or operators of facilities are responsible for penalties and cleanup costs. There may be civil or criminal enforcement or monetary damages. Local and state governments may actively enforce OPA and the CWA, but the federal government more actively enforces both acts.

State enforcement

In order to obtain approval from the EPA to administer the NPDES permit program, a state must provide enforcement equivalent to EPA's. The state enforcement program does not need to be the same as EPA's. It can vary, but authorized states need not provide a mechanism for citizen suits. States only need to allow citizens to intervene. The state must respond to citizen complaints. Even if an authorized state has taken action against a violator, the EPA can still intervene. If the EPA holds that permit violations are widespread within a state, and that the state has not enforced its permits, the EPA must assume responsibility for enforcing the state permits.

Compliance, reports, and enforcement of water regulations

The holders of NPDES permits have to report their compliance or violations to the state agency or EPA/Corps/Coast Guard, etc., on standardized discharge monitoring reports (DMRs). They must describe all discharges and how they exceed permit limitations. Noncompliance must be reported within 24 hours, and any anticipated noncompliance also must be reported. CWA is a *strict liability statute*, meaning that intent is irrelevant and liability is connected to a violation. Whether the cause was negligence or purposeful intent does not matter.

Anyone having an interest that can be affected by the release of contaminants can initiate a civil action. NPDES permit violations, OPA violations, or others can be settled under a consent agreement. There may be penalties, fees and costs, compliance schedules, payment of money to support an environmental activity in the public interest, or other requirements.

Chronology of CWA

1948:	Federal Water Pollution Control Act (FWPCA), 62 Stat. 1155; Pub.L. 845
1952:	FWPCA Amendments, Ch. 927, 66 Stat. 1155
1960:	FWPCA Amendments, Pub. L. 86-624, 74 Stat. 411
1965:	FWPCA Amendments, Pub. L. 89-234, 79 Stat. 903
1972:	FWPCA Amendments, Pub. L. 92-240, 86 Stat. 47
1977:	Clean Water Act (CWA), Pub. L. 95-217, 33 U.S.C. 1251
1981:	CWA Amendments, Pub. L. 97-117, 95 Stat. 1623
1983:	CWA Amendment, 33 U.S.C. Section 1251 (a)(2)
1985:	CWA Amendment, 33 U.S.C. Section 1251 (a)(1)
1987:	CWA Amendments, Pub. L. 100-4, 33 U.S.C. 1254
1990:	CWA Amendments, Pub.L. 101-596, 1, 104 Stat. 3000, 33 U.S.C. 1269
1994:	CWA Amendments, Pub. L. 103-431, 108 Stat. 4396.

CHAPTER 10

Drinking Water

Safe Drinking Water Act (SDWA)

Overview

- The EPA has major responsibilities in administering the SDWA.

- National primary and secondary drinking water standards are developed.

- Maximum contaminant levels are recommended.

- Groundwater is protected, and technologies applied to the purification of groundwater must be proven and field tested.

- State water well protection is ensured through the regulations. Every five years, a list of contaminants that are not regulated but are known to occur in public drinking water systems is published.

- Public notices must be distributed to alert the immediate population about contaminated water.

- Fines may be assessed for violations of the act.

- Waterworks infrastructures may be improved with state revolving funds. These may be partially financed with federal monies.

- A continuing research program identifies groups at risk from exposure to contaminants in drinking water.

- Radon and arsenic in water are targeted.

Background

The Safe Drinking Water Act (SDWA) preceded the Clean Water Act (CWA). National standards for levels of contaminants in drinking water were established, and water wells and sole source aquifers were protected.[45] Under the Superfund, or the Comprehensive Environmental Response, Compensation and Liability Act (CERCLA), the goals for safe water in the SDWA were adopted for contaminated and abandoned hazardous waste sites. The drinking water standards were also adopted for corrective action at waste sites designated for cleanup under the Resource Conservation and Recovery Act (RCRA).[46]

National standards for drinking water are created by the EPA and required to be enforced by the states. These standards ensure uniformity of water quality from municipal drinking water purification plants. In this manner, all states have safe drinking water. The SDWA regulates drinking water by establishing a national primary drinking water standard and setting a secondary drinking water standard. The primary standard regulates contaminants that may cause adverse health effects, with secondary standards advisory only (unenforceable) and limited to protecting the public welfare from bad odor or the unusual appearance of drinking water. A single contaminant might be subject to both a primary and a secondary standard under the SDWA. The act specifies that EPA must propose and promote recommended maximum contaminant levels (RMCLs) and a final primary drinking water standard.[47]

Under the 1986 amendments, the EPA set MCLs for 83 priority contaminants with the intent to add 25 more every three years. Requirements were set for disinfecting and filtration, and other types of treatment; groundwater protection; strengthened enforcement; and required

Exhibit 9: Common sources of drinking water are rivers, streams, lakes, and wells. Since purifying water is costly, regulations attempt to keep water free from contamination prior to its entering the treatment plant. (Photo: author)

monitoring of unregulated contaminants in public water systems. Technical assistance to smaller POTWs with histories of chronic noncompliance is provided.[48] There are hazardous waste injections that must have ground water monitoring. A sole source aquifer demonstration program protects critical ground water supplies and requires assessments of the effectiveness of the demonstration programs. The drinking water standards have established national *primary drinking water regulations*. The RCML, or recommended maximum contaminant level, is now MCLG, or *maximum contaminant level goal*. EPA increased its enforcement powers over public water systems and ground water protection with mandated quick action.

Under the 1996 amendments to the Safe Drinking Water Act, an additional $725 million was added to the drinking-water revolving loan fund.[49] The amendments also included a user right-to-know modification, water source protections, revised requirements for special contaminants (radon, arsenic, and others), a provision for health-effects drinking water research; and state funding for improvements to infrastructure.[50]

Regulating drinking water in public water systems

Only public drinking water systems are covered under the SDWA. By definition, these water systems are piped water to serve the public for human consumption. The system must have 25 or more service connections or must serve at least 25 persons. Public water systems include collection, treatment, storage, and distribution facilities and also applies to any collection or pretreatment storage of water used in connection with that system.

EPA issues minimum contaminant levels (MCLs) that are as close to the minimum contaminant level goal (MCLG) as is feasible. The term *feasible* means using the best technology available for treatment while taking the cost of meeting the MCLG levels into consideration.[51] If a MCL is not feasible, the EPA must promote a national primary drinking water regulation for that contaminant that requires using a treatment technique in lieu of establishing a maximum contaminant level.

According to the EPA's definition, *field tested* means that the technology has been used before without problems, or that laboratory or pilot studies show that the technology could work for those contaminants. The efficiency and economies in removing the contaminants are criteria in selecting alternative technologies. The major factors in setting MCLs (including carcinogens) are the facility itself, and whether the levels or presence of a contaminant can be detected. Large water systems are based on parts-per-billion levels.

Practical Quantification Levels (PQLs) are "the lowest concentration of a contaminant that most laboratories would be able to accurately quantify in a sample of drinking water."[52] The PQLs are reviewed on the basis of acceptable good science. The Science Advisory Board was established under the Environmental Research, Development, and Demonstration Act of 1978[53], prior to proposing MCL goals and the national primary drinking water regulations.[54]

A list of contaminants that are not regulated, but are known to occur in public drinking water systems must be published every five years. Hazardous substances listed under CERCLA must be listed, as well as those pesticides under the Federal Insecticide, Fungicide, and Rodenticide Act (FIFRA). At least five contaminants from the list must be considered for regulation and listing based on the best available public health information and the occurrence database.

In making regulatory decisions, the EPA must use the best available, peer-reviewed science and supporting studies, conducted according to scientific practices and using data collected by acceptable methods. For each regulated contaminant, the populations affected must be addressed by estimating public health risks. When any national primary drinking water regulation includes a MCL, the EPA must develop and apply analyses that will determine the following:

- Health risk reduction benefits likely to occur
- Health risk reduction benefits likely from reductions in multiple contaminants that can be attributed solely to complying with the MCL
- Costs likely to occur from complying with the MCL
- Incremental costs and benefits associated with each alternative MCL considered
- Identification of target populations and subpopulations and the effects of the contaminant on them
- Risks connected to compliance, and risks associated with multiple contaminants
- Uncertainties in the analyses, degree, and nature of the risk, and other factors.[55]

EPA publishes a determination about their decisions on tested contaminants based on costs and benefits when a standard is proposed.[56] Any determinations about contaminants that disinfect or contain byproducts of disinfectants for cryptosporidium also are published. In its determination of monitoring requirements for public water treatment systems, the EPA reviews contaminants and disseminates the information so that other public water treatment systems can make the necessary modifications. Unregulated contaminants must be monitored, and the EPA develops a list of no more than 30 contaminants to be monitored by public water systems and included in the occurrence database.

Variances may be granted for systems that cannot meet an MCL due to the characteristics of the raw water sources available to the system. Exemptions may be granted for not meeting an applicable MCL but only for three years. However, if an unreasonable risk to public health could occur, an exemption cannot be granted.

Water system enforcement

The EPA enforces through judicial actions. A public water system may be given fines per day of violation, but there are no criminal penalties. Owners or operators of (public or private) water systems must give notice to the people they serve if the system fails to comply with an applicable MCL or treatment technique, fails to perform required monitoring or testing, or fails to comply with a prescribed schedule demanded in its granted variance or exemption. Notices of violations are published in periodicals, news releases are issued to the media, and alternative water supplies are arranged for until the violation is corrected. Moreover, if a contaminant level is exceeded, the EPA requires owners or operators to give notice to all persons served.

1996 Amendments to CWA

Under the 1996 Amendments to the CWA, EPA's enforcement duties for violations of drinking water standards were extended. Fines are assessed only after public notices of impure water are given and after public comments are received. Also in the amendments, there are new funding methods to improve compliance and water works' infrastructures, improve water source quality, increase research on the potential adverse health effects of contaminants, and improve system operating procedures.

State Revolving Fund

One billion dollars were authorized for a State Revolving Fund (SRF) to improve drinking water infrastructure. States can receive grants, loans, or letters of credit. To qualify, a state first develops its own program for a water treatment revolving loan fund according to EPA requirements. Each state must have the technical, management, and financial capability to meet the requirements of its program and must already comply with primary drinking water regulations. A needs survey for the state becomes the basis for the grant awards. All amounts deposited into the state's SRF must be used only for loans, loan guarantees, or as sources of reserve and security for leveraged loans.[57] Water systems can only spend the money to help meet national primary drinking water regulations, install water treatment equipment, or further protect health. SRF funds can also be used to alter the structure of a municipal or other interstate agency in the state, purchase insurance for a bond, or as security for revenue or general obligation bonds issued by a state.

The state loan fund may be combined with another revolving fund to avoid administrative costs. Funds cannot be used for monitoring, operating costs, maintenance, or buying land. The SRF sets aside 15 percent of the fund for loan assistance to those water treatment systems serving fewer than 10,000. A state must submit a report to EPA every other year, and the EPA must audit the state loan funds.

To receive a water system grant, a state must prepare and submit a plan that describes the intended use of the SRF funds. The plan has to be developed with citizen participation or presented for public comment before adoption. This plan is an *intended use plan*, describing a yearly list of projects, terms of assistance, size of the communities, criteria for distributing the funds, status of the state loan fund, and the goals for the fund. Annually, a state must publish a list of projects eligible for funds, priorities, and an expected funding schedule. Repayments, with interest, are required for each loan.

Under the SRF, there are provisions for special assistance for *disadvantaged communities* (the area served by a public water system meeting affordability criteria developed by the state). For these communities, a state can forgive interest and principal. *Matching state funds* may total 20 percent of the total amount of the grant. Prepayments by the state must be placed in escrow in advance of the contributions.

Other 1996 amendments

State *ground water protection grants* ensure a coordinated, comprehensive protection of ground water resources. Both innovative protection programs and technical projects must be evaluated for their potential effectiveness in protecting groundwater. Grants cannot exceed 50 percent of costs, and the state must pay the balance.

A *source water assessment program* delineates boundaries of areas where public water systems obtain their drinking water supplies. When a state wishes to permanently modify its contaminant monitoring program, the source water assessment program requires adding a timetable, a statement on the availability of state funds, a list of the contaminants for which monitoring is required, and the origins of the contaminants identified within each delineated area.

Exhibit 10: Ground water is a major source of drinking water. The top of this well has had its valving and piping removed, and the owner neglected to cap the well as required by water regulations. Other wells that use the same ground water can be contaminated.

The *source water petition program* is a quality protection partnership between a state and the community water system. It is a voluntary, incentive-based partnership between the waste system operators, interested persons, and the government. Only those contaminants that are detected at levels above the MCLs are part of the petitions.

Water system capacities

Water capacity is another issue addressed by the CWA. States must prepare *capacity development strategies*. These strategies contain methods and criteria to be used by the states to identify and set priorities for public water systems according to need. Resources are provided to assist public water systems in meeting national primary drinking water regulations. The EPA publishes guidelines to ensure that all new community water systems meet federal standards (national primary drinking water regulations). States must annually compile a list of their community water systems, and their nontransient and noncommunity water systems, that have histories of not complying with provisions of the CWA.

Operators of water systems must be certified. The EPA specifies standards to certify and improve operators. The guidelines consider the current state programs, system complexities, and other factors. Users must receive a *consumer confidence report* on the source of the water being provided, whether regulated contaminants have been detected, the levels of contaminants, information on the systems's compliance with the drinking water regulations, and whether required monitoring is being performed according to EPA requirements. A state is not required to mail consumer confidence reports to communities having fewer than 10,000 persons, but in those cases, the consumers must be informed by newspaper notices.

Contaminant risks to special groups

There is a continuing research program to identify those groups at risk from exposure to contaminants in drinking water. Subjects must include women, children, infants, pregnant women, the elderly, and people with serious illnesses. Research results must be reported to the U.S. Congress. Biomedical research about absorbing, distributing, metabolizing, and eliminating the contaminants from the human body must be developed to provide more accurate health models. EPA is encouraged to study complex mixtures in drinking water to determine the synergism of chemicals (if any), and adverse effects resulting from combinations of chemicals or biological agents. Toxicological studies must be conducted by the EPA to determine exposure levels from disinfectants and disinfecting by-products used in water treatment. Dose-response curves must be developed for pathogens (including cryptosporidium and the Norwalk virus).[58] The Centers for Disease Control and Prevention and the EPA must develop and perform a joint waterborne disease occurrence study. National health care provider training and public education campaigns must be completed to inform the public about waterborne disease and the symptoms caused by infectious agents, such as microbial contaminants.

Current contaminants under EPA consideration for regulation

Radon is present in groundwater in some places and common in the Western U.S. Waterborne radon can affect people who drink this contaminated water or inhale the airborne tap water containing it. Currently, radon is being studied so that EPA can adopt a national MCLG and a national primary drinking water regulation for radon. EPA must also publish guidelines for states to develop their own multimedia radon mitigation program.

Arsenic is a naturally occurring contaminant in groundwater in many places. There is a current standard of 50 ug/l—with indication that high levels of arsenic in drinking water can increase the occurrence internal organ cancers. Because there is controversy over how much arsenic is harmful, new research for risk assessment and risk management for low level exposure to arsenic is required. A number of federal agencies are combining to fund the research on this chemical and private funds have been applied also.

Sulfates also occur naturally in water. The MCL for sulfates is 250 mg/l, based on odor, not health effects. Studies are being performed to assess the dose-response that is harmful to human health. By the year 2001, EPA will decide whether sulfates should be regulated.

Disinfectants and disinfecting by-products are commonly used to chlorinate water. When it is used as a disinfectant, chlorine may combine with other compounds to form chlorinated organic compounds.[59] All of these chlorine by-products and compounds are considered disinfecting by-products.

Underground Injection Control (UIC)

When any liquid that is listed as a hazardous waste is injected into the ground, it is regulated under the Resource Conservation and Recovery Act (RCRA). If hazardous wastes have not been treated according to the best available technology, then in-ground disposal is limited. Most of the wastes are disposed of as wastewater.[60] Since so much of the wastewater is injected underground (especially oil and gas wastes), a lot of regulatory attention is paid to injection. EPA estimates that about 400,000 injection wells are subject to UIC requirements. There are about six times more UIC wells than dischargers of wastewater given permits (under the CWA).[61]

A simple garden hose pushed into the ground is considered a well, under the UIC program. Underground sources of drinking water (USDW) are identified by three criteria:

1. They are aquifers, or portions of them, that supply any drinking water system (but not individual household wells).
2. Contain enough water to supply a drinking water system.
3. Contain less than 10,000 mg/l total dissolved solids (TDS).

The UIC program deters polluting water meant for human consumption. Any situation that could create any contaminated fluid movement into the drinking water source is prohibited. It should be noted that dissolved solids can only be tasted in drinking water at levels beginning around 1,000 mg/l. Moreover, the secondary drinking water standard for total dissolved solids (TDS) is 500 mg/l, and much of the water consumed in the nation has even lower levels."[62]

Classification of wells

There are 5 classes of wells in the UIC program:

Class I for injections of hazardous, industrial, and municipal disposal wastes into the lowermost drinking water formations (issued for 10-year period)

Class II for the oil and gas industry, salt water injection wells, liquid hydrocarbons storage wells, natural gas plant wells, and enhanced recovery wells (issued for life)

Class III for extracting minerals, such as sulfur, uranium, potash, salts (issued for life)

Class IV for hazardous or radioactive waste into a formation within 1/4 mile from an USDW

Class V for any other injection well: geothermal wells, septic system wells from dwellings, drainage wells, air conditioning return flow wells to return aquifer water from a heat pump, cesspools, cooling water return flow wells.

A report is required for Class V wells only if drinking water sources are threatened with contamination.[63] By contrast, Class I wells have closely imposed operating requirements. There are basic construction and operating requirements for Class I, II, and III wells to help eliminate the potential for leaking wells:

* Areas around a well must be analyzed to prevent open holes or abandoned wells from facilitating the movement of fluids from the injection zone to the groundwater.

* Construction, such as cementing and logging, must be performed to prevent fluids from traveling behind the well casing.

* Any leaks of fluid from the well or any boreholes must be stopped immediately.

- Financial capabilities of owners or operators must be verified to be certain that the well can be plugged or repaired if it fails.
- There must be mechanical integrity so that the well does not leak.
- There must be monitoring of injection pressures, along with the volume and rate of fluid injected.
- Records must be kept and fluid injections reported in order to be certain about the size of leaks, if any.

The state usually issues permits and enforces the UIC regulations. Class I hazardous waste injection wells are under the SWDA and RCRA. The land disposal restriction program, under RCRA[64], makes for very strict construction and operating requirements for those wells. Listed and common hazardous wastes are regulated by EPA under a series of recommendations for the best available technology (BAT) standards. In many instances, BAT applications that change liquids to solids or vapors may be approved. The land disposal restriction can be lifted when an owner or operator can prove that no hazardous waste will migrate.

No migration is a common criteria accepted and promoted by EPA. Mathematical models must be submitted, and a 10,000- year containment requirement is on the horizon.

Class II wells are oil and gas injection wells. The major wells are saltwater disposal wells and enhanced recovery injection wells. Often, the water on top of the oil is salty and contains

Exhibit 11: Drilling is performed for new wells of all types and for taking core samples. The drill bit is connected to machinery mounted on a truck. In this photo, cover material and shovel are shown in the steel drum.

high levels of TDS. As an oil field is emptied, water mixes with the oil and may become salty. Finding places to dispose of this water is difficult. Enhanced recovery wells are those where water or other fluids are injected to push the oil upward out of the well. Again, by-products of salt water or other kinds of contaminated water can be expected.

Class III wells are used in mining, and have stringent operating requirements controlled by the states. Class IV wells may not be used for injection, especially injecting above or into an USDW. In these latter wells, waste injections are particularly prone to leaks. Class V wells include a broad range of potential wastes. No permit is needed for a Class V well unless there is a danger that it could leak into an USDW. Gasoline service stations having Class V wells near them have been particular problems. Leaking oil pits, hydraulic lifts, steel drums, or the washing of the oil-containing floors into drainage pipes were endangering many USDWs. EPA has categorized Class V wells into ten general categories:

1. **Beneficial Use Wells**: those wells that improve the quality or flow of aquifers to provide a benefit.

2. **Cesspools**: those wells receiving untreated household wastes.

3. **Drainage Wells**: wells that drain surface and subsurface fluids such as agricultural runoff and storm water.

4. **Experimental Technology Wells**: or any injection well that is not proven to be safe as yet.

5. **Fluid Return Wells**: wells that contain spent fluids used in producing geothermal energy for heating or power, heat pump operations, extracting minerals, or from aquaculture.

6. **Industrial Waste Discharge Wells**: wells to injected with wastewater from industrial, commercial, and service businesses.

7. **In-situ and Solution Mining Wells**: wells that extract oil and gas from underground formations and bring them to the surface.

8. **Mine Back Fill Wells**: wells that bury underground slurries of sand, gravel, cement, mill tailings, refuse, or fly ash.

9. **Septic Systems**: wells composed of septic tanks and fluid distribution systems such as leaching fields for household wastes only.

10. **Sewage Treatment Effluent**: wells used to contain wastes from public or private treatment facilities.

Critical aquifer protection area demonstration program

A critical aquifer protection area is one that contains an aquifer designated as a sole or principal source aquifer. The area has had an areawide ground water quality protection plan approved for it under section 208 of the CWA. The quality of the ground water in this critical protection area must be maintained to protect health, the environment, and ground water resources. When an application is approved for this demonstration program, the EPA can enter into an agreement with an applicant to establish the demonstration program and grant 50 percent of the costs of implementing the plan. The EPA can also reimburse a successful applicant and recipient of an approved plan for up to 50 percent of the applicant's costs for developing the plan.[65]

State wellhead protection programs

A wellhead protection area is a surface and subsurface area that surrounds a water well, or a field containing many wells that supplies water to a public system. This area is one through which contaminants can move and taint the ground water well, or well field.[66] Each state is required to protect its wellhead areas from contaminants. Criteria are developed for acceptable radii of effect, depth of drawdown of the water table, time or rate of travel in different hydrologic conditions, distance from the well or well field, engineering pump tests and comparable data, field reconnaissance, topographic information, and the geography of the formation. The state must develop and submit a program for approval by the EPA that meets these requirements:

- Describes assistance programs for financial assistance, controls, education, training, and demonstration projects
- Determines the wellhead protection area for each wellhead
- Identifies all potential sources of contaminants
- Includes contingency plans for locating and providing alternate drinking water supplies
- Includes consideration of all potential sources of contaminants, within the wellhead area, of a new water well serving a water supply system
- Specifies the duties of state and local government agencies and their water supply systems.

If a state has more than 2,500 active injection wells, the state program must certify to the EPA that drinking water is protected from contamination by oil and brine injection or surface disposal.

Chronology of SDWA

1974:	Safe Drinking Water Act, Pub.L. 93-523, 42 U.S.C. 300
1977:	Safe Drinking Water Act, Pub.L. 95-190
1986:	Safe Drinking Water Act Amendments, Pub. L.104-182
1996:	Safe Drinking Water Act Amendments, Pub. L. 104-182, 42 U.S.C. 300

CHAPTER 11

Oil Spills into Water

Oil Pollution Act (OPA)

Overview

* Oil spills into water bodies have been a serious problem for many years.

* There have been many spills in ship channels, rivers, lakes, bays, and oceans.

* Vessels having single hulls with no oil-leak protection systems are particularly subject to leaks, but double-hulled vessels also can be damaged.

* Double-hulled vessels are mandatory for vessels that transport oil.

* Financial liability for spill cleanups is an important public policy issue.

* Under OPA, those owners or operators responsible for the spills are financially liable.

* Many of these spills are so costly that insurance carriers are needed to ensure payments for cleanups.

* An oil spill liability trust fund is established.

* Federal government holds first-strike responsibilities for cleanups of oil spills.

* U.S. Coast Guard evaluates the manning, training, qualifications, and watch-keeping standards.

* The National Contingency Plan (NCP) and the National Response System require coordination with oil spill responses.

* State authority is dominant in oil spill removal.

* Vessels and facilities must have approved spill response plans.

General

A series of major oil spills provided legislators with good reasons to develop and pass this federal act. The act establishes oil pollution liability and compensation, ensures strict liability for comprehensive damage, controls oil spills into the water from vessels and industrial facilities, describes the authority of the federal government to direct and manage oil spill cleanup operations, and compels vessel and facility operators to file detailed oil spill response plans for private sector clean up and removal. Vessel operators must work actively to prevent oil spills and replace vessels with double-hulled oil tankers and barges. The Act promotes tanker safety requirements in order to prevent spills in water. Compensation by owners or operators is required for spills at sea or in ports.

The federal government holds first-strike responsibility for cleaning up oil spills from vessels and facilities. There are claim procedures, financial responsibility requirements, and provisions about how the Oil Spill Liability Trust Fund is to be used. A vessel (pleasure craft or cargo ship) that spills oil or a dangerous cargo substance is potentially liable for cleanup costs or criminal charges. Double hulls are required for vessels that transport oil only. Both onshore and offshore facilities that are used for exploration, drilling, production, storage, handling,

Exhibit 12: Rocks near the coast are threatening to ships and can injure their hulls. The scenic beauty, marine wildlife, and recreational potential are protected by the regulations from cargo and bilge spills, oil and gas drilling, and accidents from ship transfers. (Photo: author)

transfers, processing, or transport of oil are regulated. Each responsible owner or operator is liable for all removal costs paid by the government. Removal costs under OPA can include the costs incurred by any agency or department of government to avert a release, ensure containment, prevent dispersal, or remove a contaminant. Removal costs also include those incurred for actions taken to protect fish, shellfish, wildlife, property, shorelines, beaches, or other natural resources.

Measuring natural resource damages under OPA

Each government agency develops a plan to repair environmental damages from a spill. The plan must include a provision for paying the costs of repairs. The federal government develops and administers the methods for assessing damages. The National Oceanic and Atmospheric Administration (NOAA) is the federal agency that prepares and publishes regulations on natural resource damage assessments (NRDA). There are three major components of a damage assessment:

1. Preassessment
2. Restoration planning
3. Restoration implementation

In the first component, preassessment, a preliminary determination is made as to whether there has been injury to the environment. The second, restoration planning, identifies a number of restoration alternatives. Methods to evaluate the restoration alternatives are prescribed to help decide on the most appropriate course of action. In the third component, restoration implementation, the responsible parties must complete and fund the cleanup.

Oil Spill Liability Trust Fund

This fund can be used for cleanup costs and damages. Currently, there is a $1 billion limit per incident on government and private uses of this fund. Private uses of the fund can pay for uncompensated removal costs and damages submitted according to claims procedures. Uncompensated claims can draw from this fund.

Provisions of OPA

Any foreign country that issues vessel documents for operating in U.S. waters must have U.S. Coast Guard evaluation of the manning, training, qualifications, and watch-keeping standards before those vessels may enter U.S. waters. This provision insures that the other country's standards are equivalent to those of the United States or international standards. The Coast Guard conducts periodic reviews of each country's manning standards and performs post-casualty reviews of any spills for which the country might be responsible. The Coast Guard also formulates many standards for navigation, cargo handling, and maintenance of tank vessels. Officers and crew members are restricted to working no more than 15 hours in any 24-hour period and no more than 36 hours in any 72-hour period.

Marine casualty reports of significant harm to the environment are required to be submitted to the U.S. Coast Guard. Tankers weighing over 1,600 gross tons must have a licensed master or mate on the bridge in addition to the pilot. In certain waters in the Northwest, single-hulled tankers are required to be escorted by two tugboats.[67] Non-United States and non-Canadian flag vessels of any type (not just tankers) must retain a Canadian or United States pilot on the Great Lakes.

The Act specifies thickness of hull plates for particular types of vessels and establishes minimum standards for overfill, tank level, and pressure-monitoring devices. Radio equipment is regulated. Double hulls are specified for tank vessels, and a phaseout schedule for single-hulled tankers runs until the year 2015. Under the phaseout, the older and larger vessels are retired first. If a vessel is newly constructed and weighs less than 5,000 tons, it must be built with a double-containment system that is determined by the Coast Guard to be as effective as a double hull. All single-hulled tank vessels are required to have written bridge procedures, training for sailors, ship charts that contain enhanced shore and bottom surveys, on-board cargo and mooring system surveys, working auto pilot alarm systems, completed maneuvering tests, and calculated keel clearances. Notice must be given to the harbormaster or the U.S. Coast Guard prior to entering ports.

The Department of Transportation is authorized to make loan guarantees to construct replacement vessels or reconstruct existing vessels according to Coast Guard criteria. The OPA oil spill response system relies on private resources to minimize or remove spills. Immunity from spill liability is given to those helping, rendering care, giving assistance or advice in response to a spill. Federal authorities must remove or insure removal of a discharge and prevent the substantial threat from a discharge. Spills or threats in waters or other places where natural resources are affected are also under federal removal authority.

National Contingency Plan (NCP) and the National Response System

The National Contingency Plan and the National Response System require that any cleanups of oil spills be coordinated with the NCP. Even though there is federal dominance in directing or initiating oil spill responses, state authority presides over significant aspects of oil spill removal. The NCP is placed under the CWA, which describes methods for containing, dispersing, and removing oil and hazardous substances. The NCP assigns duties to various federal departments and agencies and other levels of government and establishes Coast Guard response teams. A national surveillance and notice system provides warnings of spills, threats of spills, and a national coordination center is established. The NCP, which must protect fish and wildlife, requires that federal and state officials work together to use dispersants and other chemicals and calculate appropriate amounts and use of chemicals. The National Planning and Response System, under the CWA, establishes a multilevel governmental hierarchy to respond to spills, and it creates the National Response Unit, Coast Guard Strike Teams, Coast Guard District Response Groups, Area Committees, Area Contingency Plans, and vessel and facility response plans.

Local Area Committees are composed of federal, state, and local agencies which prepare contingency plans for worst-case discharges from a source. These plans are federally reviewed and approved. The plans are to be integrated with the procedures of the National Response System, other area plans, and vessel and facility response plans. Area plans describe and list all available equipment and personnel available.

Vessel and facility response plans

Owners and operators of tank vessels and facilities must prepare response plans to remove any oil releases into waters. Their plans must be coordinated and consistent with the NCPs and Area Contingency Plans. The person in charge of initiating and ordering spill removals must be identified. The vessel or facility response plans must be periodically updated, and they must describe training, equipment testing, unannounced drills, and response actions by personnel to decrease or prevent discharges. A vessel response plan must contain these provisions to be approved by the Coast Guard:

- Discharge notices and procedures
- Drills and training described in detail
- Private finances available to respond to a worst case discharge
- Responsible individual as well as an alternate
- Worst-case discharge quantities

There are two different planning standards: one for oil cargo vessels and the other for oil as a secondary cargo on a vessel. A response must be initiated within two hours of discovering a spill, and equipment and manpower must be in place within 12 hours in high-volume port areas; within 24 hours in river, inland, near shore and offshore areas; and within 24 hours plus travel time for spills occurring on the open seas more than 50 miles from shore. Tier 1 resources must arrive at the scene within 12 hours in high volume port areas or within 24 hours in other areas. Tier 2 and 3 resources must be capable of arriving within 24-hour increments thereafter.

Vessels that are 400 feet or more in length must be able to contain and remove on-deck cargo spills of at least 12 barrels. Those vessels under 400 feet must be able to remove at least 7 barrels. Inland oil barges have to be able to handle an on-deck spill of at least one barrel, and vessels carrying oil as secondary cargo must be able to handle a spill of one-half barrel.

For facilities, the regulations vary. If more than 250 barrels of oil are transferred over water, owners or operators must develop an approved response plan. The factors determining which facilities must submit a plan are as follows:

- type of facility
- storage capacity and material stored
- number of tanks, their age, and secondary containment
- proximity to navigable waters and public drinking water supplies
- proximity to sensitive environmental areas
- spill history
- likelihood of natural disasters
- number of annual tank barge or tank vessel transfers
- type or quantity of petroleum product transferred each year
- multiple transfer ability
- any other risk factors

Methods for containing and cleaning a worst-case discharge must be described, along with the methods for handling the loss of the entire facility or tank. Onshore pipelines must be designed for worst-case discharges and their design and engineering materials approved.

Chronology of OPA

1990:	Oil Pollution Act, 33 U.S.C 2701-2761
1995:	Oil Pollution Act Amendments, Pub. L. 104-55, 1, 109 Stat. 546, 33 U.S.C 2704-2716

CHAPTER 12

Ocean Dumping

Marine Protection, Research, and Sanctuaries Act (MPRSA)

Overview

+ MPRSA prohibits ocean dumping of material that can endanger human health or marine animals and their environment.

+ Dumping of industrial waste or sewage sludge is not allowed.

+ Most dumping today consists of dredged material—sediments removed from water bottoms to maintain navigation channels.

+ Permits must be issued prior to ocean dumping.

+ Decisions on permits are made by the U.S. Army Corps of Engineers, using EPA criteria.

+ EPA recommends the disposal sites for use under the permits.

Purpose and programs

Ocean dumping is regulated beyond three miles from shore. Transporting wastes to be dumped into the ocean is prohibited. MPRSA protects the marine environment, its ecology, and its economic future.[68] The common name of this act is the Ocean Dumping Act. The act regulates the dumping of waste into the ocean, promotes and maintains research programs, and requires the designation and regulation of marine sanctuaries. Wastes and other materials that cannot be dumped include the following materials:

- biological and laboratory wastes
- excavation debris
- chemicals
- warfare agents
- industrial, municipal, agricultural, and other wastes
- wrecked or discarded equipment
- rocks and sand
- sewage sludge
- munitions

Sewage from vessels or oil is not included, and disposal by pipes is covered under other federal regulations.[69]

For ocean dumping to be approved, owners or operators must apply for a permit issued by the EPA or the U.S. Army Corps of Engineers. In order to keep ship channels and river beds at the appropriate depth, dredging of the bottoms must be performed regularly. Disposing of such material is permitted at sea sites designated by the EPA.[70] Other fed-

Exhibit 13: Ocean wave action pulls a shoreline discharge of contaminants (dark area in right foreground) into the deeper waters. A large area can be contaminated through diffusion of concentrated chemical substances. (Photo: author)

eral agencies must coordinate places of dumping with the EPA. The U.S. Department of Commerce is responsible for designating National Marine Sanctuaries after consultation with interested federal, state, and local agencies. Sanctuaries can be located anywhere in the marine environments of the Great Lakes, ocean and coastal waters, bays, estuaries, or other submerged lands.[71]

Permits required

The EPA can issue permits for ocean dumping (from sea vessels or aircraft) after a few procedures are followed. Notice must be given and a public hearing held. Criteria for awarding of the permit include these requirements:

- The marine environment, ecological systems, economic potential, human health, welfare will not be endangered.
- There must be a need for the proposed dumping.
- The effects cannot be harmful to fisheries, shellfish, wildlife, shorelines, or beaches.
- Marine ecosystems will not be harmed.
- Species and population dynamics will not be harmed.
- There will be little effect from dumping the volumes and concentrations of the materials.
- The locations and methods of disposal must be considered, as well as the land disposal alternatives.[72]

There are different permit categories, sites may be specified, and time periods and sites may be restricted in the permits. Dredge material disposal sites must have site management plans containing a baseline assessment of conditions at the site, monitoring, special conditions or practices, specified quantities of materials to be disposed of, assurance of biodegradability of the waste, and anticipated use of the site over the long term.

Sewage sludge and industrial wastes

The dumping into the ocean of industrial wastes or sewage sludge may be allowed in emergencies. The EPA must determine that there are no alternatives, that there does exist an emergency requiring the dumping of the waste, and that dumping it elsewhere poses an unacceptable risk to human health.[73]

Radioactive material

The dumping of radioactive material may be permitted with approval of Congress after the applicant submits an acceptable Radioactive Material Disposal Impact Assessment. This assessment includes details about the containers to be disposed of, the number of containers to be dumped, structural diagrams of each container, the number of curies in each container, and the exposure levels, in rems, on the inside and outside of each container, along with many other requirements.

New York Bight Apex

In the waters of the Atlantic Ocean, about 18 miles from Long Island, are two restricted dumping areas, known as the New York Bight and the 106-Mile Ocean Waste Dump Site. No one who had not been approved prior to earlier court orders may apply for a permit to dump in these areas. Formerly, municipal sludge had been approved for ocean dumping.

Enforcement

Fees must be paid to obtain the dumping permit. Additionally, an agreement to comply with the terms of the permit must be signed. An enforcement agreement includes a plan negotiated by the owner or operator that, if adhered to by that company official, will result in the phaseout of ocean dumping and the transporting of wastes for ocean dumping. Each state that is a party to a compliance or enforcement agreement must establish a separate Clean Oceans Fund for deposit of all fees and penalties connected with ocean dumping permits and violations. The Coast Guard must perform constant surveillance to deter ocean dumping.[74] Annual reports on ocean dumping are to be made to Congress by the EPA.

Research and science

The U.S. Department of Commerce (DOC), in coordination with the U.S. Coast Guard, must maintain a continuing program of monitoring and research on the effects of the dumping of material into ocean and coastal waters (or the Great Lakes). The long-range effects of pollution, overfishing, and man-induced changes to the ocean ecosystem must be addressed.[75] Regional management plans are to be examined to ensure proper regulation of the disposal of waste materials. Sewage disposal in the New York Metropolitan Area which is related to landfilling, incineration, ocean dumping, or recycling must be reported to Congress.

Chronology of MPRSA

1972:	Marine Protection, Research, and Sanctuaries Act, 33 U.S.C. 1401- 1445; 16 U.S.C.1431, 33 U.S.C. 1271
1988:	MPRSA Amendments, Pub.L. 100-688, Title I, 1001, 102 Stat. 4139. Also named Ocean Dumping Act

Waste
and
Tanks

CHAPTER 13

Solid Waste

Solid Waste Disposal Act (SWDA)

Overview

- SWDA contains provisions for solid and industrial nonhazardous and hazardous wastes.

- The Act includes regulations for state or regional solid waste plans, research and demonstration programs, underground storage tanks, and medical waste tracking.

- Solid and hazardous waste differences are defined.

- Some solid wastes are not hazardous, but it is difficult to predict if they can remain harmless.

- Solid wastes can transform into hazardous wastes, under certain conditions.

- Federal policies promote safety through attempts at long-term conversion from landfills and dumps to other methods of treatment, storage, and disposal.

- Recycling and reusing are methods that can reduce the need for space in land waste storage.

- Definitions of many waste terms are provided.

- The relationship among waste acts is explained.

- Small town environmental planning for solid wastes is a program to help cities of less than 2,500 comply with the federal regulations.

Waste and the environment

Many believe that household wastes are not harmful nor can they create any environmental problems other than spreading disease from insects, rodents, or birds feeding on that waste. In the past, to stop the potential for human and animal infections, many communities filled over their daily waste deposits with dirt. Thus, the land areas used for this dumping were called landfills. The dirt covering supposedly made them sanitary by shielding the waste from the insects and animals; therefore, the term *sanitary landfill* became common. For many decades, most communities have disposed of household wastes in sanitary landfills. So the areas where trucks dump out their collected waste materials are called variously dumps, landfills, or sanitary landfills that are filled with intermittent layers of waste and earth cover.

But household waste is only one form of solid waste. The other forms are defined by the Solid Waste Disposal Act (SWDA):

> The term *solid waste* means any garbage, refuse, sludge from a waste treatment plant, water supply treatment plant, or air pollution control facility and other discarded material, including solid, liquid, semisolid, or contained gaseous material resulting from industrial, commercial, mining, and agricultural operations, and from community activities....[1]

Solid waste becomes the general term for all kinds of waste—liquid and solid—and the term, itself, does not indicate whether the waste is hazardous to human health or the environment. As the term is used in the federal regulations, household and solid industrial waste are considered benign and are regulated accordingly. However, some solid waste might be hazardous waste, or become hazardous over time. The chemical composition of a benign solid waste can change, or a waste could mix with another to become harmful. Since there are so many kinds, random mixtures, and consistencies of waste requiring different treatment, storage, or disposal methods, the federal regulations provide ways to handle the many kinds of wastes under different kinds of conditions. Under the SWDA-RCRA provisions, no clear distinction can be made between treatment, storage, and disposal of benign wastes as opposed to hazardous wastes. While the regulations try to make the distinction, they are not clear. Thankfully, some state regulations have clarified these differences in support of the intentions of SWDA-RCRA.

Exhibit 14: Discarded materials, or wastes, are dumped in a landfill by the truck (left-center). The dark areas of wastes are hazardous, and the lighter soil will be used to cover those wastes. Strict operational requirements are specified in waste handlers' permits.

Municipal and private solid waste storage areas (landfills) are final resting places for household waste. Even though some household waste may be hazardous, the landfills are operated as if the wastes are not hazardous but might become so. In some parts of the United States, there are few land areas remaining that are geographically suitable for landfills. Also, residential and other land uses have consumed many thousands of acres to accommodate housing needs, leaving the least suitable lands for land-based waste storage areas. For these reasons, and because of the questionable long-term safety of landfills, the EPA promotes alternative methods for treating, storing, and disposing of solid waste.

Solid waste handling and disposal

There are different requirements for treating, storing, and disposing of solid and other kinds of waste in the SWDA-RCRA. The programs vary, and include specific provisions for municipal solids (landfills and dumps), hazardous solids and liquids, medical wastes, and underground storage tanks. If a waste storage site is abandoned and leaks hazardous substances, then it may be subject to government cleanup and subsequent prosecution of responsible parties.[2] Not only are planning and management methods suggested to avoid future leaks, but research and demonstration projects are promoted as a means to find better ways to do things. States are guided to develop statewide and regional waste plans and given both technical advice and grant assistance.

Waste policies and programs

Each program within the solid waste regulations targets an expressed federal policy. For example, land is recognized to be too valuable to be polluted by discarded waste. Dangers can occur if solid and hazardous wastes are improperly disposed of on the land. Open dumping without cover and earth linings harms health and pollutes drinking water and the air. Hazardous waste must be managed properly to suppress the risks. Safe, long-term containment of wastes on the land must be assured. Storage of waste on the land must be minimized (because the more land area consumed, the greater the chance of soil or water contamination and the creation of dead zones). Hazardous wastes should not rely on permanent land storage. New and innovative methods of waste disposal need to be developed in response to the lack of suitable storage places throughout the United States. Additionally, the government recognizes that millions of tons of usable material are needlessly buried annually when the materials could be used for other purposes. Solid waste is a potential source of fuel, oil, or gas that can be converted into energy in support of our national policy to promote alternative energy sources.

The U.S. Environmental Protection Agency (EPA) is the major agency responsible for managing and controlling wastes. EPA develops rules

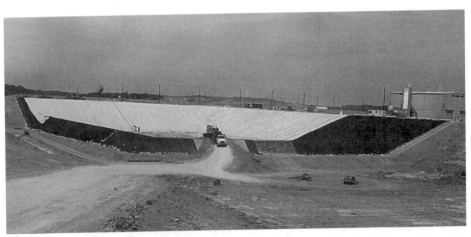

Exhibit 15: A top layer of soil has been graded to receive the next load of wastes in a large landfill. Note the sloping of the earth on all sides as a method of waste containment. Under this landfill lies a protective membrane (impermeable layer) and a pipe system to carry away any methane or other gases that might collect.

and programs to meet the intent of Congress. The agency promotes partnerships among all levels of government. (Some waste programs are delegated downward to state and local governments.) Furthermore, the EPA coordinates with other federal agencies such as the Departments of Energy, Transportation, Commerce, Navy, and Coast Guard through an Interagency Coordinating Committee. Broadly summarized, the EPA, through the SWDA-RCRA regulations, provides the framework to direct both technical and financial help to state and local governments for waste disposal planning, defining the differences between benign and hazardous wastes, and improving methods of collecting, treating, and disposing of wastes.

Waste management, recycling, or reusing wastes

Recycling and reuse of solid wastes are promoted by SWDA. If different processes can be used that can recover usable materials, a manufacturing operation should adopt it. Waste management is the planning, recycling, and reuse of wastes and the use of innovative technologies for processing wastes. For these programs, the goal is to reduce or eliminate, wherever possible, hazardous waste at its source. To reach this goal, a national research and development program targets waste management and conservation, improved organizational productivity, and better transport, recovery, treatment, storage, and disposal methods. When there are no other options and waste must be produced, that waste must be treated, stored, or disposed of to minimize danger to the environment.[3]

Terms

The federal regulations concerning solid waste use some terms that need definition:

Disposal is the discharge, deposit, dumping, injection, spilling, leaking, or placing of solid, liquid, or hazardous waste into the land, water, or other media.

Hazardous waste means a liquid, solid waste, or combination of solid and liquid waste that, due to its quantity, concentration, or chemical, physical, or infectious characteristics, can harm humans. Waste that may present hazards to health when improperly treated, stored, transported, or disposed is hazardous waste.[4]

Hazardous waste management is the control (using set procedures) of the collecting, separating at the source, or transporting, treating, storing, disposing, processing, or recovering of hazardous waste.

An *open dump* is one that is not a sanitary landfill and one that is not operating under a government permit for disposing of hazardous waste.

Resource recovery is the extraction of materials or energy from solid waste.

Sludge is solid, liquid, or semisolid waste generated from a wastewater, water supply, or air pollution facility.[5]

Exceptions

Some definitions in the regulations do not follow logically. For example, there are exceptions in the regulations that should be noted. Some of the exceptions are these:

- ❖ household wastes
- ❖ agricultural wastes used as fertilizer
- ❖ mining spoils returned to the mine
- ❖ utility wastes from coal combustion
- ❖ oil and gas exploration drilling waste
- ❖ ores, coal, and other extracted minerals
- ❖ cement kiln dust
- ❖ arsenic-treated wood wastes
- ❖ chromium bearing wastes
- ❖ certain petroleum-contaminated debris and media

Hazardous waste lists

Lists of hazardous wastes are developed and numbers assigned to each waste. One list contains general sources. Another contains specific sources of waste. Yet another has commercial chemical products, such as residues, containers, and other items that must be treated as hazardous wastes when discarded. Hazardous wastes not mentioned on any of these three lists (general, specific, or commercial chemical products) that are *ignitable, corrosive, reactive,* or *toxic* are also regulated.

Relationship among waste acts

As discussed in this chapter, there is a fine line between handling solid wastes as benign and considering them hazardous wastes. Given certain conditions, their chemical and biological composition can change. The Solid Waste Disposal Act (SWDA) had been amended with many new provisions that subtly adjust to this potential to shift classification, such as a rename of the act to the Resource Conservation and Recovery Act (RCRA)—stressing the handling of hazardous wastes in innovative ways. SWDA, with its RCRA Amendments, provides the protective framework for managing household and industrial solid and liquid wastes, hazardous wastes, medical wastes, and leaking sites and facilities. Under the RCRA amendments to the SWDA, the treatment, storage, and disposal of wastes are controlled to reduce wastes at their sources, promote high technology treatment, and designate safe methods to store those wastes. RCRA applies to all treatment, storage, and disposal (TSD) facilities. To complement RCRA, leaking, abandoned, and inactive waste sites of questionable ownership are protected under the Comprehensive Environmental Response, Compensation, and Liability Act (CERCLA), also known as Superfund.[6]

Exhibit 16: Landfills are constructed according to careful engineering practices and dug to various depths. A synthetic fabric liner is laid completely under the area to be filled. Each joint is properly sealed to prevent leaks. To further protect from leaks, clay cover may be placed over the liner, as shown.

If there is combined storage of industrial solid waste or household waste with hazardous waste, owners or operators of some landfills are required to comply with the provisions of the hazardous waste regulations. SWDA-RCRA imposes a "cradle-to-grave" system for the EPA and the states to work together to identify hazardous wastes and their constituents; identify sites and facilities; and notify the generators of waste, waste transporters, and owners and operators of TSD facilities (or sites) that they must comply with the federal regulations. Each actor within this system—that is, the generators, truckers, and owners/operators of sites and facilities—must obtain permits for which they help set the standards. Also, these actors are subject to inspections and enforcement, if necessary.[7]

Small town environmental planning

The SWDA contains a program to assist small communities in planning and financing new and improved facilities needed for environmental protection. Compliance with federal environmental laws has been difficult for small towns (less than 2,500 population). In recognizing this problem, the Small Town Environmental Planning program was developed. New ways to improve working with the EPA are defined, including the potential to revise the regulations (or develop and implement new ones) to more easily comply. All small town environmental planning must promote regional waste treatment and regional infrastructure systems. Additionally, the EPA must notify all small communities about applicable federal programs through an Office of the Small Town Ombudsman. Multimedia permits are to be examined that could benefit small towns.[8]

Chronology of SWDA

1965: Solid Waste Disposal Act

1970: SWDA certain sections amended as the "National Materials Policy Act of 1970," Pub. L. 91-512

1976: SWDA certain sections amended as "Resource Recovery and Conservation Act of 1976," RCRA Amendments, Pub. L. 94-580

1980: SWDA Amendments to the Solid Waste Disposal Act, Pub. L. 96-482, 42 U.S.C. 6901

1984: SWDA amended entirely as the Resource Conservation and Recovery Act (RCRA), 42 U.S.C. 6901, Subtitle D amended by 42 U.S.C. 6941-6949a

1984: Harzardous and Solid Waste Amendments, Pub. L. 98-616, 42 U.S.C. 6917 et seq

1991: Federal Agency Recycling and the Council on Federal Recycling and Procurement Policy, Executive Order 12780

1992: Federal Facility Compliance Act, Pub.L. 102-386, 106 Stat. 1505

1993: Federal Acquisition, Recycling, and Waste Prevention, Executive Order 12873

1996: Land Disposal Program Flexibility Act, Pub. L. 104-119, 1, 110 Stat. 830

CHAPTER 14

Hazardous Waste

Resource Conservation and Recovery Act (RCRA)

Overview

* Relationships between household and industrial solid wastes (nonhazardous) and hazardous wastes are discussed in the previous chapter.

* EPA lists hazardous wastes according to toxicity, persistence, degradability, potential for accumulating in human tissues, flammability, corrosiveness, and other hazardous characteristics.

* Methods of treating, storing, and disposing of wastes are discussed.

* Medical wastes are hazardous wastes having special provisions and requirements.

* Waste minimization (planning, reusing, and recycling) is preferred to increasing the land areas needed to permanently store waste.

* Truckers who haul hazardous waste are regulated by both the EPA and DOT.

* Liquid hazardous wastes must be placed in containers prior to disposing of them in landfills.

* Permits are required for owners or operators who generate or handle hazardous solid or liquid wastes.

* Permits are required for hazardous waste research, development, and demonstration.

* Compliance orders can be issued to enforce the regulations in the act, and civil and criminal penalties can be assessed to owners and operators for violations.

* State and regional solid waste disposal plans must be submitted to EPA.

* Demonstration facilities and projects are promoted.

Programs and requirements

Those persons generating and transporting waste, and owners and operators of treatment, storage, and disposal (tsd) facilities are regulated under SWDA-RCRA.[9] This act prohibits the careless handling or permanent storage of hazardous wastes. It only applies to companies or individuals generating over 275 tons (550,000 pounds) of hazardous waste per year.

Hazardous wastes must be reduced in quantity or volume at their sources, treated with high technology equipment, or securely contained in land disposal areas to minimize present and future risks to the population. In order to meet the act's expectations, there are provisions for each of the following tasks:

- properly storing and managing hazardous wastes
- developing state and regional solid waste plans
- managing resource and recovery
- handling federal responsibilities
- meeting requirements for research, development, demonstration, and information dissemination
- regulating underground storage tanks
- establishing a medical waste tracking program

Owners and operators of TSD facilities have to comply with performance standards, adhere to monitoring requirements, install air emission controls, and be prepared to perform corrective actions. Land disposal is prohibited unless the hazardous wastes are treated. RCRA permits are issued that specify the operating conditions for each site or facility.

A state can administer the RCRA program as long as it meets the conditions established by the EPA. One condition is that the state must administer and enforce a program that is consistent with the federal program. Methods must be adopted to compile an inventory of all hazardous waste sites in each state.

It is not just industries and facilities with large waste volumes that are regulated. EPA regulates about 200,000 companies producing less than 1,000 kilograms per month. USTs containing petroleum or other hazardous substances are regulated, and landfills containing liquid and other hazardous wastes are regulated. Every industry and business producing hazardous waste is regulated under RCRA. Grants for tire shredders are provided as a way to reduce the problems of storing whole tires, which become breeding places for insects and vermin. Also, whole tires take up more room in permanent storage. Tire pieces have greater potential for reuse.

Annually, the SWDA requires that the EPA transmit to the President and Congress a report containing all activities of the past year. It must include an explanation of how the EPA met the objectives of the environmental regulations, opinions about EPA effectiveness, descriptions of outstanding solid waste problems, and EPA's plans for the next year for solid waste activities.[10]

Identifying and listing wastes

The EPA has the responsibility to identify and list hazardous wastes according to toxicity, persistence, degradability, potential for accumulating in human tissues, flammability, corrosiveness, and other hazardous characteristics. Most hazardous wastes fall into one or more of the categories shown in the list below. Note that the list is a dynamic one, and there are regular additions.

Requirements, restrictions, and controlling wastes

Hazardous wastes that are either produced, stored, disposed of, or treated at a facility are subject to a number of requirements. The facility must have a permit that describes its operating restrictions. Some

Categories of Hazardous Waste

bottom ash waste	flue gas emission waste from burning fossil fuels
bromacil	fly ash waste
carbamates	halogenated dioxins
cement kiln dust	halogenated-dibenzofurans
chlorinated aliphatics	inorganic chemical industry wastes
chlorinated aromatics	linuron
chlorinated dioxins	lithium batteries
chlorinated-dibenzofurans	ore and mineral processing waste
coal slurry pipeline effluent	organo-bromines
coke by-products	paint production wastes
dimethyl hydrazine	refining wastes
dioxin	slag waste
drilling fluids	solvents
dyes and pigments	toluene diisocyanate (TDI)

of them may be unique to that facility alone. No open dumping of solid or hazardous waste is allowed, unless it is dumped into a sanitary landfill. Every facility must maintain accurate records. Any containers used for hazardous waste must be designed and labeled to safely contain the material. Manifests must state the chemical composition of those wastes, and permits must be obtained for persons working with them. Summaries of the total quantities of wastes

Exhibit 17: Hazardous waste landfills may be constructed differently depending on the types of waste to be contained. In this landfill, composite liner material is required for safe storage.

generated per year must be developed and maintained by the EPA for every facility that is issued a permit.

In order to reduce the total amount of hazardous wastes generated, each facility owner or operator must develop a method to treat, store, or dispose of their wastes in ways that will reduce the amount of wastes. (This reduction effort is commonly called *waste minimization.*)

Transporters of hazardous waste must adhere to standards developed by both the EPA and the DOT. Records and manifests must be kept. Wastes need to be labeled. Owners or operations of treatment, storage, and disposal facilities must meet these responsibilities:

- report
- monitor and inspect
- use safe methods approved by the EPA
- design, locate, and construct facilities after a permit is secured
- operate according to safety requirements
- develop contingency plans for emergencies
- maintain the financial ability to perform emergency repairs

Hazardous waste may not be placed in a salt dome formation, salt bed formation, underground mine, or cave if it is determined to be unsafe or threatening to the environment.

Liquid hazardous waste may not be poured onto landfills. If disposed of in a landfill, liquid hazardous waste must be placed in containers. Solvents and dioxins also require containers and may not be injected underground. Land disposal of hazardous waste is defined as the placement of waste in a landfill, surface impoundment, waste pile, injection well, land treatment facility, salt dome formation, salt bed formation, or underground mine or cave.[11] Land disposal of hazardous waste is prohibited due to the long-term uncertainties of almost any disposal technique. Air emissions are controlled at all hazardous waste TSD facilities, such as open tanks, surface impoundments, and landfills. All hazardous waste landfills require double liners prior to receiving any deposits. Ground water must be monitored around the impoundments, waste piles, land treatment units, or landfills.

Domestic sewage transport through a sewer system to a publicly owned treatment works requires certain controls. Wastewater lagoons are regulated, as are landfills and surface impoundments. The potential pathways of human exposure to hazardous wastes or their constituents from releases and the potential magnitude and nature of the human exposure make constant vigilance imperative.

Permits for hazardous wastes

In order to enforce the environmental regulations, permits are issued by the EPA or a state. An owner or operator must apply for a permit, giving estimates of quantities and concentrations of any hazardous waste identified or listed by the EPA. The site intended for the waste disposal must be described *completely* to substantiate its ability to safely contain them. The EPA reviews the permit application for compliance with its criteria and issues the permit accordingly. If a state has an EPA-authorized RCRA hazardous waste program, that state may handle permit application reviews and approve or reject the permit applications. As a condition for approving a facility permit, the generator of hazardous waste must certify annually that there is a program in place to reduce the volume and toxicity of the waste to an economically practical level. The TSD method at that facility must minimize the threats to health and the environment. Any enforcement authority of a state having an approved hazardous waste program has the same force and effect as that of the EPA.

Exhibit 18: A core sample of potentially hazardous material (from 15 to 17 feet below grade) is being inspected during this EPA facility visit.

Permits for research, development, and demonstration

Permits can be issued for research, development, and demonstration. A hazardous waste treatment facility proposing to use innovative and experimental hazardous waste treatment technology or processes may be issued a permit for one year. Criteria are stated in the permit application as to how the applicant will determine the efficacy and performance capabilities of the process or technology in that year. Any EPA protections may be added as conditions for the permit.[12]

Facility access and entry

Inspectors from the EPA or state environmental protection agency must have access to a permitted facility at reasonable times. These inspectors have powers to enforce environmental regulations and can inspect and obtain samples, review records, and make all records, reports, or other information available to the public.

Enforcement of the SWDA

EPA can issue a *compliance order* that assesses a civil penalty for any past or current violation. Compliance is required immediately, within a specified time period, or a civil action may be initiated in a U.S. district court. Any of these compliance orders can include suspension or revocation of an operating permit. The EPA or a state can conduct a *public hearing* and issue subpoenas for the attendance and testimony of witnesses. If a violator fails to make corrections within the specified time, the EPA can assess a *monetary penalty*. Also, *criminal penalties* can be imposed in any of these situations:

- hazardous waste is transported without a permit
- hazardous waste is treated, stored, or disposed of without a permit
- conditions of the permit are knowingly violated
- material information is knowingly omitted from a permit application
- false statements are made in a permit application
- wastes are mishandled
- wastes are transported without a manifest
- wastes are exported
- used oil is not identified or listed as a hazardous waste

Hazardous waste site inventory

There are two inventory programs: state and federal site inventories. Each EPA-approved state must maintain a continuing program to compile and publish an inventory that describes the location of each site

Exhibit 19: A portion of the core sample has visible contamination, as indicated by the circled dark areas.

where hazardous waste has been stored or disposed of. The inventory must include the following information:

- location
- amount, nature, and toxicity of the waste
- name and address of the owners of each site
- techniques of waste treatment or disposal used at each site
- current site status.[13]

The EPA may carry out the inventory program in a nonapproved state.

State and regional solid waste plans

Federal environmental regulations require each state to plan for the disposal of solid waste. Plans must include recovering energy and materials and conserving resources. Both funds and technical advice are available to state and regional authorities for comprehensive planning. Guidelines for comprehensive solid waste plans suggest these responsibilities:

- analyze regional geology, hydrology, climate and other factors to protect ground and surface waters from leachate contamination and surface runoff
- protect air quality
- improve methods of collecting, storing, processing, and disposing of wastes
- enforce the closing or upgrading open dumps
- provide population density, distribution, and growth information
- describe type and location of transportation
- develop a profile of industries
- list the composition and amounts of waste
- examine political, economic, organizational, financial, and management problems that could affect solid waste management
- consider alternative types of resource recovery facilities and systems
- search for new and additional markets for recovered material and energy, as well as methods for conserving materials and energy[14]

Within each state plan, one or more agencies must be designated to implement the plan, the state must be divided into regions with boundaries mapped, and both the planning and implementation agencies are to be identified.[15] If a state provides assistance to a city having a population under 5,000 (not within a metropolitan area) for solid waste management facilities, the state may qualify for federal grants.

Resource recovery and technology

In order to encourage greater commercialization of proven resource recovery technology, the U.S. Department of Commerce has the responsibilities to provide specifications for the recovered materials; stimulate markets for these materials; promote the technologies; and provide forums to exchange technical and economic data about resource recovery.[16] Recovered materials can be divided into post-consumer waste and manufacturing waste as shown in the table below for paper waste.

Operating requirements and environmental enforcement

All federal agencies are required under the SWDA to cooperate with the EPA in administering and enforcing all environmental regulations, rules, and codes. Conversely, the EPA must supply NIOSH and the U.S. Department of Labor with any information that it may have about hazardous waste treatment, storage, and disposal sites; sites where cleanup is planned or in progress; hazards to persons working at hazardous waste sites and facilities; and incidents of worker injury or harm at

---

Two Categories of Paper Waste

Post-Consumer Waste	Manufacturing Waste
◆ mixed waste paper	◆ bag, box, and carton manufacturing wastes
◆ old magazines	
◆ old newspapers	◆ bindery trimming
◆ tabulating cards	◆ butt rolls, mill wrappers, and rejected stock
◆ used cordage	◆ envelope cuttings
◆ used corrugated boxes	◆ fibers recovered from waste water
	◆ fibrous wastes
	◆ finished paper from obsolete inventories
	◆ other waste from converting operations

---

those kinds of sites. The EPA must encourage public participation in developing, revising, and enforcing regulations. If additional training is required by environmental regulations, the EPA may award grants and contracts to another organization to administer that training. Training may be required to develop or carry out a program, improve the competence of instructors and supervisory personnel, or assist other government agencies that may be enforcing a portion of some regulation.

Exhibit 20: Samples of potentially hazardous material are prepared for testing. The material has been taken from the completed monitoring well located at the feet of the EPA inspectors.

The EPA must perform many activities that relate to its environmental protection mission. EPA must conduct research, investigations, experiments, training, demonstrations, surveys, public education programs, and studies. EPA must conduct research to determine the effects of contamination on human health and the economy, and it must disseminate information about how to operate and finance solid waste management programs. EPA is also responsible for all of the following:

- developing methods for resource recovery and conservation systems
- implementing hazardous waste management systems
- marketing of recovered resources
- producing fuel from solid waste
- reducing the total amounts of waste materials
- improving collection and disposal methods

- identifying the components of solid waste and their recoverable materials
- identifying low technology and small-scale solid waste identification
- improving the performance of recovered resources from solid waste
- improving land disposal practices
- mitigating any adverse effects on air quality

Demonstration facilities and projects

The EPA can contract with public agencies, companies, or persons to construct and operate a working demonstration facility. In addition, the EPA can conduct studies or initiate demonstration projects to recover useful energy and materials from solid waste. The studies and their recommendations can include the following information:

- recovering materials and energy from solid waste
- recommending uses of the wastes
- finding potential markets for recycled waste
- understanding the impact of distributing that waste on existing markets
- discovering the potential for energy conservation and recovery

---

EPA's Teaching Role

In addition to its enforcement role, the EPA also has teaching mission. It must maintain a library to serve as a resource and develop programs to disseminate information.[17] The EPA must develop, evaluate, and coordinate information about these waste-control activities:

- Methods and costs of collecting solid waste
- Cost, operation, and maintenance of a solid waste management program
- Amounts and percentages of resources that can be recovered from solid waste using different methods
- Methods to reduce the amount of solid waste generated
- Existing and emerging technologies to recover energy and materials from solid wastes
- Hazardous solid waste resulting from the disposal of wastes
- Methods of financing appropriate facilities, landfills, or treatment facilities
- Available markets to purchase materials or energy recovered from solid waste
- Research and development projects for solid waste management

---

- reducing waste during manufacturing
- collecting, separating, and containing waste
- using federal procurement to develop market demand for recovered resources
- recommending incentives to accelerate recycling and reclamation of materials from solid wastes
- applying economic incentives
- imposing charges on disposing, packaging, using containers, vehicles, etc.
- examining legal constraints and institutional barriers to acquire land for wastes
- consulting with the USDA about agricultural waste management problems and practices
- consulting with the USDOI about mining waste management problems and practices

Regulating hazardous liquid wastes in underground storage tanks (USTs)

If a tank or combination of tanks and their connections contain a regulated substance and are at least ten percent under the ground, the tank is subject to the federal programs and controls explained in the next chapter. Some underground tanks are excluded from regulation regardless of their contents:

- farm and residential tanks of 1,100 gallons or more
- tanks used for storing heating oil on the premises
- septic tanks
- pipeline facilities and their gathering lines
- surface impoundments (lagoons, pits, and ponds)
- storm or waste water collector systems
- flow-through process tanks
- liquid traps for oil or gas production
- tanks located above the floor surface in underground areas such as basements, tunnels, or shafts

Under the SWDA, all owners of USTs must report them to the appropriate state or local agency, indicating their size, type, age, location, and uses. Rules are established to detect the release of a tank's contents and to prevent and stop the leaks. Within the rules, certain requirements must be developed:

- leak detection methods
- inventory controls
- tank tests
- record keeping
- reports of any leaks and stoppages to government agencies
- closing of tanks to prohibit any more leaks
- methods of maintaining financial responsibility, or the ability to pay to fix leaks from accidents.[18]

New tanks must meet specified performance standards with release detection equipment and design and construction standards. Petroleum storage tanks, such as gasoline service stations, are the major targets of the UST regulations.

Medical wastes

A medical waste tracking program is required by the EPA in response to Atlantic Ocean beach pollution where medical wastes washed ashore. The types of waste that are tracked include the following:

- infectious agents from laboratories
- pathological wastes, such as tissues and cultures
- human blood wastes
- needles, pipettes, broken glass, and scalpel blades
- contaminated animal carcasses and human body parts
- surgical and autopsy wastes
- laboratory research wastes that had been in contact with infectious agents
- dialysis wastes
- discarded medical equipment and parts that were in contact with infectious agents
- biological waste and discarded materials contaminated with blood or excretion
- other waste materials that could be threatening[19]

Owners, operators, and other persons who store medical wastes are subject to inspections, and they must adhere to requests for records and allow monitoring by EPA or other designated public agencies. If there is any violation, a *compliance order* is issued that assesses a penalty and requires immediate compliance or compliance within a specified time period. Also, the EPA can begin court action against a person or company. Within 30 days of the issuing of a compliance order, a public hearing may be requested by the alleged violator. Both civil and criminal court proceedings can be applied to a violator.[20] State agencies have the same powers to enforce federal medical waste rules and regulations.

Chronology of RCRA for Hazardous Waste

1976:	Resource Conservation and Recovery Act (RCRA), Pub.L. 94-580; 7 USC 1010 et seq, 40 CFR 280 and 281
1984:	Hazardous and Solid Waste Act (HSWA), 40 CFR 261, 262, 267, 268, 271, and 272

CHAPTER 15

Storage Tanks

Resource Conservation and Recovery Act (RCRA)

Overview

* While EPA regulates underground storage tanks (USTs), some states have aboveground storage tank regulations.

* Owners or operators of tanks containing regulated substances must notify the designated state agency or the EPA with descriptions and characteristics of the tanks.

* Leaking tanks must be replaced with nonmetalic tanks or metal tanks having cathodic protection.

* Service station gasoline storage tanks made of steel have been the most common type of leaking underground storage tank.

* Some tanks are excluded from the tank regulations.

* Violators of the provisions of the UST-RCRA are served with compliance orders, civil actions, or permanent injunctions.

* Reports and records must be submitted for USTs.

* Tank and pipe connections must meet construction product standards.

* Release detection devices must be installed on USTs.

* Action plans for cleanups must be developed and submitted to the appropriate regulatory agency when requested.

* When USTs are closed, they must follow procedures and meet requirements.

Tanks, locations, problems, and the need for protection

Storage tanks can be found above and below the ground almost any-where. They are used to hold either harmless or harmful gases and liquids for various periods of time. Some of the most common storage tanks are those below ground that hold gasoline at retail filling sta-tions. In addition to the service station tanks, there are other sub-stance-containing tanks. For example, tanks holding liquid chemicals at factories that make synthetic fibers, plastic food wraps, or packaging materials contain many kinds of fluids. Along with their associated pip-ing and electronic control mechanisms, below- and aboveground stor-age tanks are systems that can fail and leak liquids into the soil, surface water, or ground water. Owners, operators, and other private parties are likely to be diligent and attempt to keep their tank systems intact and safe from both spills and accidental releases of fluids or gases. However, no matter how careful these parties are, tanks and their con-nections can fail. Corrosion of the tank materials, unexpected impacts, or leaky valves can cause problems. In the worst cases, gases can be released into the air and make bystanders seriously ill.

Storage tanks must be designed, engineered, and installed in a manner that will prevent serious environmental problems. Tanks must

Exhibit 21: Note that these aboveground storage tanks have a concrete curbed contain-ment area. The facility owner or operator must plan for potential leaks from the tanks. Liquid material can be seen under these tanks.

be sturdy and composed of materials that are noncorrosive and cannot react with the tank's contents. Without environmental controls on tanks, leaks can wreak havoc over large land areas. Due to changes in the direction, structure, and composition of the soils, it is difficult to predict the direction of underground flow once a liquid contaminant penetrates the ground. In places, the land may not be level or may consist of a variety of soils. Different soils, such as gravel or sand, may be located at different angles to one another at different depths. As a result, if a liquid contaminant moves along a line between these different layers, it may move in directions that one cannot predict. Water wells, surface water drinking supplies, or land may be contaminated far from the source of contamination. The locations and extent of contamination may be unexpected. For all of these reasons, federal environmental protection from leaking tanks is considered important for protecting public health, safety, and welfare.[21]

Nationwide, there are over two million underground storage tanks and an additional two million aboveground storage tanks. The EPA believes that about 75 percent of the USTs can dangerously leak.[22] To date, an emphasis has been placed on the cleanup, fix up, or replacement of these leaking petroleum tanks, rather than on tanks containing other potential pollutants. Current federal regulations require registering all USTs by submitting information to either the EPA or the delegated state agency. The extent of the problem is vast. There may well be as many as 400,000 UST sites containing about 1.1 million federally regulated UST tanks nationwide. At these sites, there were 341,773 confirmed releases at the tanks, and 292,446 cleanups initiated, with 178,297 completed.[23] As many as 220,000 more USTs are not regulated (of which about 25,000 may be holding hazardous substances), and these must now be registered.[24]

Aboveground storage tanks (ASTs)

Many states regulate above ground storage tanks, particularly those containing petroleum substances. While many tanks are used above the ground to store chemicals and other substances, the stored product can present an environmental problem if the contents leak or are accidentally released. Pipe systems are linked to most ASTs with many connectors, such as valves, right-angle joints, pressure reducers, and automatic diverters. If the AST is constructed of a metal that can corrode, it could leak. Under many of the provisions and programs of the Clean Air Act, Solid Waste Disposal Act, Toxic Substances Control Act

Exhibit 22: Aboveground storage tanks are common in facilities that process chemicals, such as this one. The tanks and their valves, fittings, and pipes must be engineered to prevent liquids from leaking.

and others, ASTs are accommodated in the federal framework of environmental protection.

Cargo tanks that are used to transport liquid petroleum products that are flammable, but not classified as hazardous wastes, are allowed to be of any construction and are not subject to federal specifications. Both leaded and unleaded gasoline is classified as a marine pollutant when transported by highway.[25]

Responsibilities for underground storage tanks (USTs)

Owners or operators of all tanks that contain regulated substances must provide notification and documentation to the EPA or its designated state agency. In a sense, notification with the required descriptions is equivalent to registering the tank. Through this notification requirement, the government can closely track compliance with its underground storage tank regulations. The Resource Conservation and Recovery Act (RCRA), which is part (amendment) of the Solid Waste Disposal Act (SWDA), establishes regulatory controls on existing and proposed tanks. As a result of this environmental control legislation, over $5 billion had been spent to fix or replace leaking USTs. New USTs require government notification prior to installation. Existing tanks must be modified to meet design and operating standards or be closed. For example, it is common for service stations to replace older or leaking metal tanks with tank systems having synthetic materials. Existing tanks that have leaked and caused environmental problems must be fixed according to stated standards. Both the filling and draining of tanks must be conducted in a way that will prevent spills or leaks.

Reports based on site investigations that document any releases and their cleanups must be prepared and submitted. Other reports are required to substantiate financial capability to support cleanups of spills, leaks, or potential tank system replacements, if needed.

> ...[Office of Underground Storage Tanks] has adopted the franchise model as its implementation approach in managing the national UST program. The state, as franchisee, operates dependently, under a signed agreement with EPA, to operate the UST program. Regions serve as the field representatives or liaisons between EPA Headquarters and the states to relay ideas, need, and information between the EPA and the states. The states, therefore, run their programs using a management style that is tailored to

Exhibit 23: Portions of this and other tanks are underground. Not only are there cracks in the concrete containment area, but liquid wastes can be noted floating in the foreground.

meet the specific needs and demands of their own regulated community.

The demand for service and support varies in each state, and is affected by such factors as UST population, groundwater usage, weather and climate conditions, and financial conditions of owners and operators. The aim of state program approval is to develop the state-federal partnership that will allow both parties to focus on preventing leaking USTs from causing further environmental contamination.

Subtitle I of the Resource Conservation and Recovery Act (RCRA) establishes a federal program for the regulation of underground storage tanks (USTs). Subtitle I of RCRA also allows EPA to approve state programs to operate in place of the federal UST requirements if those state programs have standards that are no less stringent than the federal requirements and provide adequate enforcement of compliance with those standards. States with approved UST programs will have primary enforcement responsibility with respect to UST program requirements in their states.[26]

The RCRA UST programs are delegated to the states. To qualify for delegation, a state must adopt laws, regulations and rules to meet or exceed the RCRA UST provisions.[27] States then become the primary permitting authority for USTs, and the EPA passes on its responsibility.[28] For about half the states—those that do not qualify or do not submit for RCRA responsibilities—the designated EPA regional office performs those functions. In 1998, there were only Puerto Rico, District of Columbia, and 25 states with approved UST programs (Alabama, Arkansas, Connecticut, Delaware, Georgia, Iowa, Kansas, Louisiana, Maine, Maryland, Massachusetts, Mississippi, Montana, Nevada, New Hampshire, New Mexico, North Dakota, Oklahoma, Rhode Island, South Dakota, Texas, Utah, Vermont, Washington, West Virginia). At this time, the RCRA responsibilities of the remaining states and U.S. islands are handled by EPA.[29] If a state fails to perform its RCRA duties satisfactorily, EPA may withdraw that state's authorization.

Local governments (cities, townships, or counties) may have stricter regulations than their states, but local intervention to control the environment is uncommon. Storage tanks are one of many responsibilities that local governments like to leave to their states for a number of reasons.

Controls on USTs

Underground storage tanks contain many different kinds of liquids, gases, and compounds. Any of these substances can be contained in the UST, but controls are focused on those regulated and unregulated substances that could leak into the environment. Regulated substances are dangerous liquids and gases as defined in the Comprehensive Environmental Response, Compensation, and Liability Act (CERCLA, or Superfund) and petroleum products. Those same substances are controlled under RCRA's UST regulations for underground storage tanks.[30] Also, fuels and petroleum substances are regulated under RCRA. Even though some of the regulated substances are harmless if safely contained in the proper tank system, they may be harmful if released to the air or water, or if they are mixed with other substances.

Generally, UST systems are required to have leak detection and inventory control systems. Records must be kept of monitoring, testing, inventory control results, and owner or operator continuing financial responsibility. Corrective actions and cleanups must be promptly performed and reported by owners and operators. Under some situations, tanks must be closed to prevent future releases of regulated substances. Compensation must be available to third parties if they are harmed by accidental releases caused by operating a UST system.[31]

Exhibit 24: Hazardous liquids have leaked onto the ground at this industrial facility. The plastic chain barrier around the pool of liquids serves as a warning to employees.

Tank Systems Excluded from RCRA

Primary Exclusions

The primary list of exclusions contains many tanks that could cause environmental problems, but which nevertheless are not regulated.

- farm or residential tanks of 1100 gallons or less to store motor fuel
- heating oil tanks used on premises
- septic tanks
- pipelines regulated under other federal or state acts[32]
- surface impoundments, lagoons, pits, or ponds
- wastewater or storm water collection systems
- processing tanks that are "flow-through"
- gathering lines and liquid traps for oil or gas production
- tanks located on or above the floor of a cave or other underground area
- any pipes connected to tanks in any of the above items[33]

Secondary Exclusions

A secondary list of exclusions mentions the following items:

- hazardous wastes or their mixtures that are listed (under RCRA Subtitle C)
- wastewater treatment tank systems regulated elsewhere under the Clean Water Act
- hydraulic lift tanks, electrical equipment tanks, or other equipment or machinery needed for industrial operations that contain regulated substances
- UST systems having less than 110 gallon capacities
- UST systems containing a minimum (de minimis[34]) concentration of regulated substances under RCRA Subtitle C
- containment systems used for overflow or emergency spill containment that are quickly emptied after being filled

Tertiary Exclusions

A third list of exclusions contains "deferred" UST systems. These systems are deferred for consideration for a period of time by the EPA:

- tank systems used for wastewater treatment
- tank systems containing radioactive material regulated elsewhere[35]
- tank systems that are part of emergency generator systems at nuclear power generating facilities[36]
- airport fuel distribution tank systems
- field constructed USTs

Exclusions from RCRA

There are some tank systems that are excluded from the federal regulations as shown in the boxed item on the facing page.

Note: Each of the deferments in the third list shall be regulated in the future, supposedly. Meanwhile, no one can install a deferred UST system storing regulated substances unless these conditions are met:

- releases can be prevented from corrosion or structural failure
- electronically charged metals can be protected against corrosion
- the UST system can be constructed or lined with a material compatible with the stored substance.[37]

State implementation and enforcement of UST regulations

Even though EPA has the responsibility to designate states to implement and enforce RCRA, only 25 states (and Puerto Rico and the District of Columbia) have received EPA approval to administer their own UST programs. For this reason, there are many variations between the states. If anyone violates RCRA's provisions, the EPA can issue a civil action or compliance order, or the agency can issue permanent or tem-

Exhibit 25: Leaks of hazardous liquids from underground tanks may occur above ground through piping systems.

porary injunctions against them. Violators can request a public hearing to challenge EPA within 30 days after receipt of an EPA order or action.[38] Civil penalties may be assessed on owners or operators not complying with UST requirements. Owners must notify the EPA and submit accurate information or face civil penalties. Additionally, owners or operators can be cited for improper leak detection equipment, poor recordkeeping, not reporting to the appropriate regulatory agency, not taking actions to correct their tank's problems, improperly closing or sealing tanks, or not demonstrating financial responsibility. If a petroleum release occurs, EPA can order owners and operators of USTs to stop the leak and clean up the contamination.

Enforcement

Compliance orders and civil or criminal penalties are the major enforcement methods that can be used against violators of the UST regulations under RCRA. A *compliance order* is a written summons to perform corrections to any underground storage tank violation within a set time period or the violator could face *civil action* in the United States District Court. The court will then order a temporary or *permanent injunction*. An injunction requires a violator to obey immediately. Presently, each single day of violation after the injunction results in a $25,000 civil penalty. A *criminal action* may be initiated for a number of reasons, but *civil penalties* are more common. For example, if an owner or operator of a UST gives false information or fails to give notices to the EPA or state agency, as much as $10,000 per tank may be assessed.

UST records

Many reports and records must be submitted to the UST enforcing agency (state or EPA) and kept over long periods. In the first notification to the EPA or state agency, owners and operators have to certify that they have complied with proper installation requirements, electronic or cathodic protection, financial responsibility, and release detection. Next, they must report any suspected releases, spills, or overflows, as well as any confirmed releases. For any releases in excess of a substance's reportable quantity, reports must be submitted to the National Response Center and the RCRA-responsible agency. Any actions to correct, contain, or stop leaks have to be reported. Those reports include the character of the site at the time of the leak; the removal of the materials flowing out of the leak; results of soil and groundwater

Exhibit 26: When tanks are taken out of use, there are many regulatory requirements, such as signs, recordkeeping, monitoring, and containment.

cleanups; and, if required, action plans to correct the problems. Advanced notice must be submitted prior to permanent closing of a tank or its change in service. Lastly, submissions must be made that certify an owner or operator's financial capabilities to respond to leaks and other accidents from tank systems.

When a tank system is removed from the ground or removed from service, notice is to include the date of stopping operations; age of the tank on that date; size; type and location; and the type and quantity of substances left stored in the tank.[39]

Records can be confidential. If so, they have to be submitted separately from the public information. When metal USTs and systems are installed without corrosion protection, notice must be provided to the appropriate UST regulatory agency. Inspection and testing of cathode protection systems require the submittal of records. UST system repairs must be recorded. Performance claims made by manufacturers of release-detection equipment must be maintained along with sampling, testing, and monitoring results. Permanent closing of a tank or change in service of a tank system requires records. If a tank system site is closed permanently, closure records can be sent to the agency.

When an owner initiates the construction of a new UST system to contain regulated substances, the regulatory agency must be notified and given certification of compliance with UST requirements for installation, cathodic protection, financial responsibility, and release detection. The new tank system must be constructed of noncorrosive materials that cannot fail structurally. It must be designed to prevent a release or threat of release of any stored substance. Finally, the tank system must be composed of materials compatible with the substances to be stored. Methods used to install the system must be certified to comply with industry codes of practice and national testing laboratory standards. Anyone selling a tank to be used as an UST must inform the purchaser of the many notification requirements. When upgrading existing USTs, owners must ensure that all tanks, pipes, and valves meet new UST performance standards, tank upgrading specifications, and closure and corrective action requirements.[40]

Performance standards

In order to prevent tanks and pipe connections from failing and leaking, performance standards must be met by tanks, piping, and spill and overfill prevention equipment. Tanks or pipes may be constructed of metal without corrosion protection only if a corrosion expert determines that the site itself does not contain soils that could cause a release during the tank's operating life. Records must be kept to demonstrate compliance with tank system performance standards.[41] Spill and overfill prevention equipment must include one or more of these standard safety measures:

- automatic shutoff of the flow into a tank when it is no more than 95 percent full
- alarm device that alerts a transfer operator when the tank is more than 90 percent full and stops the flow into the tank
- flow restriction device that activates 30 minutes prior to overfilling and alerts the operator with a loud alarm one minute before overfilling
- automatic shutoff of the flow into the tank so that the fittings on top of the tank are not exposed to the liquid substance[42]

No release of a regulated substance can be made into the environment when a transfer hose is detached from a fill pipe. Industry codes of practice must be followed for installing new tanks, piping, and valves.

UST operating requirements

Underground storage tanks must be operated according to a number of requirements. The volume of the tank must be greater than the volume of the regulated substance to be poured into the tank, and this must be verified prior to filling. Transfers must be monitored constantly so that overfills and spills do not occur.[43] Any overflows or spills that occur during filling must be reported to the appropriate agency. Since so many tank systems are made of steel or another corrosive metal, corrosion protection methods must be continuously maintained to protect any components in contact with the ground. If a cathodic protection system is used, then it needs to be inspected by qualified testers, and records must be maintained for the tank system's cathode protection. Tank materials must be compatible with the substances stored in them. Repairs have to be performed in a manner that can prevent leaks, releases, or structural failure. If corrosion or damage to pipes and fittings has resulted in a substance release, the damaged parts must be replaced, not repaired.

Detecting releases of tank system substances

Methods of detecting releases must be devised that can detect a release from any portion of the tank system (tank, piping, and valves). They may include inventories that record the amount of the substance stored in a tank, use of gauges, monitoring devices for the spaces between the UST system, gas releases, and groundwater purity, tightness of pipe lines, and any other methods.[44] Each method has to detect leaks with a statistical accuracy of 95 percent.[45]

After leaks are detected, they must be stopped. Many states and the EPA maintain funds for cleanups of releases. Some states allow owners or operators who have financial problems to draw from their fund as needed and pay back later. The Leaking Underground Storage Trust Fund of the EPA is used to pay for costs of corrective action, enforcement, and cost recovery for instances where the administrator of the UST program cannot identify a UST system owner or operator.

Petroleum underground storage tank systems

If a tank contains petroleum products, it has different monitoring requirements. It must be monitored every 30 days (minimum) if it does not meet the performance standards for new and upgraded UST systems.[46] Monthly inventory control or manual tank gauging and tank tightness testing must be performed. If the tank has a capacity of 550 gallons or less, weekly tank gauging can be used instead of other release detection methods. Underground piping must be monitored also. If a regulated substance is under pressure, there must be an automatic line leak detector installed, annual line tightness testing, or monthly monitoring. If the regulated substance is under suction, the piping must have line tightness testing conducted at least every three years or have a monthly monitoring method. If the suction piping conforms with design and construction standards, it can be excused from release detection requirements.[47]

Hazardous substance underground storage tank systems

These systems have different requirements, also. Release detection methods must be installed to meet the above petroleum underground storage tank system requirements. Additionally, there must be secondary containment systems for tanks, piping, and valves. The tank system components must be monitored for a release every 30 days at a minimum. Owners or operators may obtain approvals to use their desired methods of release detection. Information about the substances stored in the tanks must be submitted, such as acceptable ways to stop leaks; the health risks of the substance; chemical and physical properties of the substance; and the nature and characteristics of the UST site.

Leak or release reports

Since so many underground storage tanks, pipes, and valves were constructed of steel and have been in direct contact with moist soils for some time, many have corroded and leaked. Leaks pose particular threats to soils, surface, and groundwater. Any suspected release must be reported to the state agency or EPA (if appropriate) within 24 hours of the event. Some conditions that require reporting are these:

- adverse monitoring reports from a release detection method
- discovery of spilled or released regulated substances at the tank system site or in the surroundings
- problems with dispensing equipment

- sudden loss of the substance from the UST system
- unexplained water in the UST system[48]

Release investigation

An investigation of a suspected release is to be conducted to confirm the problem. A *tightness test* (system test) must be conducted to determine whether and where a leak exists. If no leak is found, no further investigations are required.

If environmental contamination can be found, with no related system testing results, additional procedures must be taken. A *site check* is performed to evaluate whether a release has occurred from the UST system. If it is determined that no release has occurred, no further investigations are necessary.

If a release is confirmed, an *initial release response* is performed within 24 hours, and immediate action is taken to prevent any more substance being released. Hazards such as fire, explosions, and vapor must be eliminated at this time. *Initial abatement measures* must be performed following any release confirmation. The substance must be removed from the UST system. A visual inspection must be performed. Fire and safety hazards have to be avoided and prevented. Contaminated soils have to be cleaned if the substance has been released on the ground. The location of the release has to be determined. Finally, the hazardous substance ("free product") must be removed as soon as practical.

Contamination cleanup

If the investigation shows that the substance is present in the soil, air, or water, it must be removed and the contamination reported to the agency. Soil and water in the area of the release (and over the entire site) must be examined to determine if any of these conditions obtain:

- contaminated soils are touching groundwater or surface water
- the substance needs to be recovered
- a larger area is in danger of being contaminated
- water wells have been contaminated

As previously stated, all spills and overfills have to be contained and cleaned up at once. Reports must be submitted within 24 hours if the spills or overfills are petroleum based exceeding 25 gallons, cause a sheen on nearby surface water, and equal or exceed the reportable quantity for that substance.[49]

Cleanup action plans (Corrective Action Plans)

These plans are developed and submitted to the agency when requested. The plans address methods to clean contaminated soils and groundwater. A schedule and format is established by the regulatory agency, and owners and operators must comply. When the corrective action plan is approved, the plan must be placed in service, and then it is monitored, evaluated, and the results reported according to a set schedule and format. Owners and operators can begin cleanup of soil and groundwater before the action plan is approved, but they must first notify the agency of their intent and comply with any conditions set by the agency.

Closing a UST system

Whether a UST is temporarily or permanently closed, the same requirements apply—release detection, release reports, corrosion protection, investigation, confirmation, and corrective action. If the UST is empty, release detection is not required. For temporary closings, the vent lines are to be open and functioning, and all other lines and valves are to be secured and capped. If the temporary closing exceeds 12 months, it must be permanently closed. Permanent closings or changes in service require that an owner or operator notify the agency at least 30 days in advance. For permanent closing (closure), tanks must be emptied, cleaned, and filled with solid material or removed from the ground. If removed, the resulting hole must be backfilled. Records must be kept to indicate complete compliance with the UST requirements of the appropriate agency.

Financial responsibility must be demonstrated to the extent that an owner or operator can show its ability to pay for cleanups and for property damage or bodily injury to another party that might be caused by operating a UST. The limits to the amounts of money that must be demonstrated range from half a million to two million dollars. To meet these financial requirements, self insurance by large companies is acceptable. Large company subsidiaries can obtain guarantees, letters of credit, surety bonds, trust agreements, or EPA-approved, state-assurance funds.[50] A bond rating test may be submitted by a local government, a fund balance or guarantee may also be submitted, or an owner or operator may meet a financial test.[51] Most states have established tank system cleanup funds to help owners and operators pay for clean-ups. Records proving financial ability must be maintained and submitted. Updated copies of certification of financial responsibility, or other evidence may be required.

Chronology of RCRA for Storage Tanks

1984:	Standards for Treatment, Storage, and Disposal Facilities (TSDs), 40 CFR 264 and 265

CHAPTER 16

Federal Compliance

Federal Facility Compliance Act (FFCA)

Overview

- Federal Facility Compliance Act (FFCA) is an amendment to RCRA.

- The FFCA ensures that all government buildings and facilities comply with the same environmental controls and regulations that apply to individuals, business, and industry, or local and state governments.

- Federally owned facilities, such as military bases, airports, buildings, and munitions storage areas can be fined by the U.S. Environmental Protection Agency for violations of any environmental regulations.[52]

- All waste and tank control programs apply to every federal site.

- Criminal laws apply to federal officials violating the FFCA.

- Warships of the U.S. Navy are excluded from the regulations, except when unloading hazardous wastes in ports.

- Federally owned treatment works must comply with the same regulations as publicly owned treatment works.

Federal Facility Compliance Act (FFCA)

This act is an amendment to the Resource Conservation and Recovery Act (RCRA) to assure that federal facilities would not continue to be immune to the environmental regulations placed on the public. Both the states and the EPA may impose penalties and fines on federal buildings and facilities for violating federal, state, or local laws that regulate solid and hazardous waste. All controls and management of wastes that apply to the public sector must be respected by every federal facility. Areas of concern include public vessels, radioactive mixed wastes, munitions used by the military, and federally owned wastewater treatment works.

All criminal laws that apply to the waste management business apply to federal officials under FFCA. The EPA must conduct annual inspections of each federal facility[53] holding a RCRA Treatment, Storage, and Disposal Permit (often called a Part B permit). State agencies are also allowed to independently inspect federal facilities.

U.S. Navy warships are exempted from some FFCA requirements in the national interest. If they were not exempted, some ships that create hazardous wastes remaining at sea over 90 days would violate RCRA's restrictions. When the Navy unloads its hazardous wastes in ports, it becomes regulated according to FFCA. However, munitions stored at Department of Defense facilities could leak into soils and ground waters. Therefore, these munitions must be transported, treated, or stored according to RCRA requirements.

Flows of effluent from domestic sewage and industrial processes are handled at federally owned and publicly owned treatment works (FOTWs and POTWs, respectively) and are subject to the same requirements, enforcement, and penalties. All federal facilities must pay all fees connected with solid and hazardous waste regulatory programs.

The FFCA broadens EPA enforcement powers against federal facilities violating RCRA. Methods for calculating penalties are based on the severity of the violation—major, moderate, or minor. The severity is the extent of deviation from the regulatory requirement. Daily penalties may also be imposed. Since so many of its provisions apply to RCRA, the FFCA may be considered a part of RCRA, in many ways, rather than as a separate act.

Chronology of FFCA

1992:	Federal Facility Compliance Act, Pub.L. 102-386, 106 Stat. 1505

Safety

CHAPTER 17

Workplace

Occupational Safety and Health Act (OSH)

Overview

- While there are new concerns with indoor air in office buildings, there are many other health and safety issues in manufacturing facilities, such as dust and dirt, machinery safety, and aromatic chemicals.

- EPA and the Occupational Safety and Health Administration (OSHA) (U.S. Department of Labor) work together in many ways.

- OSHA has workplace authority and performs inspections.

- Consensus and permanent standards are established under the National Institute of Occupational Safety and Health (NIOSH) within the U.S. Department of Health and Human Services.

- Employers using chemical substances in the workplace must keep employee records and hazard communication documents such as material safety data sheets (MSDSs).

- Other federal agencies have overlapping responsibilities.

Occupational Safety and Health Act (OSH)

The primary agency administering OSH is the Occupational Safety and Health Administration (OSHA), a division of the U.S. Department of Labor.[1] This agency is an enforcement agency having both health- and labor-protecting functions. State and federal inspectors enforce its regulations and provide education about worker safety. Even though many environmental health and safety responsibilities of EPA and OSHA overlap, they do regulate different aspects of things like asbestos, vinyl chloride, cancer-causing agents (carcinogens), warning labels, and other items. Particularly, the OSH Act assures that workers suffer no harm to their health from job exposure. Employers must adhere to OSH, unless they have fewer than ten employees, or they are federal or state government agencies covered under other regulations. There is an independent panel of judges as part of the Occupational Health and Safety Review Commission that handles disagreements between labor and management. Standards for on-the-job safety and health are developed by the affiliated National Institute for Occupational Safety and Health (NIOSH) within the U.S. Department of Health and Human Services.

OSHA Standards

Regulating threats to health in the workplace is a major concern of OSHA. Some threats can be sudden and catastrophic and others slow and cumulative. As a result, for the slow and cumulative threats, OSHA may require health standards that require medical surveillance, recordkeeping, monitoring, medical examinations, and workplace air sampling. By contrast, regulating those safety threats that could

---

Scope of OSHA Regulation

OSHA Standards are established for a wide scope of worker issues on the job. For example, standards may be developed to ensure safety in any of the following areas:

- means of egress
- powered platforms, man lifts, and vehicle work platforms
- ventilation, noise, exposure, and radiation
- hazardous materials (gas, flammable mixtures, and their shelf lives)
- protective equipment (masks, respirators, etc.)
- sanitation, labor camps, and safety color codes for hazards
- available and accessible medical and first aid
- fire protection
- gas and compressed air equipment and devices
- materials handling and storage machinery
- guarding of machinery
- portable power tools and equipment
- welding, cutting and brazing
- pulp and paper
- textiles and laundry equipment
- telecommunications equipment
- electrical devices
- commercial diving
- control of toxic and hazardous substances (air contaminants, asbestos, benzene, lead, vinyl chloride, and others)
- recordkeeping[2]

---

bring immediate and violent harm is another concern. Burns, electrical shock, cuts, broken bones, loss of limbs, loss of eyesight, or risk of death are supposedly minimized by applying OSHA standards and regulations. Since there are many workplace hazards, three different methods of setting standards are used: consensus standards, permanent standards, and emergency temporary standards.

Consensus standards are those developed by other federal agencies, industries, and private groups prior to 1973. These standards list about 400 toxic chemicals and their maximum allowed air concentrations. The concentrations are listed as thresholds.

Exhibit 27: Labeling of substances stored in drums and other containers is important to workers.

Thresholds are established limits below which a worker is assumed to be safe. Since the consensus standards were not based on firm scientific evidence, but rather accepted without question from industry standards and guidelines, no testing has been performed to provide positively sound data on which to base those standards.

Permanent standards may be established by using the results of a tragedy or accident, court action, new scientific studies, or adopting the conclusions in a criteria document of NIOSH. *Criteria documents* compile all of the scientific reports on a chemical (epidemiological and animal studies) and are submitted to OSHA for adoption as a standard. Standards include suggested exposure limits, medical monitoring, antidotes, labels, and other details. To date, only a short list of permanent health standards have been enacted, due to a number of factors.[3] These standards regulate the following areas and substances:

- Asbestos
- Carcinogens: 4-Nitrobiphenyl, alpha-nephthylamine, methyl chloromethyl ether, 3,3'-dichlorolenzidine, bis-chloromethyl ether, beta-naphthylamine, benzidine, 4-aminodiphyenyl, ethyleneimine, beta-propiolactone, 2-acetylaminofluorene, 4-dimethylaminozaobenzene, N-nitrosodimethylamine

- Vinyl chloride
- Inorganic arsenic
- Lead
- Coke oven emissions
- Cotton dust
- 1,2-dibromo-3-chloropropane
- Acrylonitrile
- Ethylene oxide
- Benzene
- Field Sanitation

Other standards

Establishing an *emergency temporary standard (ETS)* is a third approach for times when the normal rule-making process would be too slow. The ETS is effective for six months, as soon as it is published in the *Federal Register*.[4]

Another standard, the *General Duty Clause*, covers times and situations when no other standards exist. Inspectors are given the authority to cite violations for any unsafe condition—even if no standard that governs that condition exists.[5]

When a company complains that the standards are unrealistic, it can seek a temporary or permanent variance. An employer may apply for a *temporary variance* when he cannot meet a standard for reasons such as these:

- necessary professional or technical personnel are not available
- technical materials or equipment are not available
- changes to the building(s) or facility cannot be completed in time

Temporary variances may be issued for less than a year, with only two six-month renewals. In order for the temporary variance to be granted, an owner or operator must prove that he or she is taking every step to ensure worker safety and has an effective compliance program that can meet the standard quickly.

By contrast, a *permanent variance* can be granted to those employers demonstrating evidence that "conditions, practices, means, methods, operations, or processes used or proposed to be used" can provide as safe a workplace as meeting the standard.

Inspecting the workplace

Ten federal regions of the Occupational Safety and Health Administration (OSHA) have the same boundaries as the EPA Regions. Each region contains from four to nine area offices, district offices, or field stations. Compliance with the OSH Act is typically handled by inspections. About 50,000 inspections are performed annually by OSHA, with about the same number performed by comparable state agencies. Random inspections are common, and there is a high priority given to inspecting highly hazardous occupations. Inspectors usually obtain voluntary entry to facilities, but when this is refused, a search warrant is obtained from a federal district court. If a hazard violation is discovered, a citation is issued depending upon the severity of the violation. The four types of violations are willful, serious, repeated, or nonserious.[6]

Records, such as accident reports, monitoring, medical records of employees, and hazard communications must be kept. Employees and their legal or union representatives are required to be given access to all facility records within 15 working days of their request. Workers have the right to refuse to work if there may be serious injury or death.[7] Workers are protected, if they complain to government officials about unsafe work conditions. Under the OSH Act, the worker can have the job restored and lost pay reimbursed.[8] Federal employees are not directly covered by the OSH Act. Under the act, responsibility for provid-

Exhibit 28: The mix of wastes, materials, and trash on this vehicle would violate many provisions of the Occupational Health and Safety Act.

Exhibit 29: This worker can easily read the hazard warning labels on the chemical drums in this loading area.

ing safe and healthy working conditions for federal employees is assigned to the head of each public agency.[9] State government employees are excluded from the protections of the OSH Act, although most states do have similar programs that cover their employees.

The OSH Act requires that OSHA encourage each state to develop worker health and safety programs. If there are any state enforcement gaps, the federal enforcement may apply. State plans for occupational health and safety must be reviewed by OSHA to assure compliance with federal intent and provisions. Typically, there are more state health and safety agencies inspecting companies than there are OSHA inspectors. Also, small employers, as well as larger ones, may request onsite OSHA consultation. At that time, the OSHA inspectors try to educate employers about how to comply.

Other federal agencies that regulate occupational safety

Other federal agencies have duties and responsibilities that overlap those of OSHA. For example, the U.S. Department of Transportation's Federal Aviation Administration and Federal Railroad Administration promote rules for the safety of work crews, maintenance personnel, and travelers. According to the OSH Act, memoranda of understanding have been signed between a number of agencies and OSHA. For example, if the EPA lists a toxic substance, such as a pesticide, OSHA may control its use by agricultural workers. The Occupational Safety and Health Review Commission (OSHRC) maintains a review process that requires the OSHRC to uphold any citation that is not challenged. NIOSH (U.S. Department of Health and Human Services) holds the training and research functions for the OSH Act. NIOSH reports to the Center for Disease Control. There is a NIOSH priority system to produce criteria documents based on severity of response needed, population at risk, current standard, and advice from other federal agencies and professional groups.

Hazard communication in the workplace

OSHA has developed the hazard communication (HAZCOM) regulation to give workers the right to know about any hazardous chemicals in the workplace.[10] Every chemical manufacturer must assess the toxicity of the chemicals it produces. The manufacturer must notify persons who purchase these products by providing them with Material Safety Data Sheets (MSDSs). All chemicals are to be labeled, and training and other educational efforts are to be provided. Chemical manufacturers must evaluate all chemicals they sell for potential worker exposure. (New Jersey has the stiffest label law in the country, and industry must label all of its chemical substances—hazardous or not—and supply the information to community groups, workers, and health officials.)

Hazardous chemical lists

All chemicals on these four lists are considered hazardous:
- International Agency for Research on Cancer Monograph
- Annual Report on Carcinogens (National Toxicology Program)
- OSHA's Subpart Z list in 29 CFR 1910
- Threshold Limit Values for Chemical Substances and Physical Agents in the Work Environment (American Conference of Governmental Industrial Hygienists)

Trade secret protection

Trade secrets are protected even though a worker is given the right to be free of exposure to any harmful chemicals. Although the identity of the chemical substance must be disclosed to a treating nurse or physician who determines that a medical necessity exists, anyone requesting such confidential information is required to sign a need-to-know statement.

Chronology of OSHA

1970:	OSHA Amendment, Pub.L. 91 - 596, 91st Congress, S. 2193
1990:	OSHA Amendment, Pub.L. 101-552, Section 3101

CHAPTER 18

Chemicals

Toxic Substances Control Act (TSCA)

Overview

- ◆ TSCA controls toxic chemical and biological substances before they can be sold.

- ◆ The Act requires tests, safety procedures, recordkeeping, and other actions.

- ◆ All manufacturers of toxic substances must provide information to the EPA prior to the start of manufacture.

- ◆ Periodic updates and reports must be submitted and approved by EPA.

- ◆ Exceptions (exemptions) may be granted for some substances.

- ◆ Biotechnology is regulated.

- ◆ Testing of any substance may be ordered by EPA for many reasons.

- ◆ Manufacturing and other facilities are inspected.

- ◆ Strict penalties can be assessed and conditions for penalty reductions are clearly stated.

Toxic substances are regulated

Toxic substances are harmful chemicals or biological agents. The Toxic Substances Control Act (TSCA) identifies and controls toxic substances before they can be sold.[12] By contrast, other federal regulations (such as RCRA, CERCLA, and OPA) control toxic chemical and biological substances after they have been released. Within this environmental regulation, there are four major sections:

1. controlling toxic substances
2. responding to asbestos hazard emergencies
3. stopping or reducing indoor radon
4. reducing exposures to lead

By far, controlling the toxic substances is one of the most difficult tasks in regulating the environment. *Toxic chemical substances* are substances of a particular molecular identity found to be harmful, and they include combinations of chemicals produced in man-made chemical reaction as well as those that occur in nature. Any element or uncombined radical can be considered a chemical substance regulated under TSCA. Some exclusions from the classification as a chemical substance are those made for commercial food, food additives, drugs, cosmetics; commercial pesticides; tobacco products; nuclear source materials and by-products; and pistols, firearms, revolvers, shells, and cartridges. Also, TSCA excludes chemical substances of small quantities manufactured for research or development; pesticides; articles having no change in chemical composition after manufacture; impurities; and by-products produced without a specified commercial purpose when another chemical substance or mixture is manufactured. Intermediate chemicals that are partially or totally consumed in the chemical reaction process are also excluded.[13]

Regulatory requirements

TSCA requires safety procedures, tests, recordkeeping, and other actions to be followed and enforced by EPA. First, suspected dangerous chemicals must be identified and tested. Next, EPA requires the review, testing, and substantiation of safety for new chemical substances before their introduction.[14] Also, the manufacture, use, distribution, or disposal of existing chemical substances can be limited or prohibited. Finally, EPA can require recordkeeping and reporting for new chemical substances, as well as export notices or import certificates. If an importer ships any chemical substance or mixture to the United States, he or she must certify to the U.S. Bureau of Customs that the shipment is either subject or not subject to TSCA.

Companies, or persons, involved with TSCA-listed chemicals are carefully regulated. Anyone manufacturing substances or mixtures of chemicals must submit tests and data to EPA. A *premanufacture notice (PMN)* must be prepared and submitted, before any unlisted chemical substance is manufactured. Records of chemical substances must be maintained, and reports on the substances must be submitted to the EPA. Companies must certify that they comply with TSCA if chemical substances are imported. If a company extracts a chemical from another substance or mixture, that company is defined as a manufacturer and is subject all of the provisions of TSCA.[15] Likewise, if a company or person prepares a chemical substance or mixture for distribu-

---

Exemptions to TSCA Regulations

Exceptions to the TSCA regulations are called exemptions. Several kinds of exemption are described below:

Test market exemption: may be granted by the EPA if it can be determined that there is no unreasonable risk to human health or the environment. By requesting a test market exemption, a company can spend some time collecting data and demonstrating the product's safety

Research and development exemption: may be granted when small quantities of new chemicals are used solely for research and development under qualified technical supervision

Low volume exemption (LVE): may be granted during a 30-day review. Low release, low exposure chemicals are exempted if the volumes do not exceed 10,000 kilograms per year. For the LVE, there can be no dermal exposure, no inhalation exposure, and no drinking water exposure

Polymer exemption: is given if no unreasonable risk of injury to health or the environment is present. Polymer exemptions do not require an application, but an annual report that indicates the number of new polymers that are manufactured or imported for the first time during the previous year must be submitted to EPA

Polaroid exemption: allows the Polaroid Corporation to be exempted for any new chemical substances used for instant photographic and peel apart film

Also, exemptions, or exceptions, are made for the following substances:

- new chemicals imported in articles that contain fluids or particles not intended to be removed from the article and having no separate commercial purpose
- impurities by-products, nonisolated intermediates, and chemicals formed incidentally when exposed to the environment or to other chemicals
- chemicals formed during the manufacture of an article, such as those chemicals formed from using adhesives, curable plastic, inks, drying oils, or rubber molding or metal finishing compounds[17]

tion in commerce, or merely distributes it, the company or person is considered a processor and is subject to TSCA.

Chemical reviews

EPA continuously updates and maintains the inventory database of new chemicals that have cleared TSCA PMN review. Every four years, reports are required for all chemical substances listed on the TSCA Inventory except for polymers, microorganisms, naturally occurring substances, and inorganic substances.[16] As a result of this requirement, the TSCA inventory has become very large (about five volumes of listed substances). A registry number is assigned to each chemical substance. New chemical reviews are made to determine whether the chemical substance complies with the *premanufacture notice (PMN)* requirements prior to manufacturing. Under PMN, EPA has to determine the risks from manufacturing, processing, distributing, using, and disposing of the new substance, based on information supplied by the PMN submitted.

Over 20,000 new chemical substances have been reviewed through the PMN process. There are four types of PMN:

- *standard PMN*, for a single chemical substance
- *consolidated PMN*, for two or more substances having similar molecular structures and use patterns
- *joint PMN*, for use when two companies must submit data together
- *exemption PMN*, for low-volume, low-release, low-exposure substances or those that are manufactured for test marketing

A *significant new use* (SNUR) is a chemical substance that can result in increased production volume, a change in exposures of individuals or populations, a different disposal method, or a different manufacturing site.

TSCA and biotechnology

EPA has placed the regulation of biotechnology under the broad authority of TSCA. PMN requirements are required for new microorganisms, and there are reporting requirements for all microorganisms. Only informal guidance from EPA is available at this time.[18] EPA has proposed that a premanufacture notice (PMN) for a new microorganism be required using a *microbial commercial activity notice (MCAN)*. Certain

Exhibit 30: Treatment lagoons, such as this one, are used for the treatment of biological wastes. Note the murky nature of the liquid.

microorganisms that do not present unreasonable risk are to be exempted from the MCAN requirement. Presently, more research and development are necessary to further refine the MCAN and PMN requirements for regulating biotechnology.

The testing of chemical and biological substances under TSCA is the responsibility of manufacturers and processors. They must develop safety and environmental data when a chemical or biological substance could present unreasonable risk of injury or when substantial quantities of the chemical or biological substances are produced with the possibility for substantial human or environmental exposure. An Interagency Testing Committee (ITC) makes recommendations to the EPA about those substances and mixtures that should have priority consideration.

Triggers, tests, and rules

Two situations, called *triggers*, that demand testing are the risk and exposure triggers. The *risk trigger* exists when a determination is made by EPA that the chemical or biological agent may present an unreasonable risk (both in toxicity and exposure). An *exposure trigger* exists when a chemical substance is produced in substantial quantities or is reasonably expected to be released into the environment in substantial quantities, or when there are insufficient data or experience to predict the environmental effects and, therefore, testing is necessary to develop data on the substance.[19] Both *substantial production* and *substantial releases* are defined as the potential for one million pounds total per year to be produced or released. *Substantial human exposure* is defined as a general population of 100,000 people; a consumer population of 10,000 people; and a worker population of 1,000 workers.

If tests are required, then a *test rule* is developed for the chemical substance, and the applicant must perform that test or combination of tests. Test rules are formalized and placed in EPA records for review by those submitting applications to the EPA. Applicants must follow those instructions, submit a PMN, maintain records, document or certify compliance with TSCA requirements, and submit reports to the EPA. If a chemical substance is questioned for any reason, decisions on allowing it to be listed may be accepted based on the test rule adopted for that chemical substance. If a significant risk is uncovered by the test data, a finding must be published and communicated to the public. Reporting and recordkeeping requirements are more rigorous for certain substances. A detailed description of the manufacturing process, health and safety information, and environmental exposure data may be required to be submitted to EPA for some listed chemicals.

Thirty days after a chemical is placed on the ITC Priority Testing List, that chemical is added to the *Preliminary Assessment Information Rule (PAIR)* list. More detailed information is needed for a more narrow group of chemical substances, and those substances are subject to the *Comprehensive Assessment Information Rule (CAIR)*. Records of *significant adverse reactions*[20] must be kept, along with allegations of any problems submitted by employees or others. There are only six chemical-specific regulations. They are the ones governing the following substances:

* asbestos
* chlorofluorocarbons
* dioxins
* hexavalent chromium
* metalworking fluids
* polychlorinated biphenyls (PCBs)

Requirements for these problem substances are precise and carefully crafted.[21]

Facility inspections

EPA carries out a six-step process in inspecting a facility for the suspected handling or manufacturing of a chemical or biological substance that is not listed in TSCA.

1. **Pre-inspection preparation**

   The regional office delivers a written notice in advance of a visit. Usually, the notice discusses the EPA's procedures and intent and allows the party to make a declaration of *confidential business information* (CBI).

2. **Notification and entry**

   This can be performed with or without a search warrant (if a company gives permission).

3. **Opening conference**

   The conference is usually conducted with facility officials to explain the inspection purpose, scope, and procedures.

4. **Sampling and documentation**

   The inspector reviews records and may take samples.

5. **Closing conference**

   The EPA inspector presents the facility manager with an itemized receipt of all samples, records, and documents taken. At that time, the inspector may discuss observed deviations and problems or may offer suggestions based on his preliminary findings.

6. **Report preparation and follow-up**

   This procedure includes the inspection report or final audit report. The regional EPA office then decides whether it should enforce TSCA through civil or criminal prosecution or take other actions.[22]

Exhibit 31: EPA inspectors look for labeling, methods of storing, handling of unlisted chemical or biological substances, and conformity to previous facility reports and requirements.

TSCA, FIFRA, and the FDCA

Other federal regulations relate to TSCA. FIFRA states that chemicals must meet TSCA pesticide exclusions to be classified as a pesticide, fungicide, or insecticide. The Federal Food, Drug, and Cosmetic ACT (FDCA) covers those substances excluded from TSCA for being foods, food additives, drugs, devices, or cosmetics. If the EPA adopts a test rule for a chemical, state or local governments cannot adopt a different one. TSCA governs state and local actions.

Violations and Penalties

There are nine conditions that a facility owner or operator must satisfy in order to relieve penalties for violations of TSCA. All nine conditions must be satisfied to achieve full penalty reduction.

1. **systematic discovery**: a company must discover violations through due diligence or an environmental audit
2. **voluntary discovery**: not required by an order or permit condition
3. **prompt disclosure**: violations must be reported within 10 days of discovering them
4. **independent discovery**: a company must discover and disclose before a government inspection occurs
5. **correction and remediation**: violations must be certified as corrected within 60 days
6. **prevent recurrence**: steps must be taken to prevent the violation from happening again
7. **no repeat violations**: no similar or identical violations can occur at the same place within three years, nor can the violation in question fit into a pattern of company violations
8. **other violations excluded**: no serious harm or present endangerment could have occurred, nor could the violation be the same kind of violation that has resulted in previous penalties
9. **cooperation**: company must cooperate with EPA in its investigations of violations and related compliance issues.[23]

Chronology of TSCA

1976:	Toxic Substances Control Act, Pub. L. 99-519
1977:	TSCA Amendment, 15 U.S.C. 2601 - 2671
1986:	TSCA Amendment, creates "Asbestos Hazard Emergency Response Act of 1986"
1992:	TSCA Amendment, creates "Lead-based Paint Exposure Reduction Act," Pub. L. 102-550, 1021(c) Stat. 3924

CHAPTER 19

Pesticides

Federal Insecticide, Fungicide, and Rodenticide Act (FIFRA)

Overview

* Pesticides, herbicides, insecticides, fungicides, and rodenticides must be registered with the federal government prior to manufacture and distribution for sale.

* The EPA is responsible for developing and maintaining labeling requirements for these substances.

* EPA coordinates and works with the Food and Drug Administration (FDA) of the U.S. Department of Agriculture and the Occupational Safety and Health Administration (OSHA) to prevent lingering residues and worker exposures.

* In order to assure product safety, all contractors and applicators are certified.

* Labels must be printed with safety warnings.

* Trade secrets are protected.

* Carriers of disease are eradicated according to special means.

* Experimental use permits may be issued.

* Scientific review of products may be required.

* Records must be kept.

* States can enforce FIFRA but do not really have responsibility for the act.

* Onsite inspections are performed and penalties are assessed to enforce the act.

Insect, pest, and rodent controls

Controlling the use of pesticides, insecticides, and rodenticides is important for protecting the environment. Insecticides control or kill insects. Fungicides protect vegetation against diseases or insects. Rodenticides control or kill mice, rats, or other rodents. *Pesticides* are any substances that prevent, destroy, repel, or decrease the numbers of any pest (including insects), or any chemicals that function as plant regulators, defoliants, or desiccants. *Pests* may include any insects, rodents, worms, fungi, weeds, plants, viruses, bacteria, microorganisms, and other animal life harmful to humans or beneficial plants and animals. Since there are so many insects, bacteria, fungi, and other pests, the use of these eliminators and retardants may be warranted for many situations, but they are also potentially harmful. Many ingredients in these products and mixtures may be safe in certain doses, but harmful to agricultural crops, people, animals, fish, or vegetation in other doses.

Manufacturer and contractor requirements

Before any pesticide regulations are decided or published, the EPA must solicit opinions from the U.S. Department of Agriculture and the U.S. Department of Health and Human Services. Both domestic and foreign producers of fungicides, insecticides, and pesticides are subject to the provisions of FIFRA.[24] Each state may be federally authorized to conduct a program to certify the contractors or applicators of pesticides as long as the state's program conforms with FIFRA.[25] But states do not register the pesticides. Registration is granted by the EPA if a pesticide can perform its intended function without harmful effects on the environment and can be used in a common manner; that is, repeatedly, without unreasonable adverse effects.[26] Pesticides that are identical or very similar to other registered products (such as generic drugs), are called *me-too pesticides* and are expeditiously approved. Tests must be performed and documented by the applicant prior to submittal for registration. A balancing test (considering costs and benefits) may be used to decide whether to allow the continued use of a chemical known to produce cancer in laboratory animals. The EPA can stop the sale or use of, or remove and seize, pesticides that are not registered. It may do the same for pesticides that are adulterated, misbranded, or mislabeled. Coloring or discoloring may be required for identifying a pesticide or insecticide. Misbranded pesticides can be removed from sale when pesticide claims are unsup-

❖ Federal Insecticide, Fungicide, and Rodenticide Act (FIFRA)

ported by the registration information.[27] Special storage, disposal, and transportation are required, and certain pesticides or insecticides may be recalled or confiscated at any time. Container design must provide for proper sealing and otherwise meet EPA requirements. Violators of FIFRA are subject to civil and criminal prosecution.

Regulatory process for pesticides

The EPA and the U.S. Department of Agriculture must conduct research into integrated pest management and initiate a national monitoring plan. The plan must be detailed. *Integrated pest management* is defined as a sustainable approach to pest control incorporating biological, cultural, physical, and chemical tools to minimize environmental and health risks.[28] After a pesticide has been registered, the registrant must report any additional factual information about adverse effects on the environment.[29]

A scientific advisory panel must comment on the impact on the environment of any regulations that are adopted. The panel must evaluate and recommend operating guidelines for scientific studies that lead to decisions about pesticides and insecticides. To support this advisory panel, a science review board assists in reviews conducted by the panel. The Food and Drug Administration (USDA) and the Occupational Safety and Health Administration (OSHA) are consulted for information about pesticide residues and disinfectants. The EPA delegates the primary enforcement responsibility of pesticide or insecticide use violations to the states. Comment on a pesticide or insecticide may include an agricultural impact statement assessing the effects on production and prices of agricultural commodities, retail food prices, or other agricultural factors.

A pesticide or insecticide may be suspended from use. In FIFRA, *suspension* means an immediate ban on a pesticide. By contrast, *cancellation* only initiates administrative proceedings that lead to decisions about a pesticide, but does not stop its use.

Registration procedures

Before any pesticide is manufactured, distributed, or imported, it has to be approved by EPA. Approval is called *registration*. Labels listing the contents and warnings are required as the primary control device. In order to have the fungicide, insecticide, or pesticide registered, the manufacturer must submit the necessary paperwork, which includes laboratory tests and many other details. An approved label constitutes proper registration.

At this point, some comment on labeling may be in order. Labeling as a primary regulatory device is questionable, according to some authors.[30] Yet, federal policy is full of notification and open record requirements for chemicals, biological agents, and chemical substances.[31] Also, warnings are important to the many who read labels. Therefore, registration of a pesticide or insecticide with restrictive labeling seems very sound.

FIFRA and other environmental regulations

Other federal regulations control fungicides, insecticides, and pesticides. The *Food Quality Protection Act (FQPA)* has affected pesticide and insecticide regulation in recent years. The EPA, Food and Drug Administration, and the U.S. Department of Agriculture monitor pesticide residues in food.[32] Any pesticide traces on food are considered unsafe unless a safe level is specified for that substance and the trace elements or residues fall below the specified safe level.

The Clean Air Act requires that hazardous pollutants be listed. Many are fungicides, insecticides, and pesticides. The Federal Water Pollution Control Act requires that pesticide manufacturers apply for discharge permits prior to releasing contaminants into any body of water and that they use the best available control technology (BACT). Soil contamination from fungicide, insecticide, and pesticide runoff or discharge into waters is a concern of the water regulations. The Solid Waste Disposal Act requires special storage, treatment, and disposal methods for pesticides. The Occupational Health and Safety Act protects farm workers and other pesticide and insecticide users from harmful exposures. The U.S. Department of the Interior and the National Oceanic and Atmospheric Administration (U.S. Department of Commerce) monitor pesticides in water, air, and fish. Finally, the U.S. Department of Transportation regulates the transportation of pesticides and insecticides.[33]

Chronology of FIFRA

1947:	Federal Insecticide, Fungicide, and Rodenticide Act, 7 U.S.C. 136 et seq.
1978:	Federal Pesticide Act, Pub.L. 95-396, U.S.C. 136 et seq.
1988:	FIFRA Amendments, Pub.L. 100-532
1991:	FIFRA Amendments, Pub.L. 102-237

CHAPTER 20

Land

Surface Mining Control and Reclamation Act (SMCRA)

Overview

- ◆ SMCRA primarily regulates coal mining.

- ◆ The mining of any kind of minerals must be performed according to the provisions of this act.

- ◆ Both surface mining and underground mining can harm the environment.

- ◆ Large open pits resulting from scraping coal from the surface can contaminate water supplies, denude the landscape, and accelerate runoff during rains.

- ◆ Public hazards are created that could be avoided through mining land regulation.

- ◆ The Bureau of Land Management (BLM) of the Department of Interior (DOI) is primarily responsible for administering SMCRA.

- ◆ Both abandoned and existing mines are regulated.

- ◆ Open tunnels and caves must be filled, waste piles removed or covered in a natural manner, and vegetation planted to make the surface-mined land appear as natural as possible.

- ◆ Mining research is promoted through state mining and mineral resources research institutes.

- ◆ The Abandoned Mine Reclamation Fund is administered by the DOI to reclaim abandoned mines.

(Overview continued on next page)

- ♦ Each state that has coal mines must prepare and submit a State Reclamation Plan.

- ♦ An owner or operator cannot engage in surface mining without a permit.

- ♦ Site reclamation plans must be part of every permit application.

- ♦ Mines must comply with performance standards for environmental protection.

- ♦ There are many surface requirements for surface and underground mining.

Purpose and programs

Coal is mined from the surface and below the ground. Both mining methods have the potential for harming the environment. Underground coal mining can result in land subsidence if performed improperly. Surface coal mining can scar the landscape, destroy or diminish the usefulness of the land for commercial, industrial, residential, recreational, agricultural, or forestry uses. Landslides or erosion resulting from poor mining practices can contribute to floods, pollute waters, or destroy fish and wildlife habitats. The mining of land can destroy the natural beauty of an area and greatly diminish property values. Even other government programs to conserve soil, water, and other natural resources can be ruined by poor surface mining practices. Since energy needs create pressures to increase coal production, there is an urgency to establish standards that minimize environmental damage. SMCRA sets those standards.[34]

Surface mining methods to reclaim the land have been advanced by new concepts, techniques, and successful demonstration projects. State, local, and federal government controls can now draw upon these innovations to decrease the overall problems that could occur if surface mining is left unchecked. Because there are unique local geographic characteristics, state responsibilities are promoted under SMCRA. Authority is available from the Bureau of Land Management (BLM) for each state to develop its own version of SMCRA. The surface mining of other minerals is controlled by regulations based on coal surface mining. SMCRA establishes a program that protects the land from the adverse visual and physical effects of surface coal mining. Rights of adjacent landowners are protected by requiring that surface areas of mines be reclaimed to a state of environmental health as close as possible as that of adjacent and contiguous areas. Sheet runoff of rain is not allowed to flow onto adjacent lands, nor can existing surface waters be so diverted.

The national coal supply must be assured as a continued major source of energy while, at the same time, the environment is protected. As a result, surface and subsurface mines are licensed prior to their initial operations. Monthly unannounced site inspections are performed.[35]

Problems from the past

When SMCRA was passed, there were many surface coal mines that had not been reclaimed and had been abandoned by mining companies. Not only were they huge visual scars on the landscape, but they damaged adjacent parcels with their runoff of chemical substances. Underground mines would often deposit waste materials near the mouths of entry tunnels, cave entrances, or on mountainsides. SMCRA has provisions to reclaim these abandoned areas. Additionally, safe subsurface mining is promoted in the act by encouraging new underground extraction methods. There are requirements for research, experiments, and demonstration projects for extracting, processing, developing, and producing minerals and for the training of mineral engineers and scientists. The U.S. Department of Interior (DOI) Office of Surface Mining Reclamation and Enforcement is assigned these program responsibilities.

Exhibit 32: Lands scarred by surface mining must be returned to normal conditions. Where surface drainage must be accommodated, waterways, ditches, or ponds must be engineered to respect the surrounding environment.

Mining research

SMCRA established state mining and mineral resources research institutes. The DOE and the U.S. Bureau of Mines, in conjunction with the National Academy of Engineering can designate 13 universities as coal research laboratories. At these laboratories, research is to be promoted with federal and state funds, and fellowships are to be awarded for coal mining studies.

States that participate could receive federal funds for mining research university projects. These funds are to be used for demonstrations and experiments of basic, theoretical, and practical mining and mineral resource research.[36] A center for cataloging all current and projected scientific research in mining and mineral resources was created at the DOI. The Committee on Mining and Mineral Resources Research is composed of members from the DOI, U.S. Geological Survey (USGS), National Science Foundation (NSF), National Academy of Sciences (NAS), National Academy of Engineering (NAE), and others. One important duty of the committee is developing a national research plan.

Funds for land reclamation

Abandoned mines are to be reclaimed through a trust fund (Abandoned Mine Reclamation Fund) administered by the DOI. State abandoned mine funds are to be stimulated from this federal fund. The sources of funding are reclamation fees, user charges, donations, recovered moneys, and interest earned. Funds can be used for reclaiming and restoring land and water resources damaged by past coal mining practices; acquiring and filling holes and sealing tunnels, shafts, and entryways; performing studies and research and demonstration projects; awarding state grants; and other purposes.[37] In the SMCRA, the trust fund grows with reclamation fees, penalties, and civil actions that can be taken to recover fees. Priorities are set for spending from the fund, and these priorities include protecting public health, safety, welfare, and property from the physical and esthetic dangers of surface mining.[38] Lands and water that are eligible for reclamation or drainage trust fund moneys are those that have been mined for coal, waste banks, coal processing, or other coal mining.

State coal mine reclamation programs

Each state having coal mines must submit a state reclamation plan and a list of annual projects. The state reclamation plan must contain information about the relationships between the reclaimed land and the areas around it, specify the criteria for ranking and identifying the projects that need funding, and describe the state's capability to perform the work. Lands of Indian tribes qualify for funds from the Indian Lands Coal Mine Reclamation Program.

Agreements must be secured from landowners to control and prevent erosion and damages from sediments from the unreclaimed mined lands. Conservation and development of soil and water resources affected by coal mining must be promoted in the state plan to receive federal approval. The USDA must review and comment on conservation and development plans. If a coal mine has removed or disturbed a water-bearing stratum and the water rights or water supply to a tenant or landowner have been adversely affected, the plan can propose methods to enhance the water quality or quantity through joint action with other affected landowners.[39]

Requirements for land acquisition

Any state can acquire any land adversely affected by past mining practices if it can determine that the land will serve recreational, historic, conservation, or reclamation purposes or provide open space benefits. Permanent facilities such as a water treatment plant or a relocated stream channel can be constructed. If not, the coal waste disposal sites must be converted to public ownership in order to have a responsible party to meet emergency situations and prevent recurrences of contamination.

Filling mine voids and sealing tunnels

The SMCRA requires that voids, tunnels, shafts, and entryways be filled to avoid hazards to public health and safety. Federal or state funds may be used to fill and seal openings if mine owners or operators are delinquent or cease to exist. When mine waste piles are reworked, they can be used to fill voids and seal tunnels. Land may be acquired to meet the objectives of SMCRA. Reclamation projects can protect, repair, replace, construct, or enhance public utilities. Improvements to water supply, roads, or other public service facilities that have been harmed by mineral mining and processing are major objectives.

Standards and the permit program

No owner or operator can engage in surface coal mining without first receiving a permit. Permits cannot exceed five years.[40] Each applicant for a permit must include a reclamation plan for the site. The reclamation plan has to include provisions for public agency inspections, insurance certificates, and blasting plans. The DOI requires that all abandoned coal waste sites be reclaimed and that permits be issued for onsite reprocessing of abandoned coal waste. Provision for the inspection of sites must be made in developing site-specific permits. States may assume exclusive jurisdiction over the SMCRA provisions and issue the permits as long as the state meets all SMCRA requirements. There must be adequate state staff to administer and enforce the necessary programs. A performance bond or another kind of financial assurance of the applicant's ability to perform must be submitted before the permit is approved.

Reclamation plan requirements

Each reclamation plan submitted as a part of a permit application must include details sufficient to indicate that reclamation can be accomplished. Boundaries of lands for surface coal mining must be indicated, along with phasing, timing, etc. The condition of the land prior to any mining that is covered by the permit must be described in the reclamation plan. The description of conditions must include the following details:

- existing land uses
- capability of the land, prior to any mining, to support a variety of uses considering soil and foundation characteristics
- topography and vegetative cover
- productivity of the land prior to mining
- use of land after reclamation, including capacity of the reclaimed land to support different uses
- post-mining land use and how it will be achieved
- engineering techniques to be used in mining and reclamation, along with a description of the major equipment to be used
- water drainage plan
- backfilling plan
- timetable

❖   Surface Mining Control and Reclamation Act (SMCRA)

- consistency of surface mining and compatibility with surrounding land uses
- steps that will be taken to comply with air and water pollution regulations
- ownership of contiguous land parcels

Performance standards for environmental protection

Permits will be issued to only those applicants who can meet performance standards for environmental protection. These standards include the responsibility to perform the actions shown in the box, "Land Reclamation Performance Standards."

Additionally, there are requirements to restore the land to the original contours, meet those contours, and adjust to those contours. There are steep-slope surface coal mining standards. Permit variances may be granted that may not require restoring the land to its original contours. The variances depend closely upon meeting local government requirements for land use planning.

Land Reclamation Performance Standards

- Ensure maximum conservation of the solid fuel (or coal) resource.
- Restore the land to a condition capable of supporting any mining, or a higher or better use.
- Backfill, compact, insure stability, prevent leaching of toxic materials, slope the land, and grade to the approximate original contour of the land with all high walls, spoil piles, and depressions eliminated.
- Stabilize and protect all surface areas including spoil piles.
- Remove soil from the land in a separate layer and replace it on the backfill area.
- Restore the topsoil or the available subsoil which is best able to support vegetation.
- For all farm land, perform special soil placement.
- Create, if authorized in the permit, impoundments of water on mining sites only when it is demonstrated that the size of the impoundment is adequate for its intended purpose and the dam of the water is stable and safe.
- Conduct any boring operations to recover the mineral reserves remaining after the operation and reclamation are complete.
- Minimize the disturbances to the prevailing hydrology at the mine site and at offsite areas.
- Stabilize all waste piles.
- Refrain from surface coal mining within 500 feet from active and abandoned underground mines.
- Ensure that all debris, toxic materials, or inflammable materials are treated or buried and compacted.
- Assume the responsibility for successful revegetation.
- Protect offsite areas from slides.

Surface requirements for underground coal mining

According the SMCRA, there are distinct differences in the regulations for underground as opposed to surface mining. Each permit for underground coal mining requires the owner or operator to assume the following responsibilities:

* Prevent subsidence and material damage, maximize mine stability, and maintain the value and future use of surface lands.
* Seal all entryways, drifts, shafts, tunnels, or other openings between the surface and underground mine when no longer needed.
* Fill or seal exploratory holes no longer necessary for mining.
* Stabilize all surface waste piles.
* Ensure that new coal mine waste piles (mine wastes, tailing, coal processing wastes, or other liquid and solid wastes shall be designed, located, constructed, operated, maintained, enlarged, modified, and removed, or abandoned in accordance with standards and criteria.
* Regrade disturbed surface land areas and establish a vegetative cover.
* Protect offsite areas from damages.
* Eliminate fire hazards and health hazards.
* Minimize water (hydrology) balance at the mine site and offsite areas.
* Use existing roads as much as possible for site access.
* Use the best technology available to minimize disturbances and impacts on fish, wildlife, and the environment.
* Locate openings for all new drift mines and working acid or iron-producing coal seams in a manner to prevent gravity discharge of water from the mine.
* Suspend any underground coal mining operations in urbanized areas to minimize the chance of any subsidence.

Inspections of surface coal mining and reclamation

In order to administer approved state programs or enforce federal SMCRA administration, inspectors have the right to enter any mining or reclamation operation. Records and reports must be made available to the inspectors, and monitoring system records must be maintained. The federal or state permit authority specifies the particular monitoring sites to be used to record the quantity and quality of surface drainage; potential zone of influence; and the level, amount, and samples of ground water and aquifers potentially affected by the mining. Also, records must be kept of all well logs, bore hole data, and monitoring sites for recording the rainfall at the site. Inspections must be held at least once a month, they must occur without prior notice, and they must include the filing of inspection reports for the mine. Each permittee must maintain a conspicuous sign at the entrances to the surface coal mining and reclamation operations. The sign must be clearly visible and display the name, business address, phone number, and permit number.

Notice of any violations may be issued by the site inspector, and penalties assessed. Any willful violations of the SMCRA may result in imprisonment. Corporations are subject to the same civil penalties, fines, and imprisonment as individuals.[41]

Designation of land unsuitable for noncoal mining

Federal land areas may be reviewed, if requested by a state, to determine if they are unsuitable for the mining of minerals or materials other than coal. Criteria submitted must include urban or suburban character, land use, mineral estate in the public domain, and the impact on land for alternative land uses.[42]

Chronology of SMCRA

1977:	Surface Mining Control and Reclamation Act, Pub.L. 95-89, 30 USC 1201 et seq

CHAPTER 21

Nuclear Safety

Atomic Energy Act (AEA)

Overview

- The Nuclear Regulatory Commission (NRC) of the U.S. Department of Energy is the primary agency regulating radioactive materials.

- Similar to other federal acts, the AEA mandates federal and state cooperation in controlling atomic energy emissions.

- Since radioactive materials are so hazardous to health and the environment, sources, by-products, special nuclear materials, and wastes require substantial regulation for safe disposal.

- Not only can soils and water become irradiated, but the soils and water can transfer radioactivity to people, animals, and plants.

- Long-term impacts of storage and disposal are considered, including the engineering for storage and disposal.

- Scientific research is promoted through demonstration projects.

- Many regional low-level radioactive waste disposal sites are designated throughout the United States.

- Safety in processing, possessing, transferring, and disposing of radioactive materials is promoted by licensing each activity.

Purpose and programs

There have been changes in responsibilities under the AEA. The Atomic Energy Commission has been abolished and all duties were transferred to the Nuclear Regulatory Commission and the Administrator of the Energy Research and Development Administration of the U.S. Department of Energy (DOE). The federal government cooperates with the states for the peaceful uses of atomic energy. Controlling radiation hazards and dealing with the by-products and sources of radioactive and special nuclear materials is a major purpose of the regulations. The Act develops radiation standards for the application of controls by federal agencies and the states. Agreements with the states are considered (when submitted) for by-products, sources, and special nuclear materials of a critical mass.[43]

Regulatory controls and demonstration projects

The NRC, not any state, regulates the construction and operation of any nuclear or uranium enrichment facility, the export or import of any nuclear material, disposal into the ocean or sea of nuclear waste materials, and the disposal of any nuclear material and the licensing of that disposal. Radiation standards are developed for each material in order to protect the environment and people against radiation hazards. The EPA coordinates its radioactive materials programs with the NRC, the National Academy of Sciences, and experts in biology, medicine, and health physics. Inspections are performed by the NRC as deemed appropriate anywhere and at any time. Agreements between the federal and state agencies can be suspended at any time if the NRC or EPA determines that there are dangers, or if a state has failed to take necessary steps to contain or eliminate the cause of danger in a timely manner.[44] States must comply with all health and environmental protection standards. They must follow NRC procedures for licensing, rule making, and license impact analysis. Each license application has to consider an assessment of the radiological and nonradiological impacts to the public health. Applications must also consider impacts on waterways and groundwater resulting from the operations proposed in the license application. Alternatives need to be considered, such as alternative sites and engineering methods. Long-term impacts must be considered in the license application, including decommissioning, decontamination, and reclamation impacts in relation to the granting of such a license.

The armed services must dispose of weapons in a safe manner, and the NRC must approve their plans for permanent disposal of waste from atomic energy defense activities. Demonstration projects for storing radioactive wastes are promoted. For example, one such project was the West Valley Demonstration Project at the Western New York Service Center in West Valley, New York. The project demonstrated solidification techniques for the permanent disposal of high-level radioactive wastes. At the Service Center, the NRC also controlled for the disposal of low-level radioactive waste (not high-level radioactive waste, spent nuclear fuel, or by-product material).[45]

Regional low-level radioactive waste disposal

A regional disposal facility is to be established by each state or group of states to store low-level radioactive waste.[46] Regional compacts may be established for this purpose. Any waste owned or generated by the federal government and disposed of at a regional disposal facility or nonfederal disposal facility is subject to the same conditions, regulations, requirements, fees, taxes and surcharges imposed on others by those regional agencies.

Regional Disposal Compacts

The following regional disposal facility compacts have been approved:[47]

- Appalachian States Low-Level Radioactive Waste Compact Consent Act (PA, WV)
- Central Midwest Interstate Low-Level Radioactive Waste Compact Consent Act (IL, KY)
- Northwest Interstate Compact on Low-Level Radioactive Waste Management (AK, HI, ID, MT, OR, UT, WA, WY)
- Central Interstate Low-Level Radioactive Waste Compact (IL, KY)
- Southeast Interstate Low-Level Radioactive Waste Compact Consent Act (AL, FL, GA, MS, NC, SC, TN, VA)
- Midwest Interstate Low-Level Radioactive Waste Compact Consent Act (IA, IN, MI, MN, MO, OH, WI)
- Rocky Mountain Low-Level Radioactive Waste Compact Consent Act (AZ, CO, NV, NM, UT, WY)
- Northeast Interstate Low-Level Radioactive Waste Compact Consent Act (CT, NJ, DE, MD)
- Southwestern Low-Level Radioactive Waste Compact Consent Act (AZ, CA)

Health and environmental standards for radioactive materials

Protecting public health is a major objective of the NRC in disposing of by-product materials. Safety in processing, possessing, transferring, and disposing of radiation hazards are reasons for regulating. Ownership and custody of certain by-product material and disposal sites require obtaining a license. Licensing allows for adherence to decontamination, decommissioning, and reclamation standards for sites where ores were processed for source material content and where such by-product material is deposited.[48]

Chronology of AEA

1954:	Atomic Energy Act, 42 U.S.C. 2014, 2012-2021d, 2022, 2111,2113, and 2114
1978:	Atomic Energy Act Amendment, Pub.L. 95-604
1982:	Nuclear Waste Policy Act (NWPA), 42 U.S.C. 10101-10270

Responding to Contaminant Releases

CHAPTER 22

Public Notice and Spill Planning

Emergency Planning and Community Right-to-Know Act (EPCRA)

Overview

- States must establish local government chemical emergency spill response programs.
- These programs require state and local emergency response committees and committed spill cleanup teams.
- Public announcements of accidental spills must be made immediately.
- Methods of prompt cleanup must be in place.
- Reports must be filed and available to the public about existing chemical or biological substances contained in buildings and facilities.
- Any amount of toxic chemical release must be recorded in permanent public records.

Responding to spills

EPCRA requires that states develop, prepare, and establish local chemical emergency programs, and communicate information to the public about those hazardous chemicals located within their communities.[1]

These chemicals may be potentially air- or waterborne, or they may reach the environment through soils, foods, or even direct human contact. This act requires that the potential for risks from accidental chemical spills be disclosed to everyone.[2] There are four major components to EPCRA for responding to potentially dangerous releases of chemicals:

1. Plans must be developed that are capable of quick execution.
2. Both chemical and biological substance releases (and emergency releases) must be promptly advertised.
3. Public reports must be filed containing information about existing chemicals in buildings and facilities (recognizing that the community has a "right to know").
4. Any amounts of toxic chemical releases must be recorded in permanent records.

Each of these four components has special reporting requirements.

Public notice and response to spills

EPCRA assumes that, given the knowledge, people may be able to make decisions for themselves about how best to take care of themselves. The Act requires that local governments have methods in place to stop or clean up the spills. When a chemical or biological accident occurs, the public must be notified. Information must be distributed so that residents in states, towns, and cities can understand the potential chemical hazards around them. The governor of each state designates a state emergency response commission (SERC) and appoints a local emergency planning committee (LEPC). The SERC must designate emergency planning districts within each state to prepare and implement emergency plans. The LEPC must develop and specify methods for cleaning up spills, protecting residents, and distributing information about the spills. The owner or operator of a facility that produces, uses, or stores a hazardous chemical must notify the SERC and the LEPC immediately whenever a listed hazardous substance is released in amounts that exceed the reportable quantity (RQ).[3]

Required recordkeeping

Under EPCRA, minimum threshold quantities are established by EPA for reporting the kinds and amounts of hazardous chemicals at a facility. Material safety data sheets (MSDSs) must be prepared and submitted to the government from each owner or operator of a facility storing a federally listed hazardous material. MSDSs are report forms that contain the quantities and names of chemicals stored on site or used for any industrial activities. The MSDSs are required under the Occupational Safety and Health Administration's (OSHA's) hazard communication standard regulations described in Chapter 17. MSDSs must be submitted to the SERC, the LEPC, and the local fire department (LFD) having jurisdiction over the facility.

Under EPCRA, owners or operators of certain manufacturing facilities must submit annual reports on the amounts of EPA-listed toxic chemicals that are released from their facilities. These reports must be submitted regardless of whether the chemical or biological release is accidental, intentional, or routine. All releases to the air, water, or soils must be reported. Discharges from publicly owned treatment works (POTWs) and transfers to offsite locations for treatment, storage, or disposal also must be reported. In order to avoid violations or prosecution, any facility subject to these reporting requirements, or any others, must develop written information management programs, plans, and implementation methods.

Spill emergency plans

Emergency plans must be comprehensive, specify the kinds of facilities subject to EPCRA requirements within an emergency planning district, and identify the safest routes for the transportation of hazardous substances. The plans must detail the methods and procedures to be used in responding

Exhibit 33: Emergency response, or cleanup teams, must promptly arrive at the scene of the spill. This crew is wearing clean suits to protect them from the dangers of the hazardous material.

to all kinds of releases. The area or population likely to be affected by a release must be defined. A community emergency coordinator, such as a fire department or cleanup company under contract to the community, has to be designated. There must be procedures mentioned in the emergency plans to provide reliable and timely notice of a chemical release to the public. Emergency equipment, storage sites, staging areas, or facilities to be used in cleanups must be designated. Evacuation plans (including precautionary evacuations), training programs, and schedules for medical and cleanup personnel must be included in the spill emergency plan. Finally, methods must be clearly stated about how to initiate and schedule the emergency plan.

Notices of a release

Release notices must be submitted to the LEPC and must include the following information:

- chemical or substance name
- whether the substance is listed by the EPA
- estimate of the quantity released
- time and duration of the release
- anticipated acute or chronic health risks
- precautions to be taken (such as evacuations, barrier construction, etc.)
- name and telephone number of a contact person(s)[4]

As soon as possible after a release of a chemical or other substance, there must be a follow-up emergency notice given, actions must be taken to avoid any threats or health risks, and medical advice must be given when appropriate. The toxic chemical threshold amount for reporting is 10,000 pounds of the toxic chemical used in a facility per year. If a toxic chemical is manufactured or processed at a facility, the threshold amount for reporting is 25,000 pounds per year.[5]

Medical needs for chemical information

If a chemical is requested by a health professional for the purposes of diagnosis, treatment, or a medical emergency, or if the knowledge of that chemical could assist in diagnosis or treatment, then the owner or operator must promptly provide the information. A written request is required.[6] A confidentiality agreement may have to be signed by health professionals to ensure that the information will be used only for diagnosis or treatment and will not be otherwise disclosed. There are civil, administrative, and criminal penalties for not complying with EPCRA.

Chronology of EPCRA

1986:	Emergency Planning and Community Right-to-Know Act, Pub.L. 99-499, 42 U.S.C. 11001 - 11050
1990:	Pollution Prevention Act, 42 U.S.C. 13101 - 13109

CHAPTER 23

Hazardous Waste Spill Cleanup

Superfund

Comprehensive Response, Compensation, and Liability Act (CERCLA)

Overview

- Superfund and CERCLA are two different names for the same act.

- Sometimes, the word Superfund is used to describe the actual fund that is used to pay for hazardous waste spill cleanups.

- CERCLA pays for cleaning up spills when responsible persons cannot be identified to pay.

- There are many more sites in need of cleanup than there are funds available to pay the cost of cleanup.

- For sites leaking hazardous wastes, funds are allocated by a ranking system.

- Waters of the United States are protected by requiring all owners and operators to have financial ability to clean up their own spills.

- Sites can be either completely cleaned or modified to prevent leakage.

- Engineering requirements for preliminary site status are strict.

- Hazardous substances are those listed in other federal acts, such as TSCA, SWDA, RCRA, CWA, CAA, etc.

- Compliance orders may be issued to those parties responsible for leaks.

- Civil and criminal penalties may also be issued.

Superfund scope

The Comprehensive Environmental Response, Compensation, and Liability Act (CERCLA) is called both *CERCLA* and the *Superfund.*[7] CERCLA, or Superfund, is a program that attempts to minimize contamination from releases of hazardous substances. It provides for compensation for cleanups of hazardous waste spills until responsible parties are identified and payment can be arranged. The act protects the public and the environment from abandoned and leaking hazardous waste sites not otherwise controlled under existing laws. The Superfund is funded by a combination of the taxes on the petroleum and chemical industries, general tax revenues, and a specially levied environmental tax on corporations.

These funds are sufficient to pay for cleaning only a limited number of hazardous substance spills (when the responsible owner or owners of the leaking sites cannot be determined easily), due to the high costs of planning, design, engineering, and contracting. The EPA can recover its cleanup costs from private parties, and it can obtain judicial orders to require liable parties to reduce any dangers to health or the environment. There is no requirement that blame for the release of a hazardous substance be declared or discovered. CERCLA is retroactive and costs may be assessed to previous owners, a series of owners, or officers of defunct companies even when the vessel, site, or facility is 50 or more years old. When the EPA can do so, it may require a potentially responsible party (PRP) to undertake and pay for the cleanup without committing any moneys from the Superfund. Since the available funds appear to the public to be so large and the provision of providing funds for such emergencies so innovative, *Superfund* has become the most common name for the program.

Parties responsible for spills

CERCLA applies to any owner or operator of a vessel or facility in its entire history. Anyone who, at the time of disposal of any hazardous substance, owned or operated either a vessel or facility can be a responsible party. Anyone who agreed to dispose of or treat the wastes, or anyone accepting any hazardous substances for transport to another place, can be a responsible party. In any of these instances, all costs of removal or remedial action may be levied against a responsible party or parties. There may be damages assessed for injury or destruction of natural resources, costs for any health assessment or health

Exhibit 34: This transporter of hazardous materials uses a truck that can securely seal and contain wastes. After hauling, the operator safely cleans the containment area.

effects study needed, or any other related costs for responding to the leak.[8] However, if a registered pesticide product is applied improperly, no damages may be recovered.

CERCLA requires that financial responsibility be maintained by owners or operators of vessels that carry hazardous substances or cargo. Bonds, insurance, guarantees, surety bond, or self-insurance are allowable evidence of financial responsibility. If a vessel owner or operator is not financially responsible, that vessel may not enter the waters of the United States.[9] Financial responsibility for facilities must be initially established by the owner or operator, recorded at the EPA, and amounts adjusted as necessary to meet changes in the facility. States can impose any additional liability or requirements for the accidental or known releases of hazardous substances.

Before adopting any plan or proposal for taking cleanup action by the federal or state governments, public notice must be given and time for written and oral comments allotted.[10] The final plan must be published and made available to the public before adopting it.

Connection between priorities and funding

Even though most EPA actions under CERCLA relate to hazardous substance dangers, the program requires that EPA develop nationwide criteria for assigning priorities for releases or threats of releases. EPA develops the criteria based on risks to public health, welfare, and the environment. In applying this risk criteria, EPA scores and ranks different sites on its Comprehensive Environmental Response and Liability Information System (CERCLIS)[11] for possible listing on the National Priorities List (NPL).[12] If a site is listed on the NPL, it is merely an annual listing that needs further investigation. Liability is not assigned to responsible parties through the act of listing. The NPL designation does not require the EPA to take action.

There are two sections to the NPL, the General Superfund Section, and the Federal Facilities Section. The Federal Facilities Section of the NPL lists sites that are the responsibility of federal agencies other than the EPA.[13] After collecting site information, EPA conducts a preliminary assessment (PA) to determine the extent of the leaks. If further site investigations need to be performed, the site may be investigated further and scored to determine its potential to be added to the NPL. The NPL is part of the National Contingency Plan (NCP), and the NCP is the major guide for CERCLA responses and actions. A hazard ranking system is used. Criteria for ranking are as follows:

- quantity, toxicity, and concentrations of hazardous substances in the waste
- potential or extent of the release into the environment
- degree of risk to the public and the environment

A site may be added to the NPL if it scores high on the Hazard Ranking System (HRS). There are four paths: ground water, surface water, soils, and air. EPA policy is that a score of 28.5 or greater on the HRS makes a site eligible for the NPL. Each state can designate a single site as its top priority, regardless of its HRS score.[14] Even if a site does not score high enough on the HRS, it can be listed on the NPL if it meets all of these conditions:

- the Agency for Toxic Substances and Disease Registry (ATSDR) issues a health advisory
- there is a significant public health threat, according to the EPA
- EPA anticipates that it will be more cost effective to respond immediately to the release than to wait.[15]

EPA can remove sites from the NPL when it determines that no further response is necessary under Superfund.[16] The NPL has a construction completion list (CCL).[17] This list was developed by EPA to communicate the successful completion of site cleanups. By 1998, there were 155 sites deleted from the NPL, with seven sites deferred to other authorities.

Removal or remediation?

EPA can remove or remediate. *Removal* means that wastes are taken away. *Remediation* means that dangerous waste sites are modified, treated, or redesigned to safely contain the wastes. Environmental emergencies can require removal of contaminants. *Remedial actions* are usually long-term, permanent cleanups. After a cleanup, the EPA recovers its costs from potentially responsible parties (PRPs), or compels PRPs to perform the cleanup themselves—after administrative or judicial proceedings. In any remedial action, timing and coordination are major concerns. Swift actions made in a competent and cost-sensitive manner are desired.

After a site is identified on the NPL, the remedial action process requires a *Remedial Investigation/Feasibility Study (RI/FS)*, during which the EPA chooses the best alternative. During the RI, the amount and composition of hazardous substances are determined and site areas needing attention are pinpointed. The RI provides EPA with good information that can be used successfully in developing the FS. The FS develops a range of alternatives for consideration.

Clearly, the RI/FS process can take a long time. A site cleanup can be total or partial, depending on the RI/FS findings. Any remedy that leaves hazardous materials on a site must meet all *Applicable or Relevant and Appropriate Requirements (ARARs)*. ARARs are any criteria, limitations, requirements, or standards under any federal environmen-

Exhibit 35: Superfund sites may not look different from any other site. This drainage area may contain contaminants that need to be tested for toxicity. The toxicity levels could determine whether this site is listed on the National Priority List.

tal program, act, or law, or under any state law stricter than a federal one. The ARARs include the following information:

- purpose of the remediation
- medium of contamination
- regulated substances
- action planned to be taken
- land use
- structure size and type
- potential site use in the future[18]

To select a remedy, ARARs are applied to provisions in the NCP that require consideration of cost effective remedies. Other considerations are just as important, however. CERCLA suggests that remedies consider these factors:

- cost
- ability to carry out the selected alternative
- short- and long-term effectiveness
- reductions in toxicity, movement, or volume during treatments
- public acceptance

Acceptance of the remedial method by the state and the residents living around the site is a very important criterion. For example, if there is strong public opposition to a particular method, it may be abandoned in favor of another.

After completing the RI/FS, a *Record of Decision (ROD)* is issued by the EPA. The ROD states the facts, site determinations, remedy, applicable ARARs and how they were obtained or why they were waived, and establishes its cost-effectiveness and permanence. Public comments about the chosen remedy must be included in the ROD. When the ROD is issued, EPA develops a *remedial design (RD)* for the site, facility, or vessel. In summary, responding to spills with government action, using the emergency funds, allows for swift cleanup when the public is endangered.

Hazardous substances, releases, liability, and compensation

Under CERCLA, EPA may conduct a cleanup of hazardous substances and later recoup costs from a potentially responsible party (PRP), or it may compel the PRPs to clean up the site themselves. Hazardous substances refer to those substances listed by the EPA or designated under other environmental programs. The number of substances of concern in CERCLA is very large. Hazardous substances include those listed in the Toxic Substances Control Act, Solid Waste Disposal Act, Resource Conservation and Recovery Act, the Clean Water Act, Clean Air Act, and any other substances that can be dangerous to health or the environment. A long list of hazardous substances is provided in CERCLA.[19] Any pollutant or contaminant that is released to the environment, or poses a substantial threat of being released to the environment, is covered under CERCLA. But according to the act, EPA is entitled to recover its cleanup costs from private parties only if the release is a hazardous substance. Petroleum is excluded as a hazardous substance, but it is included under RCRA as a hazardous substance. Therefore, the provisions of CERCLA do not apply to cleanups of petroleum or its products.[20]

Useful definitions for protecting the environment

The phrase *protecting the environment* can be confusing. In some federal acts, environment is not defined, nor do some of the programs require strict definition of the components of the environment. For hazardous substances, the *environment* is defined as:

> ...the navigable waters, the waters of the contiguous zone, and the ocean waters of which the natural resources are under the exclusive management authority of the United States...and any other surface water, ground water, drinking water supply, land surface or subsurface strata, or ambient air within the United States or under the jurisdiction of the United States.[21]

By contrast, *natural resource* is defined as

> land, fish, wildlife, biota, air, water, ground water, drinking water supplies, and other such resources belonging to, managed by, held in trust by, appertaining to, or otherwise controlled by the United States, state or local government, any foreign government, Indian tribe.[22]

Yet another definition of importance is that of *owner or operator*. Anyone owning, operating or chartering a vessel is subject to CERCLA.

An *owner/operator* may be defined as anyone owning or operating an onshore facility, building, or site, or anyone who holds title or control of that site, which was conveyed—due to bankruptcy, foreclosure, tax delinquency, abandonment, or similar means—to a unit of state or local government. In determining the PRPs, actions of previous owners or operators are balanced against factors for each PRP that include the following:

- volume of hazardous substances contributed
- toxicity contributed
- time during which each party was involved at the site
- care exercised in handling
- cooperation by the parties with government officials to prevent harm to the public or environment

The definition does not include a person who did not participate in the management, but holds ownership only to protect his security interest in the vessel or facility. If a lender does not participate in management, he or she is excluded from cleanup liability. If a lender did not participate in management prior to foreclosure, and tries to sell, release to another, or otherwise divest the person of the vessel or facility

Exhibit 36: This landfill contains many different kinds of leaking, hazardous wastes. Changes in site ownership over the years or decades make it difficult to find a responsible party. Using Superfund money for making the site safe insures quick and long-term protection of public health, safety, and welfare.

at the earliest practical time (taking into account market conditions and legal requirements), he or she is considered liable. There are a number of definitions of participation in management, but generally, lenders that are partial owners are exempt from financial responsibility for cleanup unless they had decision-making control over the environmental compliance of the facility, site, or vessel, or exercised control comparable to a daily manager with respect to compliance and operational functions. If a party only monitors or inspects a facility, he or she is not participating in management. Also, merely providing financial or other advice or counsel, to prevent a decrease in the economic value of a vessel or facility is not participating in management.

Releases of contaminants

Contaminated material can be difficult to contain. *Release of a contaminant* may be defined as any discharging, dumping, emitting, emptying, escaping, injecting, leaching, leaking, pouring, pumping, spilling, or disposing of a substance into the environment (including abandoning or discarding barrels, containers, and other closed containers holding any hazardous substance, pollutant, or contaminant). Release of a contaminant does not apply to those releases that expose persons located entirely within their workplace. Also, releases of contaminants are not defined as emissions from engine exhausts of motor vehicles, rolling stock, aircraft, vessels, or pipeline pumping station engines, or sources, by-products, or special nuclear materials from a nuclear accident.

Responding to a spill

To *respond to a spill* means to remove or remedy or take remedial action.[23] Responsible parties must be aware of the EPA guidelines for reportable quantities. The definitions for reportable quantities of hazardous substances can be changed at any time by the EPA.[24] As soon as a person in charge of a vessel, offshore, or onshore facility has knowledge of any release of a hazardous substance, notice must be given to the National Response Center established under the Clean Water Act.[25] If the National Response Center is not notified, criminal prosecution can result. At every facility, vessel, and site, records that identify the location or condition of a facility, characteristics, quantity, origin or condition of any hazardous substances contained or deposited in a facility must be kept for 50 years.[26]

Removal action

Any action that could lessen the threat from a spill is a removal action. For example, the EPA can remove a hazardous substance, provide alternate water supplies if needed, clean spills from containers, or erect fences around hazardous waste sites. Usually, more actions are needed after the removal if an immediate risk exists. The removal could be part of a broader set of remedial actions to be taken, and even more actions would be necessary.

Remedial action and the National Contingency Plan

When there is a substantial threat, or release, of a hazardous substance, then the EPA or another federal agency may be engaged to remove the threat or cleanup the release. These actions are long-term and permanent cleanups. Sometimes a remedial action could take a number of years to complete and require a number of steps. At any time, special powers may be exercised under Presidential or EPA orders. For some sites, no RI/FS (remedial investigation or feasibility study) needs to be performed, unless the President orders it. Public health threats are the major reason to seek immediate Presidential action. The President will not order the removal of a hazardous substance in the following situations:

- ◆ the release or its threat is from a naturally occurring substance in its unaltered form
- ◆ the substance has altered solely through naturally occurring processes or phenomena
- ◆ the substance has been released from a location where it is naturally found
- ◆ the substance has been released from parts of the structure within residential, business, or community structures
- ◆ the substance has been released into drinking water supplies due to deterioration of the system through ordinary use

Investigations, monitoring, coordination, or other actions may be ordered at any time when an illness, disease, or complaints can be attributed to a hazardous substance. The President may promptly notify the appropriate federal and state natural resource trustees of the potential damages to natural resources from releases and have them proceed with planning for cleanup or other remedial actions.

Selecting a remedial action

A state may be granted a credit against the share of the cleanup costs for a facility listed on the NPL. Under the National Contingency Plan, amounts expended for remedial action may be covered according to agreements with the President. If state expenditures are required for a remedial action, or if the total expenses exceed 10 percent of all costs, prior approval must be secured from EPA. In order to better chose the remedial action, the EPA can enter a facility, site, or vessel and obtain information (or documentation) at any time from any owner or operator. Requested information can include the quantity and nature of the substance released, extent of the release or threatened release, and information about the ability of a person to perform a cleanup. Samples may be requested and obtained from any location for any suspected hazardous substance.

Compliance orders

When danger from a leak occurs, the EPA or Attorney General's office may enforce or require actions to reduce that danger. Fines may be levied, or criminal prosecution pursued. An order may be issued that directs owners or operators to comply with the regulations. If an owner or operator interferes with the entry or an inspection by the EPA, the courts must direct the owner/operator to allow access. If information or documents are requested, the courts can mandate availability or possession, unless the request is found to be arbitrary and capricious, or an abuse of discretion. High-cost civil penalties may be imposed on anyone who interferes with inspector entries or access to records.

Information disclosure

All information obtained under a compliance order is considered confidential unless the President (or the state) deems it proprietary. It may not be protected or confidential if the site's substance under question has a trade name, common name, generic class, or category of the hazardous substance. Other breaches of protection may be ordered due to boiling points, melting points, flash points, specific gravities, vapor densities, solubility in water, or vapor pressures at 20 degrees Celsius. Other triggers for disclosure by owners or operators are when the substance poses a hazard to health and the environment; potential routes of human exposure are a problem; the location of the leak is dangerous; or any groundwater monitoring, hydrogeological, or geological data discloses threats.

Agency for Toxic Substances and Disease Registry (ATSDR)

CERCLA establishes the Agency for Toxic Substances and Disease Registry (ATSDR) within the U.S. Public Health Service.[28] The ATSDR cooperates with the states to develop a national registry of diseases and illnesses related to toxic substance exposures and keeps records of affected persons. It performs field tests and studies on sites suspected of having contaminated persons living around them. Another list is maintained that designates areas closed to public use or restricted because of contamination. A major function is preparing a priority list of hazardous substances commonly found at sites on the National Priorities List (NPL).

This agency supports all of the environmental protection programs in all agencies in important ways. Toxicological profiles (evaluation of the potential harm of different substances) are developed on the health effects from human exposure according to EPA and ATSDR.[29] Also, the ATSDR provides medical care and testing to exposed people, and conducts periodic surveys, determines relationships between exposure to toxic substances and illnesses, takes tissue samples, and performs epidemiological studies. When people are exposed, they are eligible to be admitted to hospitals and other facilities and services operated or sponsored by the Public Health Service. The ATSDR maintains a library of information, materials, research, and studies on the health effects of toxic substances.[30]

National Contingency Plan (NCP)

The NCP is developed and disseminated annually to set priorities for contaminant releases. The plan lists sites in order of priority for cleanup. Since funds are limited, the most dangerous sites are cleaned first. The NCP contains procedures and standards to respond to problems, such as the following:

- ◆ locating and investigating potentially leaking sites
- ◆ determining which sites get cleaned and in what order
- ◆ evaluating remedies
- ◆ determining the scope of remedies

- deciding roles for federal, state, and local governments or private parties
- providing equipment and supplies for cleanups
- deciding cost-saving and effective ways to respond to spills and perform cleanups[31]

A hazard ranking system consists of a scoring method for sites to determine if they should be placed on the National Priorities List (NPL). The EPA scores prospective sites according to this system. Higher scores give higher priority for cleanup.

Demonstration programs for innovative treatments

The EPA is required to research, evaluate, test, develop, and demonstrate different technologies for treating hazardous wastes. Contracts may be negotiated with the private and public sectors to learn better ways of neutralizing the dangers from hazardous wastes. Plans, sites, and required supervision of the project or program must be submitted and approved by the EPA. The information developed from the approved demonstrations must be disseminated as a part of the funding requirements.

Responsible party settlements under Superfund

Some responsible parties at a leaking hazardous waste site may want to settle the matter by taking action or paying for a cleanup. Others may wish to delay the inevitable. Concerned parties may quickly respond to the spills when notified and take all necessary actions at their own expense. In other cases, the parties may be willing but unable to pay for anything but their own part of the cleanup. Partial cleanup may not work, so Superfund moneys may need to be allocated as part of these kinds of settlements.

> ...at every multiparty CERCLA site there are parties that wish to settle with EPA and those that cannot or do not. At the same time, there may be a vast quantity of wastes at the site that came from defunct or bankrupt companies. Waste from these defunct or bankrupt companies have traditionally been referred to as a site's "orphan

share." Thus, at most sites, those parties that settle will ordinarily account for less than 100 percent of the volume of hazardous substances at the site. In fact, it is not uncommon for many settlements to involve settlers whose cumulative volume of waste represents less than 50 percent of that present at the site.[32]

De Minimis settlements

PRPs who deposited relatively small quantities of hazardous substances at a multiparty site may receive offers of a settlement having finality by the EPA. *De Minimis* settlements are those where amounts of the hazardous substances deposited by that party are minimal compared with those deposited by the other parties. An owner of the property may not have conducted the handling, generating, or disposal of hazardous substances at the facility, contributed to releases, or even known—when acquiring the facility—that it had been used for hazardous substances.[33]

Chronology of CERCLA or Superfund

1980:	Comprehensive Emergency Response, Compensation, and Liability Act (CERCLA) - "Superfund" statute was enacted, 26 USC 4611-4682; Pub.L. 96-510, 94 Stat. 2797
1983:	CERCLA Amendments, 42 USC 9601-9657; Pub.L. 98-802, 97 Stat. 485
1986:	CERCLA Amendments, Pub.L.99-499, 100 Stat. 1613
1986:	Amended by Superfund Amendments and Reauthorization Act (SARA)
1996:	Asset Conservation, Lender Liability, and Deposit Insurance Protection Act, Pub. L. 104-208, 2501, 110 Stat. 3009-462

CHAPTER 24

Asbestos in Buildings

Asbestos Hazard Emergency Response Act (AHERA)

Overview

♦ Airborne asbestos is a recognized health hazard.

♦ Asbestos is required to be contained or removed if found to be unsafe.

♦ All contractors that contain or remove asbestos in buildings must be accredited by their state.

♦ Removal management plans must be developed after an inspection and the plans submitted to, and approved by, the state.

♦ Any removed asbestos must be safely transported in sealed containers.

Regulating for asbestos

Prior to the 1980s, asbestos was used in many building products. It was used to insulate pipes and structural members, soundproof ceilings, provide finished floor surfaces (floor tiles) or wall boards, and was mixed with compatible building materials such as vinyl. As a result of the ability of asbestos to insulate items from temperature changes and its fireproof characteristics, most large office buildings, schools, institutional buildings, and some residential buildings contained lots of asbestos. Recognition of the need to regulate or ban the product arose as information about the horrors of asbestosis, a lung disease, became known to the public. In this disease, airborne asbestos fibers become embedded in the lungs, causing extreme breathing difficulties. In the worst cases, the embedded fibers caused the lung tissue to become rigid and immovable, resulting in death.

Asbestos program highlights

This program is a subchapter within the Toxic Substances Control Act (TSCA).[34] It is not a separate act, but one of many programs within TSCA. AHERA is a program that resulted from a congressional finding that easily crumbled (friable), asbestos-containing material (ACM)[35] in school buildings is unsafe and should be contained or removed. Likewise, all public buildings are to be assessed, inspected, and monitored to contain or remove the ACM. These ACMs are commonly found in ceilings and walls, in flooring materials, and covering structural members, piping, and ducts as insulating material. Over time, the asbestos materials dry out, crumble, and turn to powder. This creates the health hazard.[36]

Contractor accreditation

A method of accrediting or qualifying contractors for safe asbestos removal is required by AHERA, and the EPA is the federal regulatory agency that delegates the responsibilities to the states for their implementation. The very act of removing asbestos can release fibers into the air, making it risky to remove the material without enclosing the work area to prevent the airborne release from being inhaled by unprotected workers or building inhabitants. EPA registers asbestos-removal contractors to ensure that damaged asbestos is not released into the air during the removal process. Contractors must be certified and can obtain their registration only by completing special courses approved by an EPA-sanctioned state agency.

Removal management plans

An inspection must be performed on a building or facility and action taken. After the contractor removes or contains the material, a periodic and long-term re-inspection of any remaining *asbestos-containing material (ACM)* must be performed. When ACMs are removed, they must be transported safely. Containers must be used to prevent scattering the ACM fibers into the air. Since the required asbestos removal always includes an inspection, the results of that inspection must be transmitted by the contractor to the approved state agency in the form of an *asbestos management plan.* The management plan includes many handling details, such as notifying building occupants and protecting them during any removal. Removal plans must be implemented by obtaining state agency approval of the management plan. Many times, plans require sealing off an area so that ACM particles do not invade occupied areas of a building. Next, emergency procedures must be established and placed in effect to respond to any sudden or accidental releases during removal. The onsite air must be constantly monitored. Safe waste transportation and disposal must be performed, and worker safety must be promoted at all times. Only accredited persons may inspect buildings, design removal plans, conduct responses, and physically remove or contain asbestos. The EPA approves all training courses for personal and contractor accreditation.

Chronology of AHERA

1976:	Toxic Substances Control Act, Pub.L. 94-469,
1986:	Asbestos Hazard Emergency Response Act (AHERA), amended by TSCA , Pub.L. 99-519

Nature
and
Natural
Resources

Wildlife,
Natural Resources,
and
Other Environmental Concerns

Section Note

There are many other federal acts that protect wildlife, marine life, natural resources, climate, public lands, waters, and wetlands than those presented in the previous chapters. All aspects of these subjects are not protected, and important related areas may well have been overlooked by Congress, the Office of the President, or federal agencies. In this section, selected nature and natural resource acts are treated more concisely because they are shorter in length and contain fewer provisions and requirements than those examined in previous sections. Each of these acts is extremely important in the structure of the federal framework of environmental regulations. For the reader's information, a list of relevant natural resource acts is presented below. The asterisk (*) indicates that a brief explanation of that act is included in one of the chapters in this section. (Natural resources are protected through many federal regulations. One of the better known programs is the National Estuary Program, NEP. It protects the environment of significant bays and estuaries. NEP requires a Comprehensive Conservation and Management Plan to correct and prevent problems. Currently there are 28 estuaries included in the NEP.)

Airborne Hunting Act
Alaska National Interest Lands Conservation Act
Anadromous Fish Conservation Act
Antarctic Protection Act *
Aquatic Nuisance Prevention and Control Act *
Bald Eagle Protection Act
California Desert Protection Act
California Wilderness Act
Chesapeake Bay
Coastal Barrier Resources Act
Coastal Zone Management Act *
Coastal Wetlands Planning, Protection and Restoration Act *
Endangered Species Act *
Federal Land Policy and Management Act *
Fish and Wildlife Act
Fishery Conservation and Management Act
Forest and Rangeland Renewable Resources Planning Act *
High Seas Driftnet Fisheries Enforcement Act
Illinois Land Conservation Act
Marine Mammal Protection Act *
Marpol Protocol
National Invasive Species Act
National Wildlife Refuge System Administration Act
Navigable Waters
Oceans Act
Oregon and California Lands Act
Outer Continental Shelf Acts *
Pacific Salmon Treaty Act
Rivers and Harbors Act
Shore Protection Act
Soil and Water Resources Conservation Act *
Submerged Lands Act
Walrus Protection Act
Whaling Convention Act
Wild Bird Conservation Act
Water Bank Act
Wilderness Act *

CHAPTER 25

Extinction

Marine Mammal Protection Act (MMPA)

Overview

♦ MMPA relies upon the National Oceanic and Atmospheric Administration (NOAA), Department of the Interior, EPA, and Department of Commerce as primary federal agencies to prevent mammal extinction.

♦ The Act depends on cooperative research, planning, field observation, coordination with commercial fishermen, other countries and the U.S. Coast Guard.

♦ Not only is it important to respond to catastrophes, but also marine research is performed to investigate all kinds of threats to the populations and habitats of marine animals and polar bears.

Purpose and focus

The purpose of this Act is to address the potential extinction and depletion of certain species of marine mammals as a result of man's activities. These species are not to be diminished beyond the point where they "cease to be a significant functioning element in the ecosystem of which they are a part."[1] Stocks of species are to be replenished, and habitats protected. These habitats may include rookeries, mating grounds, and significant areas for each species of marine mammal. *Marine mammals* are defined as any mammal adapted to the marine environment, such as seals, sea otters, walruses, polar bears, and dolphins. The Act recognizes the present lack of understanding of the ecology and population dynamics that affect breeding. It proposes that international research be negotiated for mammal protection and respects the importance and significance of the mammals themselves. The National Oceanic and Atmospheric Administration (NOAA) is the federal agency responsible for protecting marine mammals. A Marine Mammal Commission is appointed as the overseer, and the U.S. Coast Guard helps enforce the environmental regulations.[2]

Marine mammals

Preserving the health and well-being of dolphins, seals, sea lions, otters, and other marine mammals is an important goal of the MMPA.[3] The Act requires that studies be performed of mammal epidemics, international fishing entrapment of dolphins, and threats to other species of marine mammals. Since feeding can result in behavior change, feeding studies are mandated under the Act. The MMPA provides for maintaining maximum productivity and reproduction of marine mammal populations and species. Fish stocks are identified and grouped according to geographic, scientific, technical, recreational, and economic characteristics in order to promote conservation. Important concerns of the MMPA are fishing and the harming of marine mammals in the process. Restrictions are placed on the taking or importing of marine mammals or marine mammal products unless they are used for scientific research or educational purposes.

Reckless tuna fishing using drift nets is prohibited when marine mammals could be harmed.[4] But there is a "Good Samaritan" exception to this regulation. When there is a potential to injure the mammal or species, the mammal may be removed as long as the removal is reported to NOAA within 48 hours. Otherwise, no marine mammal may be taken from its habitat on the high seas or in waters or lands of the United States. Pregnant or nursing mammals may not be imported, nor may they be taken or removed from their habitats in a manner deemed inhumane by NOAA.[5] No whales of any species may be taken or removed by commercial whaling.

The ecosystem for marine mammals is protected in the Gulf of Maine and the Bering Sea. Fishing gear research and development is encouraged to avoid harming any marine mammals. Also, the DOI and the State of Alaska must consult with Russia about cooperative research and management programs to conserve polar bears in Alaska and Russia.[6] If the Secretary of the Interior determines that a species or stock should be designated as depleted (or no longer so designated), public notice must be given along with an opportunity for public comment. Conservation plans must be prepared.[7]

Science and marine life

Both the Department of Commerce and Department of Interior must form regional scientific review groups to examine population estimates and to determine a population's status. These groups must include experts in marine mammal biology and ecology, population dynamics and modeling, and commercial fishing technology and practices . A Pacific Coast Task Force and a Gulf of Maine Task Force shall perform scientific investigations to determine whether California sea lions and Pacific harbor seals are having a significant negative impact on the recovery of salmon fishery stocks. Unusual marine mammal mortality events must be researched, a National Marine Mammal Tissue Bank established, and tissue analyses initiated.[8]

Chronology of MMPA

1972:	Marine Mammal Protection Act, Pub.L. 92-522;16 USC 1361-1407; 86 Stat. 1027
1976:	MMPA Amendment, Pub.L. 94-265; 90 Stat. 360
1978:	MMPA Amendment, Pub.L. 95-426; 92 Stat. 985
1981:	MMPA Amendment, Pub.L. 97-58; 95 Stat. 979
1984:	MMPA Amendment, Pub.L. 98-364; 98 Stat. 440
1986:	MMPA Amendment, Pub.L. 99-659; 100 Stat. 3706
1988:	MMPA Amendment, Pub.L. 100-711; 102 Stat. 4755
1990:	MMPA Amendment, PubL. 101-627; 100 Stat. 4465
1992:	Marine Mammal Health and Stranding Response Act, Pub. L102-587, 3001, 106 Stat. 5059
1994:	MMPA Amendments, Pub.L.103-238, U.S.C. 1386 et seq
1997:	International Dolphin Conservation Program Act. Pub.L. 105-42, 111, Stat. 1122 U.S.C. 962 et seq

CHAPTER 26

Seacoasts

Coastal Zone Management Act (CZMA)

Overview

- CZMA protects land and water along the shorelines of the 29 coastal states.

- The act spans both the Clean Water Act and the CZMA, and is administered by both the EPA and the National Oceanic and Atmospheric Administration (NOAA).

- There are many regulations that target the control of nonpoint pollution from agriculture, silviculture, urban runoff, marinas, and other sources.

Areas and zones

A national interest in preserving coastal zones has been identified by Congress and has become a basic purpose of the CZMA.[9] The shorelines and coasts of the United States extend from the Northwest corner of Washington state along the Pacific Ocean to Southern California, the Gulf Coast from Texas to Florida, and from southern Florida northward along the Atlantic Ocean to northern Maine. The Act includes the coasts of Alaska, the Hawaiian Islands, and the island territories. Additionally, the Great Lakes have vast coastal areas that are quite important to environmental stability. These various coastal zones contain a wide variety of esthetic, ecological, commercial, natural, and recreational resources that need to be protected.[10] All of those coastal waters, lands, and their adjacent shore lands comprise the coastal zone. The coastal zone includes islands, tidal and intertidal areas, transitional areas, salt marshes, wetlands, and beaches.

CZMA assumes that, without care, the coasts will degrade. Increasingly, these lands and waters have been stressed by population growth, building development, mineral extraction, transportation and navigation, waste disposal, and fish harvesting. Over time, there has been a loss of wildlife, fish, marine mammals, wetlands, and shoreline. Habitats in the coastal zone are sensitive, fragile, and vulnerable. Land-use and water-use conflicts need to be mitigated through regulation. Global warming may well cause a rising of shorelines.

For all of these reasons, the federal, state, and local governments are encouraged by the CZMA to develop land- and water-use coastal programs. Grants are available to help states develop programs to be approved by NOAA that are consistent with the CZMA. Methods, such as mediation, for settling conflicts between diverse interests are necessary.[11]

Programs and management

To accomplish the above policies, goals, and objectives, the Act collects, analyzes, and diffuses information and research results and provides technical assistance that supports land-use controls on the coastal and ocean areas.[12] Additionally, changing circumstances can affect the coast; therefore, federal and state cooperation is expected to provide strong and effective ways to avoid environmental problems. State programs that modify federally approved programs for coastal zones may be approved for changing conditions.[13] Grants may be awarded by the EPA to any eligible coastal state to preserve or restore lands and waters for shellfish, redevelop deteriorating and underutilized urban waterfronts and ports, and provide access to public beaches and waters. The CZMA can support efforts to manage nonpoint source programs, identify land uses and critical coastal areas, monitor improvements, provide technical assistance, improve public participation and administrative coordination, and modify state coastal zone boundaries.[14] Federal and state programs must be consistent with one another.

A Coastal Zone Management Fund is created to loan funds to improve coastal areas. The funds may be used to manage land and water areas, promote demonstration projects, award emergency grants, develop or confer awards of excellence in coastal zone management, develop special programs, or apply the public trust doctrine to implement state management programs. The EPA provides technical assistance and necessary research to help states to implement their coastal zone management plans.[15]

Under the CZMA, a National Estuarine Research Reserve System is created. Priorities for coordinated research are identified, common research principles are developed, uniform methods of research are propagated, performance standards are created, and sources of funds are identified for estuarine research.[16] Finally, an advisory council of specialists in ocean and coastal resources is created. This council has representatives from academic institutions in every coastal region.

Exhibit 37: Shore lands can be damaged by human development, discharge of contaminants into waters, unexpected erosion or sand deposits, or other environmental changes. Public beach access and shoreline management are regulated by provisions of the Coastal Zone Management Act. (Photo: author)

Chronology of CZMA

1976:   Coastal Zone Management Act Amendments, 16 U.S.C. 1452

1980:   Coastal Zone Management Improvement Act, 16 U.S.C. 1453(17), 16 USC 1452(3)

1985:   Coastal Zone Management Reauthorization Act

1990:   Coastal Zone Act Reauthorization Amendments(CZARA), 16 U.S.C. 1455(b)

CHAPTER 27

Species Protection

Endangered Species Act (ESA)

Overview

- Many species have threatened lives or are totally endangered.

- They might not survive as a species unless strict regulations are imposed.

- The ESA creates scientific and management authorities.

- The act is managed jointly by the DOI and the DOC.

- A list of endangered species is published and updated every five years.

- Recovery plans must be developed for these endangered species.

- Monitoring of species is required, and civil and criminal penalties can be imposed upon violators of the ESA.

Purpose and programs

An international agreement was signed in 1973 requiring that all nations respect a treaty to protect the critical habitats of endangered species of fish, wildlife, insects, and plants.[17] The ESA determines and designates species that are endangered or threatened with extinction. *Endangered species* are defined as those that are threatened with destruction of their habitat or range, subject to disease or predators, or affected adversely by natural or man-made factors.[18] Land acquisition is authorized, if necessary, to protect animal and fish habitats. The U.S. Department of Commerce (DOC) and the U.S. Department of the Interior (DOI) cooperate with states, international governments, and other federal agencies. Scientific and management authorities are created by the Act, and many activities are prohibited, such as hunting, dumping wastes, or heating waters near the threatened or endangered species.

The DOI and the DOC have program responsibilities for the ESA. Lists of threatened or endangered species are published in the *Federal Register* by either the Department of Interior or the Department of Commerce. Once every five years, a review is performed of all endangered species, and the list is modified as needed. Protective regulations may be issued by either federal department in support of the ESA.

Methods of managing endangered species

Recovery plans must be developed and implemented to conserve and ensure the survival of endangered and threatened species. The plans must describe site-specific management requirements, measurable criteria, and estimates of the time required to carry out the actions needed to protect each species. A system must be developed to monitor the status of all at-risk species.

Each state must adhere to the ESA, and state laws cannot conflict with the ESA. Exceptions to the ESA may be made for any declared disaster area.[19] Any experimental population is treated as a threatened species. Civil and criminal enforcement can be applied, and penalties are administered for violations of the ESA. A number of enforcement provisions can be applied, ranging from massive fines to imprisonment.

Exhibit 38: Red squirrels are protected under the Endangered Species Act. These animals are more like chipmunks than squirrels. (Photo: author)

In order to review, critique, and approve recovery plans, an Endangered Species Committee has been established. At present, it is composed of the Secretaries of Agriculture, Army, and Interior, as well as the Chairman of the Council of Economic Advisors and the Administrators of the EPA and the National Oceanic and Atmospheric Administration.[20]

Chronology of ESA

1973:	Endangered Species Act, 16 U.S.C. 1531 et seq.
1978:	Endangered Species Act Amendment, Pub.L. 95-632, Stat. 3751
1979:	Endangered Species Act Amendment, Pub.L. 96-159, 4(1)(C), 93 Stat. 1225,1226

Chapter 28

Forests and Ranges

Forest and Rangeland Renewable Resources Planning Act (FRRRPA)

Overview

- FRRRPA is mainly concerned with the replacement and regrowth of forests and maintaining an ecological balance in rangelands.

- Land management and resource management are promoted by timber cutting restrictions, research programs, and surveys of conditions.

- Technical assistance is provided to the private sector.

- Extension service programs are developed.

Purpose and programs

The FRRRPA assesses renewable resources; inventories the national forest system; promotes guidelines for land management and resource management; establishes a scientific advisory committee; and requires the issuing of permits, contracts, and other legal instruments. Nonfederal lands are also protected.[21] Forest Service activities are specified to implement the act. A Reforestation Trust Fund, National Forest Transportation System, and the National Forest System are established under the FRRRPA.[22] Timber cutting limitations are established. Periodic surveys and analyses of area conditions are required, as well as general and specific research programs and studies of different kinds of forests. Technical assistance is provided to both public and private sectors. Extension programs are established to disseminate information about renewable resources.

The FRRRPA identifies the need to serve the national interest by having the Forest Service of the U.S. Department of Agriculture cooperate with other agencies to assess the nation's renewable resources and prepare a national renewable resource program which is to be periodically reviewed and updated.[23] The Forest Service must perform research in the use of recycled and waste timber products, develop techniques for substituting secondary materials for primary materials, and promote the use of recycled timber products. Public involvement, as in most federal acts, is a requirement, as is consultation with other governmental agencies.[24]

Managing, reporting, and scientific planning

The forested lands must be maintained at appropriate rates of growth with appropriate forest cover and tree species. The conditions of timber stands must be maintained to secure the maximum benefits of mul-

Exhibit 39: In the lower right corner, a monitoring well is part of this plan required to prevent contamination of forests, ground water, and soils under the Forest and Rangeland Renewable Resources Planning Act.

tiple-use, sustained-yield management.[25] An annual report on the use of herbicides and pesticides in the National Forest System must be prepared and submitted. Suitable lands must be identified for resource management. Inventories must include all renewable resources, such as soil and water. The inventories must contain maps, graphic material, and explanatory aids. Guidelines for land management plans that are environmentally sensitive and comprehensive must be developed. An interdisciplinary approach must be used to consider and integrate the physical, biological, economic, and other sciences. All regulations must be based on good science.

The Bureau of Land Management (BLM) must complete its own Forest Land and Resource Management Plans. The Department of Agriculture may use the BLM assessments, surveys, and programs to assist states and other organizations in planning to protect and manage renewable resources on private land. Both forestry and range lands are concerns of the FRRRPA, and state and private lands are also controlled.[26]

Research and science

Environmental research must be performed to protect vegetation and animal life; maintain forests; prevent fires; and control insects, diseases, noxious plants and animals, air pollutant damage, and other problems. When biological, chemical, or mechanical control methods and systems are needed, they must be used in a way that will protect people, resources, and property. A newer, related federal act, the Wood Residue Utilization Act (WRUA), makes information available that can have potential commercial application for wood residues.[27] Wood residues are wood by-products from timber harvesting and forest protection and management.

Extension programs of the U.S. Department of Agriculture (USDA) are to be used to educate private forest and range landowners, processors, and users of forest and rangeland renewable resources about environmental protection. Subjects to be taught in these extension programs range from urban forests to trees and temperatures, and shrubs as shelter belts to prevent erosion. Also, state and local programs are to be reinforced with USDA extension programs and funding.[28]

Chronology of FRRRPA

1974:   Forest and Rangeland Renewable Resources Planning Act, 16 USC sec. 1601

1978:   Forest and Rangeland Renewable Resources Research Act, Pub. L. 95-307, 92 Stat. 353

1980:   Wood Residue Utilization Act, Pub.L. 96-554, 94 Stat. 3257

1987:   Renewable Resource Extnesion Act Amendments, Pub.L. 100-231, 101 Stat. 1565

1988:   Forest Ecosystems and Atmospheric Pollution Research Act, Pub.L.100-521, 102 Stat. 2601

❖   Forest and Rangeland Renewable Resources Planning Act (FRRRPA)

CHAPTER 29

Soil and Water

Soil and Water Resources Conservation Act (SWRCA)

Overview

The SWRCA

* is a soil and water conservation program.

* protects agricultural and grazing lands and their waters.

* collects data about the land and its resources.

* provides financial and technical support.

Purpose and programs

SWRCA collects data to develop soil and water conservation programs. The Act protects agricultural and private grazing lands. Under this Act, an appraisal of land must be performed to determine its physical condition and those actions which will be needed to maintain its natural use and prevent its environmental degradation.[29] Continued evaluation is required of soil, water, and related resources. Data reviewed must include the quality and quantities of soil, water, fish, wildlife, and the capabilities and limitations of those resources for meeting the current and projected demands of the land on the resource base.[30] Financial and technical assistance are provided for conserving agricultural and private grazing lands. Annual reports covering program effectiveness must accompany the submittal of annual budgets.

Chronology of SWRCA

1977:   Soil and Water Resources Conservation Act, 16 U.S.C. 2001-2009, Pub.L.95-192

1985:   SWRCA Amendments, Pub.L. 99-198

1994:   SWRCA Amendments, Pub.L. 103-354

CHAPTER 30

Ecosystem

Antarctic Protection Act (AAPA)

Overview

- The AAPA builds upon international treaties to ensure that the minerals of Antarctica are not exploited and that the natural laboratory to study stratospheric ozone depletion is not spoiled.

Purpose and programs

Mineral resources of the Antarctic continent are protected under the AAPA.[31] The habitats of the Antarctic continent are distinctive environments having special ecosystems. The continent offers a natural laboratory to monitor critical aspects of stratospheric ozone depletion and global climate change. While Antarctica is protected by a series of international agreements, there have been poor waste disposal practices by the scientific stations of the different nations, as well as oil spills, increased tourism, and over-exploitation of marine life. The Antarctic Treaty Consultative Parties have agreed to a voluntary ban on mineral resource activities that are made legally binding in the AAPA. No one may engage in, finance, or provide any assistance for any Antarctic mineral resource activity.[32]

Chronology of AAPA

1978:   Antarctic Conservation Act, Pub.L.95-541, 92 Stat. 2048

1990:   Antartic Protection Act, 16 U.S.C. 2461-2466

CHAPTER 31

Wetlands

Coastal Wetlands Planning, Protection, and Restoration Act (CWPPRA)

Overview

+ CWPPRA protects the Louisiana Coastal wetlands by declaring priorities for preserving, restoring, and conserving that state's wetlands.

+ An appointed task force develops a prioritized list of coastal wetlands restoration projects.

+ The EPA, U.S. Army Corps of Engineers, U.S. Department of the Interior and the State of Louisiana are designated stewards of the wetlands.

Purpose and programs

CWPPRA protects the Louisiana Coastal wetlands.[33] As the largest river in the United States, the Mississippi deposits much silt and debris carried from many other states and its tributaries into its delta and the Gulf of Mexico. There are many other reasons to protect Louisiana's wetlands—sensitive coastal zone environments that serve as purification areas, transition zones, and unique aquatic environments.

Priorities are declared for restoring and conserving the state's wetland areas with grants, planning, and specially designated projects.[34] A task force is created to identify and initiate, by priority, a list of coastal wetlands restoration projects in Louisiana. All targeted wetland areas must be described, mapped, and designated. The U.S. Army Corps of Engineers, the EPA, U.S. Department of the Interior, and the State of Louisiana are involved in implementing the requirements in this Act. Existing plans are developed by each of these agencies and integrated and coordinated into an overall state conservation plan. Each project is given a priority ranking. Projects must clearly indicate their benefits as a condition for funding. National coastal wetlands conservation grants are to be used for the wetlands protection projects and for planning.[35]

Exhibit 40: Swampy, marshy wetlands may be easily contaminated. Much of the vegetation in this wetland has been killed by soil or water contamination.

Chronology of CWPPRA

1990:	Coastal Wetlands Planning, Protection and Restoration Act, 16 U.S.C. 3951 to 3956

CHAPTER 32

Nonnative Species

Nonindigenous Aquatic Nuisance Prevention and Control Act (NANPCA)

Overview

- The NANPCA regulates the introduction of nonnative species of fish and plants into established habitats.

- Diseases or parasites or unexpected nonnative species growth could destroy the native species or disrupt aquatic environments, and even the economy of near-shore areas.

- Controls include prevention of unintentional discharges into waters; research, prevention, control, and information dissemination; minimization of the economic and ecological impacts; and establishment of a research technology program.

Purpose and programs

NANPCA focuses on the problems created by the introduction of nonnative species of fish and plants into established habitats.[36] Many native species have been harmed or eliminated, and the safety of some species has been seriously threatened due to a lack of knowledge and forethought. Species have been harmed by the jettisoning and discharging of ship ballast. When conditions are favorable, nonnative species can become established and compete with, or prey upon, native species of fish, plants, or wildlife. Diseases or parasites can be introduced that could destroy the native species or disrupt aquatic environments and even the economy of near-shore areas.[37] A prime example of an introduced species is the zebra mussel whose economic disruptions to aquatic communities is estimated at over five billion dollars. Other disruptions have been caused by the ruffe, mitten crab, green crab, brown tree snake, brown mussel, Eurasian watermilfoil, hydrilla, water hyacinth, and water chestnut. These are only a few of the thousands of introduced species.

Because of the problems caused by these nonnative species, the NANPCA attempts to prevent unintentional discharges and introduction into waters; coordinates federal funding for research, prevention, control, and information dissemination; develops and carries out control methods; minimizes the economic and ecological impacts; and establishes a program of technological research.[38] Violators of any of NANPCA's regulations may be subject to both civil and criminal penalties.

Requirements

In this act, coordination is required with Canada, Mexico, and the International Maritime Organization of the United Nations. Ship ballast water is a major concern, so shipping studies must be performed to determine the feasibility of regulatory controls. Special nuisance problems must be solved in the Great Lakes, Lake Champlain, Columbia River system, and the Mississippi River system. Regional grants are made available for research in aquatic nuisance species prevention and control for the Chesapeake Bay, Gulf of Mexico, Pacific Coast, Atlantic Coast, and the San Francisco Bay-Delta Estuary. A national ballast information clearinghouse is created at the Smithsonian Environmental Research Center.[39]

Chronology of NANPCA
_____

1990: Nonindigenous Aquatic Nuisance Prevention and Control Act, Pub.L. 101-646, 104, Stat. 4761

1996: National Invasive Species Act, Pub.L. 104-332,
_____

CHAPTER 33

Land

Federal Land Policy and Management Act (FLPMA)

Overview

* The FLPMA controls the public lands of the United States to help avoid environmental degradation.

* Federally owned land consumes an incredibly large land area of the country, and environmental quality is regulated to avoid negative spillovers to adjacent private lands.

* Designated management areas are the California Desert, Yaquina Head Outstanding Natural Area (Oregon), Fossil Forest Research Natural Area (New Mexico), and lands in Alaska.

* Wilderness studies must be performed and updated periodically for these areas.

* DOI maintains a current inventory of all public lands and their resources.

* Range management is mandated, and leases are available for grazing, rights of way, pipelines, water use, electric transmission and distribution lines, roads, etc.

Purpose and programs

FLPMA is the act creating the Bureau of Land Management (BLM) to control the public lands of the United States.[40] Federal lands are vast; therefore, the need to control, manage, and regulate these lands is quite important. Careful control and management are necessary to ensure that these large undeveloped land areas do not degrade. Additionally, the environmental quality of these lands is managed to prevent negative spillovers to adjacent private lands.

The FLPMA requires land-use planning, land acquisition, and disposition. It specifies administration by creating a Bureau of Land Management, giving enforcement authority, establishing budgets, providing working capital, making loans available to states, and requiring annual reports.[41] Range management is promoted by this act, by establishing grazing fees, requiring leases, and issuing permits for using federal lands, and establishing right-of-way restrictions and requirements. Designated management areas are the California Desert, Yaquina Head Outstanding Natural Area (Oregon), Fossil Forest Research Natural Area (New Mexico), and lands in Alaska. These areas are considered extremely fragile ecosystems that are easily damaged. A wilderness study identifies wilderness areas that are to be designated special management areas.[42] The study must be updated periodically.

Regulatory requirements

According to the act, public lands and their resources have to be regularly inventoried and land-use plans developed to guide present and future use. The land-use plans have to be coordinated with state and local plans and other federal plans. The sale or lease of any federal parcel in these public lands must serve the national interest. Since there can be such a wide interpretation of the national and public interest, the disposal of these lands through sale or lease is easily justified. For this reason, the Department of the Interior (administrator of the FLPMA) must develop rules and regulations with stated criteria for land disposition. Also, areas of critical environmental concern are designated within these land areas.

The Department of the Interior is responsible for maintaining a current inventory of all public lands and their resources, including their value as scenic, recreational, or natural resources. Priorities are given to areas of critical environmental concern. Land-use plans are developed with public participation. Interdisciplinary approaches to planning must include physical, social, and economic factors. Long-term benefits to the public must be evaluated, and all pollution control laws must be considered in the plans. The plans may designate new land areas for purchase, but sufficient reasons for such acquisitions must be included.[43] New land areas can be contiguous or away from the national forest system holdings. Conversely, the federal government may convey public lands to the state and local governments.

Detailed provisions of the Act also include the establishment of trespass controls, fee schedules, a forest ranger force, and a working fund; delineation of search and rescue responsibilities; loans to states; use of Land and Water Conservation Fund to purchase lands; and range management.

Range management is an important part of the FLPMA. Grazing fees are established on public lands in 11 western states. Leases are granted for grazing based on criteria, priorities, and allotment management plans. Rights-of-way are granted or renewed for water use; pipelines; electric transmission and distribution lines; radio and telephone towers; roads and other transportation facilities; and other uses in the public interest.[44]

Chronology of FLPMA

1976:	Federal Land Policy and Management Act, 43 U.S.C. 1701 et seq, Pub.L. 94-579, 90 Stat. 2743

CHAPTER 34

Offshore

Outer Continental Shelf Lands Act (OCSLA)

Overview

- ◆ The OCSLA regulates offshore oil and gas resources.

- ◆ Activities in the ocean must be managed to prevent pollution from accidents.

- ◆ A Fishermen's Contingency Fund is established to pay for any claims from fishermen when their equipment or catches are spoiled by the extractors of oil and gas.

- ◆ There must be color coding, stamping, and labeling of equipment and tools with the owner's identification.

Purpose and programs

OCSLA regulates the oil and gas resources located on the outer continental shelf beyond the shorelines of the United States.[45] The Act recognizes that the United States has become dependent on foreign oil and that there is a decreasing supply of natural gas.[46] For these reasons, the oil and gas resources of the Outer Continental Shelf must be managed to prevent pollution from accidents on offshore drilling platforms or along their ocean pipelines. The use of the most current technologies is promoted in the Act as a means to avoid spills.[47] States are to work closely with local governments to manage the Outer Continental Shelf for safety from offshore oil spills, natural gas spills, and the adverse activities of fishermen. The marine environment (fish and shellfish) is protected by the OCSLA through mandatory regulations that manage current extraction technology. Funds are provided to clean any oil or gas spills.[48]

Regulatory requirements

Oil and gas in the oceans must be exploited with the greatest protection of the marine environment. An Offshore Oil Pollution Compensation Fund was originally established to be deposited in the Oil Spill Liability Trust Fund, but the fund has been terminated and a Fishermen's Contingency Fund created.[49] This new fund is established to pay for any claim for damages and other fees to fishermen when their equipment or catches are spoiled by the extractors of oil and gas. There must be an economic loss in order to be awarded these funds. In order to avoid potential hazards to commercial fishing caused by Outer Continental Shelf oil and gas exploration, development, and production—and any obstructions on the sea bottoms and on the surface—there must be color coding, stamping, and labeling of equipment and tools with the owner's identification prior to their use.[50] (This provision for identification is designed to encourage care during sea operations. Supposedly, careless owners and operators will be discovered more easily.) For any gas distribution lines originating on the Outer Continental Shelf, the DOE must issue a certificate of public convenience and necessity.[51]

Chronology of OCSLA

1978:	Outer Continental Shelf Lands Act, 43 U.S.C. 1331 et seq; 43 U.S.C. 1801 et seq
1988:	Outer Continental Shelf Operations Indemnification Clarification Act or OCSLA Amendments, Pub.L. 95-372

CHAPTER 35

Undeveloped Land

Wilderness
Act
(WA)

Overview

- A National Wilderness Preservation System is established.

- The U.S. Department of Agriculture (USDA) maps and develops legal descriptions of each wilderness area.

- The uses of wilderness areas are limited.

- There are definite prohibitions against any kind of development or use of machinery in a wilderness area.

Purpose and programs

Increasing population in the United States, suburbanization, and the rapidly growing use of vehicles are modifying many areas. Without protective action, in the future, there would be no lands left to preserve and protect in their natural condition. A National Wilderness Preservation System is established to include federally owned areas designated as wilderness areas.[52] These areas are to be used and enjoyed in a manner that leaves them unchanged from their natural state. These wilderness areas are to be protected and preserved in perpetuity. All of the areas within the national forests that are classified as wilderness, wild, or canoe are now designated as wilderness areas.[53] The U.S. Department of Agriculture (USDA) maps and develops legal descriptions of each wilderness area. Public records are kept that include any additions or deletions. Periodically, each area in the national forests is assessed by the USDA to determine its suitability for preservation as wilderness. Congress can increase the size of each wilderness area by 1280 acres. Every roadless area of 5,000 contiguous acres or more in the national parks is periodically reviewed, along with every roadless island, national wildlife refuge, and game range. The DOI maintains the roadless areas within the national park system. The USDA and DOI report to Congress and the President about the suitability of any area for preservation as wilderness.

Regulatory provisions

Public notice must be given, public hearings arranged, and decisions, plans, programs, and wilderness area designations submitted to the governor's office of each state and to the administrative offices of counties or boroughs for their review and comment.[54] Wilderness areas are limited to recreational, scenic, scientific, educational, conservation, and historical uses. There are definite prohibitions against roads, motor vehicles, motorized equipment or motorboats, the landing of aircraft, other form of mechanical transport, or structures or installations within any wilderness area.

Wilderness areas can be used for prospecting for minerals under certain conditions only. Wilderness areas may be restricted to ingress and egress for exploration, drilling and production of oil, and use of land for transmission lines, waterlines, telephone lines, or mining and processing operations. Mining locations within the boundaries of the wilderness areas can be used solely for mining or processing operations. Timber cutting is restricted to cutting, under sound principles of forest management. Commercial services may be performed in wilderness areas to support recreational or other wilderness activities.[55]

Chronology of WA

1964:	Wilderness Act, 16 U.S.C. 1131 et seq

The Past Fifty Years

Chronology of Federal Environmental Regulation

1940s

1947   Federal Insecticide, Fungicide, and Rodenticide Act, 7 U.S.C. 136

1948   Federal Water Pollution Control Act (FWPCA), 62 Stat. 1155; Pub.L. 845

1950s

1952   Federal Water Pollution Control Act (FWPCA Amendments), 66 Stat. 1155

1954   Atomic Energy Act (AEA), 42 U.S.C. 2014, 2012–2021d, 2022, 2111, 2113, and 2114

1955   Air Pollution Control Act (APCA), 69 Stat. 322

1960s

1960   Federal Water Pollution Control Act (FWPCA Amendments), Pub.L. 86-624, 74 Stat. 411

1963   Clean Air Act (CAA), Pub.L. No. 88-206, 77 Stat. 392

1964   Wilderness Act, 16 U.S.C. 1131 et seq

1965   Solid Waste Disposal Act (SWDA), amended 1984 entirely as the Resource Conservation and Recovery Act (RCRA)

1965   Federal Water Pollution Control Act (FWPCA Amendments),
        Pub.L. 89-234, 79 Stat. 903

1967   Air Quality Act (AQA), Pub.L. 90-148, 81 Stat. 465

1969   National Environmental Policy Act (NEPA),
        42 U.S.C. 4321–4370

1970s

1970   National Environmental Policy Act (NEPA), Pub.L. 91-190,
        42 U.S.C. 4321–4347

1970   Environmental Quality Improvement Act (EQIA), 42 U.S.C.
        4371 to 4375

1970   Federal Water Pollution Control Act (FWPCA Amendments),
        Title II, Pub.L. 224

1970   Solid Waste Disposal Act (SWDA), Pub.L. 91-512, amended
        1984 entirely as the Resource Conservation and Recovery Act
        (RCRA)

1970   Clean Air Act (CAA Amendments), Pub.L. 91-604, 84 Stat.
        1676, Pub.L. 91-596, 91st Congress, S. 2193

1970   Occupational Safety and Health Act (OSHA), Pub.L. 91-596,
        84 Stat. 1590

1972   Federal Water Pollution Control Act (FWPCA Amendments),
        Pub.L. 92-240, 86 Stat. 47

1972   Noise Control Act (NCA), 42 U.S.C. 4901–4918

1972   Marine Protection, Research, and Sanctuaries Act (MPRSA),
        33 U.S.C. 1401–1445; 16 U.S.C.1431 et seq; also
        33 U.S.C. 1271

1972   Marine Mammal Protection Act (MMPA), Pub.L. 92-522;
        16 U.S.C. 1361–1407; 86 Stat. 1027

1973   Endangered Species Act (ESA), 16 U.S.C. 1531 et seq

1974   Forest and Rangeland Renewable Resources Planning Act
        (FRRRPA),16 U.S.C. 1601

1974   Safe Drinking Water Act (SDWA), Pub.L. 93-523,
        42 U.S.C. 300

1975   National Environmental Protection Act (NEPA), (NEPA Amend-
        ment), Pub.L. 94-52, Pub.L. 94-83

1976   Resource Conservation and Recovery Act (RCRA), (RCRA
        Amendments changing the name of the Solid Waste Disposal
        Act) Pub.L. 94-580; 7 U.S.C. 1010 et seq, 40 CFR 280 and
        281)

1976   Toxic Substances Control Act (TSCA), Pub.L. 99-519

1976   Toxic Substances Control Act (TSCA), Pub.L. 94-469

1976   Coastal Zone Management Act Amendment (CZMA),
        16 U.S.C. 1452

1976   Marine Mammal Protection Act (MMPA), (MMPA Amendment),
        Pub.L. 94-265; 90 Stat. 360

1976   Federal Land Policy and Management Act (FLPMA),
        43 U.S.C. 1701, Pub.L. 94-579, 90 Stat. 2743

1977   Toxic Substances Control Act (TSCA), 15 U.S.C. 2601–2671

1977   Clean Water Act (CAA), CAA Amendment, Pub.L. 92-500,
        33 U.S.C. 1251

1977   Soil and Water Resources Conservation Act (SWRCA),
        16 U.S.C. 2001-2009

1977   Clean Air Act (CAA), CAA Amendments, Pub.L. 95-95,
        91 Stat. 685

1977   Surface Mining Control and Reclamation Act (SMCRA),
        Pub.L. 95-89, 30 U.S.C. 1201

1977   Clean Water Act (CWA), Pub.L. 95-217, 33 U.S.C. 1251

1977   Safe Drinking Water Act (SDWA), Pub.L. 95-190

1977   Executive Order 11991 42 CFR 26967 (May 24)

1977   Soil and Water Resources Conservation Act (SWRCA),
        16 U.S.C. 2001, Pub.L. 95-192

1978   Marine Mammal Protection Act (MMPA), MMPA Amendment,
        Pub.L. 95-316; 92 Stat. 380

1978   Forest and Rangeland Renewable Resources Planning Act
        (FRRRPA), 16 U.S.C. sec. 1601 et seq

1978   Forest and Rangeland Renewable Resources Planning Act
        (FRRRPA), Pub.L. 95-307, 92 Stat. 353

1978   Federal Insecticide, Fungicide, and Rodenticide Act (FIFRA),
        Pub.L. 95-396, U.S.C. 136 et seq

1978   Atomic Energy Act (AEA), AEA Amendment, Pub.L. 95-604

1978   Endangered Species Act (ESA), ESA Amendment,
        Pub.L. 95-632, Stat. 3751

1979   Endangered Species Act (ESA), ESA Amendment,
        Pub.L. 96-159, 4(1)(C), 93 Stat. 1225, 1226

1979   Aviation Safety and Noise Abatement Act, 49 U.S.C.A. 2101 et
        seq.

1980s

1980   Solid Waste Disposal Act (SWDA), SWDA Amendments, Pub.L. 96-482, 42 U.S.C. 6901

1980   Forest and Rangeland Renewable Resources Planning Act (FRRRPA), FRRRPA Subchapter: Wood Residue Utilization Act (WRUA), Pub.L. 96-554, 94 Stat. 3257

1980   Comprehensive Environmental Response, Compensation, and Liability Act (CERCLA, or "Superfund"), 26 U.S.C. 4611–4682; Pub.L. 96-510, 94 Stat. 2797

1980   Coastal Zone Management Act (CZMA), CZMA Amendments changing name to Coastal Zone Management Improvement Act (CZMIA), 16 U.S.C. 1453(17), 16 U.S.C. 1452(3)

1980   Airport Noise Abatement Act (ANAA), 49 U.S.C. 47501–47510

1981   Clean Air Act (CAA), CAA Amendments, Pub.L. No. 97-23, 95 Stat. 139

1981   Clean Water Act (CWA), CWA Amendments, Pub.L. 97-117, 95 Stat. 1623

1981   Marine Mammal Protection Act (MMPA), MMPA Amendments, Pub.L. 97-58; 95 Stat. 979

1982   Airport and Airway Improvement Act, 49 U.S.C.A. 2202

1982   National Environmental Protection Act (NEPA), NEPA Amendments, Pub.L. 97-258

1982   Environmental Quality Improvement Act (EQIA), EQIA Amendments, Pub.L. 97-258 4(b) 96 Stat. 1067

1982   Nuclear Waste Policy Act (NWPA), 42 U.S.C. 10101–10270

1983   Clean Water Act (CWA), CWA Amendments, 33 U.S.C. 1251, 42 U.S.C. 9601–9657; Pub.L. 98-802; 97 Stat. 485

1984   Marine Mammal Protection Act (MMPA), MMPA Amendment, Pub.L. 98-364; 98 Stat. 440

1984   Solid Waste Disposal Act (SWDA), SWDA amended 1976 by the Resource Conservation and Recovery Act (RCRA); name change of certain sections and amendments of the SWDA-RCRA to "The Hazardous and Solid Waste Amendments of 1984" (HSWA), 40 CFR 261, 262, 267, 268, 271, 272, Pub.L. 98-616, U.S.C. 6917. Other RCRA amendments include: "Standards for Treatment, Storage, and Disposal Facilities (TSDs)," 40 CFR 264–265 (42 U.S.C. 6901). Also, Subtitle D amendments by 42 U.S.C. 6941–6949

1985   Clean Water Act (CAA), CWA Amendment, 33 U.S.C.1251

1985   Coastal Zone Management Act (CZMA), CZMA Amendments and name change to "Coastal Zone Management Reauthorization Act of 1985"

1985   Clean Water Act (CAA), 33 U.S.C. 1251

1986   Safe Drinking Water Act (SDWA), SWDA Amendments, 40 CFR 141–143

1986   Comprehensive Environmental Response, Compensation, and Liability Act (CERCLA), CERCLA amendments, Pub.L. 99-499, 100 Stat. 1613). A new trust fund is formed, 26 U.S.C. 4611–82 changed to 26 U.S.C. 9507; certain sections may be cited as "Superfund Amendments and Reauthorization Act (SARA)"

1986   Toxic Substances Control Act (TSCA), TSCA Amendments create "Asbestos Hazard Emergency Response Act (AHERA)," Pub.L. 99-519

1986   Safe Drinking Water Act (SDWA), SDWA Amendments, Pub.L.104-182

1986   Emergency Planning and Community Right-to-Know Act (EPCRA), 42 U.S.C. 11001–11050

1986   Marine Mammal and Protection Act (MMPA), MMPA Amendments, Pub.L. 99-659; 100 Stat. 3706

1987   Clean Water Act (CWA), CWA Amendments, Pub.L. 100-4, 33 U.S.C. 1254

1987   Forest and Rangeland Renewable Resources Planning Act (FRRRPA), FRRRPA Amendments for extension services, Pub.L. 100-231, 101 Stat. 1565

1988   Forest and Rangeland Renewable Resources Planning Act (FRRRPA), FRRRPA Amendments, certain sections to be named, "Forest Ecosystems and Atmospheric Pollution Research Act of 1988," Pub.L. 100-521, 102 Stat. 2601

1988   Outer Continental Shelf Lands Act (OCSLA), OCSLA Amendments, certain sections to be named, "Outer Continental Shelf Operations Indemnification Clarification Act or OCSLA Amendments of 1988," Pub.L. 95-372

1988   Marine Protection, Research, and Sanctuaries Act (MPRSA), MPRSA Amendments, Pub.L. 100-688, Title I, 1001, 102 Stat.4139

1988   Federal Insecticide, Fungicide, and Rodenticide Act (FIFRA), FIFRA Amendments, Pub.L. 100-532

1988   Marine Mammal Protection Act (MMPA), MMPA Amendment, Pub.L. 100-711; 102 Stat. 4755

1990s

1990   Pollution Prevention Act (PPA), 42 U.S.C. 13101–13109

1990   Coastal Zone Management Act (CZMA), CZMA Amendments and certain sections to be named "Coastal Zone Act Reauthorization Amendments of 1990 (CZARA)," 16 U.S.C. 1455

1990   Aquatic Nuisance Prevention and Control Act (ANPCA), or Nonindigenous Aquatic Nuisance Prevention and Control Act of 1990, Pub.L. 101-646, 104, Stat. 4761

1990   Antarctic Protection Act (AAPA), 16 U.S.C. 2461–2466

1990   Oil Pollution Act (OPA), 33 U.S.C 2701–2761

1990   Clean Air Act (CAA), CAA Amendment, Pub.L. 101-549, 104 Stat. 2399

1990   Clean Water Act (CWA), CWA Amendments, Pub.L. 101-596, 104 Stat. 3000, 33 U.S.C. 1269

1990   Occupational Safety and Health Act (OSHA), OSHA Amendments, Pub.L. 101-552, Section 3101

1990   Marine Mammal Protection Act (MMPA), MMPA Amendment, Pub.L. 101-627; 100 Stat. 4465

1991   Federal Insecticide, Fungicide, and Rodenticide Act (FIFRA), FIFRA Amendments, Pub.L. 102-237

1991   Federal Agency Recycling and the Council on Federal Recycling and Procurement Policy, Executive Order 12780

1992   Federal Facility Compliance Act (FFCA), Pub.L. 102-386, 106 Stat. 1505

1992   Toxic Substances Control Act (TSCA), TSCA Amendments, certain sections named as "Lead-based Paint Exposure Reduction Act of 1992," Pub.L. 102-550, 1021(c) Stat. 3924

1992   Marine Mammal Protection Act (MMPA), MMPA Amendments, certain sections named as "Marine Mammal Health and Stranding Response Act of 1992," Pub.L. 102-587, 3001, 106 Stat. 5059

1993   Federal Acquisition, Recycling, and Waste Prevention, Executive Order 12873

1994   Noise Control Act (NCA), NCA Amendments, Pub.L. 103-272, 7(b) 108 Stat.1379

1994   Airport Noise Abatement Act (ANAA), ANAA Amendments, Pub.L. 103-272, 108 Stat 1284

1994   Marine Mammal Protection Act (MMPA), MMPA Amendments, Pub.L.103-238, U.S.C. 1386 et seq

1994   Clean Water Act (CWA), CWA Amendments, Pub.L. 103-431, 108 Stat. 4396

1994   Soil and Water Resources Conservation Act (SWRCA), SWRCA Amendments, Pub.L. 103-354

1995   Oil Pollution Act (OPA), OPA Amendments, Pub.L. 104-55, 109 Stat. 546, 33 U.S.C 2704–2716

1996   Safe Drinking Water Act (SDWA), SDWA Amendments, Pub.L. 104-182, 42 U.S.C. 300

1996   Aquatic Nuisance Prevention and Control Act (ANPCA), ANPCA Amendments, certain sections are named "National Invasive Species Act of 1996," Pub.L. 104-332

1996   Federal Land Policy and Management Act (FLPMA), FLPMA Amendments, certain sections are named, "Land Disposal Program Flexibility Act of 1996," Pub.L. 104-119, 110 Stat. 830

1996   Comprehensive Environmental Response, Compensation, and Liability Act (CERCLA), certain sections are named, "Asset Conservation, Lender Liability, and Deposit Insurance Protection Act of 1996," Pub.L. 104-208, 2501, 110 Stat. 3009-462. Also, certain sections apply to Resource Conservation and Recovery Act (RCRA).

1997   Marine Mammal Protection Act (MMPA), MMPA Amendments, certain sections are named, "International Dolphin Conservation Program Act of 1997." Pub.L. 105-42, 111, Stat 1122 U.S.C. 962 et seq

Notes

Number System for Federal Laws and Regulations

Laws, rules, and regulations

Federal environmental regulations are the result of deliberation and careful consideration by lawmakers, public agencies, corporate professionals, and many others. Many laws are passed, along with policy actions by environmental agencies, and together these create the federal framework. The way in which laws are enacted and then made into sets of environmental regulations requires some explanation. Environmental rules and regulations are recorded in the *Statutes at Large*, *United States Code*, *Federal Register*, *Code of Federal Regulations*, *Unified Agenda*, and the *Weekly Compilation of Presidential Documents*. Eventually, most regulations become numbered in the *Code of Federal Regulations*. To clarify the process of enacting and numbering the environmental regulations, the general process for all regulations needs to be briefly reviewed. Although the federal agencies issue their own memoranda, clarifications, and bulletins that can have the effect of a formal regulation, they are not discussed here.

Enacting and numbering the laws

Federal environmental laws are enacted by the U.S. Congress and the President to support or enforce public policy. Those bills originating in the House of Representatives are given a number and the prefix *H.R.* Those bills originating in the Senate are given a number with the prefix *S.* Bills that are passed or are allowed to become law without the President's signature are transmitted by the White House to the Archivist of the United States for numbering. A public law number is assigned for the *Statutes at Large* volume that refers to that congressional session. Law numbers are sequenced starting at the beginning of each Congress by the number of each Congress (103, 104, 105, etc.), such as Public Law 106-12 or Private Law 106-222. All laws passed by the same Congress will have the same numerical prefix.

The first publication of the law is known as the *slip law*. It is separately published as an unbound pamphlet. The Office of the Federal Register, National Archives and Records Administration, prepares the slip laws with editorial notes that give citations to other laws and any needed details. These editorial notes are called *marginal notes* giving *United States Code* numbers and classifications. The slip law contains information about the legislative history of the law (committee report number, name of the committee, date of passing the Senate or House of Representatives, reference to the *Congressional Record* by volume, year, and date, as well as other information). Then, public laws are transformed into other groups of documents and given different names, numbers, edited or annotated with comments, and placed in categories. Sometimes, comments that may change or amend the laws are added during the preparation of the different sets of documents or regulations.

Statutes at Large

United States Statutes at Large (29 Stat. 491) contains the laws and any concurrent resolutions of Congress, reorganization plans, or proclamations issued during each congressional session. Annually, the Office of the Federal Register (National Archives and Records Administration) prepares the *United States Statutes at Large*. Supplemental volumes are issued that contain tables of prior laws that have been amended, repealed, or affected by other public laws enacted. Each volume has a table of contents and index. Each of the statutes is organized, that is, numbered, in chronological order and not by subject matter. In order to organize the laws by subject matter and show the changes made to those laws, the following numbering system is assigned, the *United States Code* (42 U.S.C. 6901).

United States Code

United States Code (42 U.S.C. 6901) is the compiled, written set of laws in force on the day before the beginning of the current session of Congress. The *Code* is prepared by the Law Revision Counsel of the House of Representatives. Complete, new editions are published every six years, with supplements containing the latest additions published every year. There are 50 title headings numbered in alphabetical order according to subject matter. The purpose for this coding and its numbering is to avoid the need for users to have to work with the *Statutes at Large* and later amendments to older laws. Through codification, one volume or title can contain all the current rules and regulations. In this manner, there can be "one-stop-shopping" for users.[1] The code is updated periodically, with changes annotated to sections. Those code versions containing comments or additions for the sections, or provisions, are called *United States Code Annotated* (42 U.S.C.A. 6901). Titles may be changed as the editing is completed for each title. Changes in a section of the *Code* are made within five business days of enacting the law.

Federal Register

The National Archives and Records Administration, Office of the Federal Register, publishes the *Federal Register* each workday. It contains notices, rules, proposed rules, federal agency orders, executive orders, and presidential documents. The *Federal Register* is available on the Internet.

Unified Agenda

This agenda is a summary of those actions that are anticipated to be taken by federal agencies. It is published semiannually (April and October) and is available on the Internet, also.

Weekly Compilation of Presidential Documents

Presidential documents—proclamations, executive orders (12999), and reorganization plans (1998 Plan No. 5)—contain statements, messages, and other materials released by the Office of the President. Every Monday, the Office of the Federal Register publishes the past week's presidential documents. They can also be viewed on the Internet.[2]

Details on the multiple numbering systems

Since environmental laws and their resulting programs can originate in many places within the federal government, they may start with different numbers in different places. A *bill* is the name given to a proposed law in the Senate or House of Representatives. Prior to enactment, the House of Representatives or the Senate gives a number to the bill (S.B. 1203 or H.R. 1203). After a vote is taken that passes the bill, a public law number is assigned. If the President issues a proclamation, executive order, or reorganization plan, a document number also is assigned (12999).

Each environmental law, like any law, requires many instructions, requirements, assigned duties and responsibilities, and restrictions on behavior. The law may also designate penalties that can be changed over time. For these reasons, laws need further definition, and supplemental rules and regulations need to be written and changed to insure that there will be no misunderstandings. When these additions are made, they are announced in the *Federal Register* and may be given yet another number in order to provide a usable reference to receive comment from the public, other public agencies that might be affected, or the private sector. After the rules and regulations are published, revisions may be made to them prior to their enactment. Then, they may be again renumbered according to the *Code of Federal Regulations* (CFRs).

Where to Find Environmental Regulations in the *Code of Federal Regulations*

Title Number	Subject
5	Administrative Personnel
7	Agriculture
15	Commerce and Trade
16	Conservation
29	Labor
30	Mineral Lands and Mining
33	Navigation and Navigable Waters
40	Protection of the Environment
42	Public Health and Welfare
43	Public Lands

Under the CFR numbering system, the subject matter of each rule, regulation, or law is categorized under a *title* number. There are many titles that have constant numbers and subjects. Primarily, environmental laws are scattered among 10 of the 50 title numbers as shown in the chart on the facing page.

Under each Public Law, *United States Code*, *United States Statutes at Large*, *Code of Federal Regulations*, title or chapter numbers (Arabic: 1,2,...9, etc.) are assigned to further divide the subjects and guide the user to the desired section of the law. Subchapter numbers (roman numeral: I, II,...IX, etc.) are given to sub-items for additional directions. Finally, section numbers are assigned (1,2,...999, etc.) and divided into small letters (a, b,....z). For example:

> Pub.L. 102-389, Title III, Oct. 6, 1992, 106 Stat. 1602.

> After a Public Law is codified in the *United States Code*; for example, Title 42, The Public Health and Welfare, Solid Waste Disposal, Hazardous Waste Management, it is identified as 42 U.S.C. 6921.

Code of Federal Regulations

The *Code of Federal Regulations* (CFR) may be more detailed and contain more items than the *United States Code*. By contrast, the *Code of Federal Regulations* (CFR) has provisions that may contain rules and regulations developed over time in response to needed changes in that law. As rules are developed, they are published in the *Federal Register* for review and comment by the public (including business and industry). The subjects covered in the CFRs parallel those in the federal Public Laws, but have a different numbering system. CFRs contain very specific rules for behavior with respect to protecting the public health, safety, and welfare, and in this way, they protect the environment. The CFR numbering system is as follows:

> 40 CFR 280.

> The first number, 40, indicates Title 40—Protection of the Environment. CFR indicates *Code of Federal Regulations*. The last number, 280, indicates Part 280—Technical Standards and Corrective Action Requirements for Owners and Operators of Underground Storage Tanks (UST).

CFRs are constantly changing. Some sections and parts are expanded, others reduced, and others deleted as changes are made. Numbers are not always consecutive, and a system is maintained in which some numbers in every sequence are skipped and reserved for future use by new topics. The EPA and other responsible environmental agencies regularly require fine tuning of subjects in the regulations or major revisions of entire sections. Access to the CFRs is available on the Internet from the publisher, the National Archives and Records Administration's Office of the Federal Register, and from the Government Printing Office (GPO). Paper editions of the CFR and *Federal Register* are available through the Superintendent of Documents. CD-ROM versions with usable computer search engines, as well as bound book copies, are available from the publisher of this book.

In summary, the *Code of Federal Regulations* is an annual publication that provides users with the permanent rules, regulations, and laws previously published in the *Federal Register*. The purpose of the CFRs is to present the official and complete text of agency regulations in one organized publication. Also, it has become the one comprehensive and convenient reference for the texts of the federal (environmental and other) regulations. To keep current, the CFR must be used with the daily *Federal Register*. For most users, the most recent edition of the CFRs can be considered as the major reference to most environmental regulations. As stated above, the other compilations of documents must be studied to obtain the complete regulatory picture.

Notes to Appendix 2

1   www.gpo.ucop.edu/catalog/uscode.html; and thomas.loc.gov/home/lawsmade.bysec/publication.html.

2   thomas.loc.gov/home/lawsmade.byse/appendiz.html.

Section One: The Framework (Chapters 1 to 5)

1   Other levels of government regulate the environment, also.

2   Each federal act or program designates different agencies that are responsible for functions and provisions. Responsibilities, duties, and agencies may change.

3   There are now 10 regional offices of the U.S. Environmental Protection Agency. They are located in Boston (Region 1), New York (Region 2), Philadelphia (Region 3), Atlanta (Region 4), San Francisco (Region 9), Chicago (Region 5), Dallas (Region 6), Kansas City (Region 7), Denver (Region 8), Seattle (Region 10).

4   For example, land use is one area that has been left to the state and local governments.

5   CERCLA is the Comprehensive Environmental Response and Liability Act. The Resource Conservation and Recovery Act (RCRA) refers to amendments—new sections, deletions, and changes—to the Solid Waste Disposal Act. 42 USCA 9601 to 9675; 42 USCA 6901 to 6992k; Pub.L. 94-580, Section 1.

6   The Communicable Disease Center (CDC) is an agency within U.S. Department of Health and Human Services.

7   In some instances, a federal agency other than EPA is given responsibilities for an environmental program. In those cases, there may be delegation of some duties to state and local agencies or even required cooperation with the EPA under a program.

8   After Lynn M. Gallagher. "Clean Water Act," in Thomas F.P. Sullivan, Ed. *Environmental Law Handbook: Fourteenth Edition.* Rockville, MD: Government Institutes, Inc., 1997. 111.

9   42 USCA 6941; 4001.

10 The SWDA may be cited as the "Resource Conservation and Recovery Act of 1976." Section 1; Pub.L. 94-580.

11 By passing this act, Congress authorized a waiver of the normally granted, sovereign immunity allowing the same civil fines and penalties for the private sector (or individuals) to be assessed on the federal government.

12 42 USCA 11002(a).

13 42 USCA 11001 to 11050. The Emergency Planning and Community Right-to-Know Act (EPCRA) was enacted to further protect citizens from accidental releases of chemicals.

14 42 USCA 9601 to 9675. The first version of CERCLA was enacted in 1980. Subchapter IV and certain sections of CERCLA were included as amendments to the 1980 act, with changes and additions to other federal acts, and named the Superfund Amendments and Reauthorization Act (SARA) in 1986.

15 42 USCA 4331

16   42 USCA 4331, 101

17   42 USCA 4333, 103

18   42 USCA 4342, 201

19   42 USCA 4344, 204

20   42 USCA 6901 to 6992k

21   42 USCA 4366a(a)(b)

22   42 USCA 4369(a)(b)

23   42 USCA 4371 to 4375

24   42 USCA 4372

25   42 USCA 13101 to 13109

26   *Source reduction* is the common term used by environmental professionals.

27   42 USCA 13103

28   42 USCA 13104

Section Two: Air (Chapters 6 to 8)

1   42 USCA 7401 to 7671q. The Clean Air Act began as the Air Pollution Control Act in 1955. Short titles and years of these changes are: 1959—Reauthorization; 1960—Motor Vehicle Exhaust Study; 1963—Clean Air Act Amendments; 1966—Clean Air Act Amendments of 1966; 1967—Air Quality Act of 1967; 1967—National Air Emission Standards Act; 1970—Clean Air Act Amendments of 1970; 1973—Reauthorization; 1974—Energy Supply and Environmental Coordination Act of 1974; 1977—Clean Air Act Amendments of 1977; 1980—Acid Precipitation Act of 1980; 1981—Steel Industry Compliance Extension Act of P.L. 97-23; 1987—Clean Air Act 8-month Extension; 1990—Clean Air Act Amendments of 1990.

2   42 USCA 7408

3   49 USCA 192, 193, 195

4   42 USCA 7409, 7601(a). 50.7. Changes particulate matter in revisions, 1998.

5   40 USCA 68

6   56 Fed. Reg. 42216 (1991)

7   42 USCA 7410

8   40 USCA 51.100(o). Reasonably available control technology (RACT) is only used for secondary NAAQS and can be used in State Implementation Plans as long as the secondary NAAQS are attained as quickly as possible. Primary and secondary NAAQS are required to be met by states as quickly as possible, and delays are only granted with "good cause" as defined by the EPA. See Administrative Procedures Act 553(b)(3)(B).

9   42 USCA 7502

10   Ayers, et al., *Environmental Science and Technology Handbook*. (Rockville, MD: Government Institutes, 1994). 135.

11   40 USCA 50, 53, 58. 2.5 micrometers (PM2.5), and 10 micrometers (PM10).

12 42 USCA 9602, 9603, 9604; 33 usca 1321, 1361. Unless the disturbances result in readings greater than 7.6 picocuries per gram or pCi/g of Uranium-238, 6.8 pCi/g of Thorium-232, or 8.4 pCi/g of Radium-226.

13 Senate Report No. 91-1196, 91st Congress, 2d. Sess. 15-16 (1970).

14 40 USCA 60

15 F. William Brownell. "Clean Air Act," in Thomas F.P. Sullivan, 1997. 82-83.

16 Defined as limits of 100 or 250 tons per year (tpy).

17 40 USCA 52.21

18 Brownell, 84

19 Ibid, 85

20 42 USCA 7503

21 Not feasible for economic or technical reasons.

22 59 Fed. Reg. 21370 (1996)

23 42 USCA 7412

24 61 Fed. Reg. 31668 (1996)

25 42 USCA 7651

26 The issue of regional haze is not addressed as a SIP requirement.

27 Brownell, 95

28 OMB 2060-0345. 1998

29 Fed. Reg. 7716 (1994)

30 57 Fed. Reg. 32250 (1992); 42 USCA 7661a

31 An *affected state* is defined as one whose air quality can be degraded, is contiguous to the state containing the source, or is a state within 50 miles of the source.

32 42 USCA 7661

33 If the change is made and the minor revision denied, then the source may be liable for violating its permit.

34 Clean Air Act, Preamble. Title V.

35 42 USCA 7661c

36 40 USCA 73, E

37 Brownell, 106

38 49 Appendix 1301

39 42 USCA 4904(b)

40 42 USCA 4907

41 42 USCA 4909

42 42 USCA 4913

43 49 USCA 47504

44 49 USCA 47504

45 49 USCA 47505

46 49 USCA 47509

Section Three: Water (Chapters 9 to 12)

1   In some instances, a federal agency other than EPA is given responsibilities for an environmental program. For those cases, there may be delegation of some of their duties to state and local agencies, or cooperation with the EPA may be mandatory.

2   Lynn M. Gallagher. "Clean Water Act," in Thomas F.P. Sullivan, Ed. *Environmental Law Handbook: Fourteenth Edition.* Rockville, MD: Government Institutes, Inc., 1997. 111.

3   33 USCA 1311

4   33 USCA 1342

5   33 USCA 1341, 1342

6   33 USCA 1311, 1316, 1317

7   33 USCA 1321

8   33 USCA 1344

9   33 USCA 1319, 1365

10   Pub.L. 92-500, 86 Stat. 816 (1972)

11   Water Quality Act, Pub.L. 100-4 (1987)

12   33 USCA 1311

13   40 USCA 122

14   The nonregulatory method of coordinating federal and state groundwater pollution control is the Comprehensive State Groundwater Protection Programs (CSGWPP). EPA had approved four of them by 1997: Alabama, Connecticut, New Hampshire, and Wisconsin.

15   See the manual developed jointly by the Fish and Wildlife Service, Soil Conservation Service, and U.S. Army Corps of Engineers. *Federal Manual for Identifying and Delineating Jurisdictional Wetlands.* 1987.

16   For a full discussion of the NPDES permit program, see the *NPDES Permit Handbook: Second Edition.* (Rockville, MD: Government Institutes, Inc., 1992).

17   33 USCA 1342(b)

18   40 USCA 123

19   There are 10 regional EPA offices in the United States.

20   40 USCA 123

21   40 USCA 121

22   33 USCA 1314(e)

23   On discharge monitoring reports—DMRs

24   33 USCA 1342(o)

25   33 USCA 1314

26   33 USCA 1316(a)(2)

27   33 USCA 1313(c)(2); 40 USCA 131

28   33 USCA 1314 (l)

29   Standard Industrial Classification (SIC) codes are given to each land use. They are a uniformly accepted land use classification system intended to be a complete list of all possible uses.

30   60 Fed. Reg. 50804, September 29, 1995.

31   33 USCA 1342

32   61 Fed. Reg. 41243, September 9, 1992.

33   33 USCA 1326

34   40 USCA 228

35   Annex V of the International Convention for the Prevention of Pollution from Ships (MARPOL V) and the Marine Plastic Pollution Research and Control Act of 1987. Sewage from vessels is regulated under the Marine Sanitation Device Program, 40 USCA 140.

36   33 USCA 1342

37   33 USCA 1329(b)

38   33 USCA 1451 to 1464

39   This kind of permit to allow the discharging of dredged or fill material is commonly called a 404 Permit. It is named and numbered after the Clean Water Act's section 404 (33 USCA 1344).

40   40 USCA 230

41   33 USCA 1344(g)(h)

42   33 USCA 2701 to 2761, the Oil Pollution Act of 1990 (OPA).

43   40 USCA 112(d)(2). Exempted from the SPCC plan are facilities where the underground storage capacity is 42,000 gallons or less of oil, and the above-ground storage capacity is 1,320 gallons or less of oil, with no single container having a capacity over 660 gallons.

44   The National Response Center has additional duties to respond to pollution events under CERCLA, the Superfund Act. This center maintains the priority lists for cleanup of the Superfund sites (CERCLIS).

45   Pub.L. 93-523, December 16, 1974

46   42 USCA 6925(u)-(v); 42 USCA 6928(h)

47   42 USCA 300g-1(b)(1)

48   Pub.L. 99-339; 100 Stat. 66(1986)

49   "...EPA announced that $12.1 billion was needed immediately for water systems to meet health-based standards, $10.2 billion, or 84% needed to protect water supplies from microbial contaminates. The 1996 Amendments authorize $9.6 billion through the year 2003. More daunting, though, is EPA's estimate that $138.4 billion will be needed over the next 20 years to replace or upgrade the drinking water infrastructure, including treatment, storage and delivery, of the nation's 55,000 community drinking water systems. Whether the system were large, medium, or small, EPA estimated necessary improve-ments would cost many billions of dollars." EPA. "Drinking Water Infrastruc-ture Needs Survey: First Report to Congress." Washington DC: EPA, January 1997.

50   Pub.L. 104-182; 110 Stat. 1613 (August 6, 1996)

51   42 USCA 300g-1(b)(5)

52   Gallagher, 202

53   42 USCA 300g-1(e)

54   PQLs are used for carcinogens because the MCLG is zero and the PQL can represent the lowest feasible level.

55   42 USCA 300g-1(b)(3)

56   There are no other environmental regulations that include assessments of costs and benefits.

57   42 USCA 300j-12

58   Enhanced Surface Water Treatment Rule, Disinfectant and Disinfection By-products Rule, and Ground Water Disinfection Rule.

59   42 USCA 300g-1

60   About 95 percent according to RCRA records.

61   Gallagher, 217

62   Ibid, 218

63   40 USCA 144

64   42 USCA 6924

65   The total grants cannot exceed $4,000,000. in one year.

66   42 USCA 300h-7

67   Rosario Strait, Puget Sound (Washington), and Prince William Sound (Alaska) are waters where single hull tankers over 5,000 gross tons must be escorted by at least two towing vessels.

68   33 USCA 1401

69   See Clean Water Act, NPDES Permit process in 33 USCA 1342.

70   www.epa.gov/OWOW/OCPD/oceans/update2.html. See the "Green Book," or *Evaluation of Dredge Material Proposed for Ocean Disposal—Testing Manual.* EPA-503/B-91/001. 1991.

71   www.homer.hsr.ornl.gov/oepa/law_sum/mprsa.html

72   33 USCA 1412

73   33 USCA 1412a

74   33 USCA 1417

75   33 USCA 1442

Section Four: Waste and Tanks (Chapters 13 to 16)

1   But does not include solid or dissolved material in domestic sewage, or solid or dissolved materials in irrigation return flows, or industrial discharges which are point sources subject to permits defined as atomic energy. 42 USCA 6903

2   Funds are made available under a "Superfund" to clean up those abandoned sites before prosecution.

3   42 USCA 6902

4   Even though it may be hazardous, some wastes are excluded from being called hazardous. They are mixtures of domestic sewage and other wastes passing through a sewer system to a publicly owned treatment works, industrial wastewater discharges that are point source discharges under the Clean Water Act, irrigation return flows, and special nuclear or by-product material regulated under the Atomic Energy Act.

5   Many of these definitions follow the wording of the SWDA definitions, but most do not for purposes of clarification.

6   42 USCA 9601 to 9675

7   42 USCA 9607

8   42 USCA 6908

9   See the chronology of this act at the end of Chapter 13. The Solid Waste Disposal Act (1965) had been amended, or changed, many times. Different combinations of sections were given different short titles, such as: Resource Conservation and Recovery Act (1976); Used Oil and Recycling Act (1980); Hazardous and Solid Waste Amendments (1984); Medical Waste Tracking Act (1988); Federal Facility Compliance Act (1992); and Land Disposal Program Flexibility Act (1996).

10   42 USCA 6915

11   42 USCA 6924

12   42 USCA 6925

13   42 USCA 6933

14   42 USCA 6942

15   42 USCA 6947

16   42 USCA 6951

17   42 USCA 6983

18   42 USCA 6991b

19   42 USCA 6992a

20   42 USCA 6992d

21   "Health, safety, and welfare" are the very foundations of legislative protection granted under the U.S. Constitution. Governments at all levels operate under the premise that they are performing these sets of public services.

22   Karen J. Nardi. "Underground Storage Tanks," in Sullivan, 1997. 360.

23   EPA Office of Underground Storage Tanks. "FAQ 4: What Has EPA's Office of Underground Storage Tanks (OUST) Accomplished?" www.epa.gov/swerust1/topfour.htm.

24   EPA Office of Underground Storage Tanks. "UST Program Facts: Implementing Federal Requirements of Underground Storage Tanks" (EPA 510-B-96-007, December 1996). Also, cited in Sullivan, 1997 as Environmental Information, Ltd. "Underground Storage Tank Cleanup: Status and Outlook (1995)."

25   RSPA, 173.8(b), 1998

26   EPA Office of Underground Storage Tanks. "State Authorization Status as of December 31, 1997." (www.epa.gov/epaoswer/hazwaste/state/index.htm.)

27   42 USCA 6991C

28   One of the objectives of EPA, is to include each set of state regulations into the U.S. *Code of Federal Regulations*. U.S. EPA, Region 6 offices; August 4, 1998.

29   EPA Office of Underground Storage Tanks. "SPA FAQ 3: List of states with Approved UST Programs." August 6, 1998. (www.epa.gov/swerust1/states/spalist.htm.) See also, EPA Office of Solid Waste Internet site, August 6, 1998. "State Authorization Status as of December 31, 1997." (www.epa.gov/epaoswer/hazwaste/state/index.htm.)

30   Subchapter IX—Regulation of Underground Storage Tanks. 42 USCA 6991

31   42 USCA 6991

32   Such as the Natural Gas Pipeline Safety Act of 1968, Hazardous Liquid Pipeline Safety Act of 1979, and any state laws for gas and liquid pipelines.

33   42 USCA 6991; 40 CFR 280.12

34   This term is determined on a case-by-case basis, and regulated substances in very small quantities in a tank may be excluded from RCRA requirements.

35   Such as tanks controlled by the Atomic Energy Act of 1954.

36   Such as those tank systems regulated by the Nuclear Regulatory Commission.

37   42 USCA 6991b

38   42 USCA 6991e(b)

39   42 USCA 6991(a)(2)(b)

40   40 CFR 280.2

41   40 CFR 280.20(a)(4)

42   40 CFR 280.20(c)(1)(ii)

43   40 CFR 2809.30

44   40 CFR 280.43

45   40 CFR 280.40(a)(3)

46   After December 1998, the tanks must be upgraded or permanently closed. 40 CFR 280.41

47   40 CFR 280.41

48   40 CFR 280.50

49   40 CFR 302

50   40 CFR 280.101

51   40 CFR 280.104-107

52   By passing this act, Congress authorized a waiver of sovereign immunity allowing civil fines and penalties to be assessed on the federal government.

53   These inspections are called Compliance Evaluation Inspections or CEIs.

Section Five: Safety (Chapters 17 to 21)

1   Pub.L. 91-596; 84 Stat. 1590

2   29 USCA 654(a)(1)

3   29 USCA 655(b)

4   29 USCA 655(c)(1)

5   29 USCA 654(a)(1)

6   29 CFR 1910.20

7   29 CFR 1977.12

8   29 USCA 660

9   Executive Order 12196, 26 February 1980

10   29 CFR 1910.1200

11   51 Fed. Reg. 34590

12   15 USCA 2601 to 2692

13   15 USCA 2604

14   15 USCA 2609

15   15 USCA 2607

16   40 CFR 710.26

17   15 USCA 2604

18   Marshall Lee Miller. "Pesticides," in Sullivan. *Environmental Law Handbook. Fourteenth Edition.* (Rockville, MD: Government Institutes, 1997). 249.

19   15 USCA 2603

20   *Significant adverse reaction* is one that substantially impairs normal human activities or causes lasting or permanent damage to the environment or health.

21   15 USCA 2603

22   15 USCA 2610, 2615

23   15 USCA 2615, 2616

24   7 USCA 136 to 136y

25   7 USCA 136a

26   An application must include standard chemical descriptions, specific mention of pests and hosts, and extensive testing data. If not provided, EPA can demand additional testing.

27   7 USCA 136a(e)

28   7 USCA 136r-1

29   7 USCA 136a; 7 CFR 159.152; 152.50

30   Marshall Lee Miller. "Pesticides," in Sullivan. *Environmental Law Handbook. Fourteenth Edition.* (Rockville, MD: Government Institutes, Inc., 1997). 315.

31   See EPCRA mentioned earlier in this chapter.

32   21 USCA 342

33   16 USCA 1500

34   30 USCA 1201, 1202, 1211

35   30 USCA 1202

36   30 USCA 1221. Mining and Mineral Resources Research Institute Act of 1984 (MMRRIA).

37   30 USCA 1231. Surface Mining Control and Reclamation Act of 1977 (SMCRA).

38   30 USCA 1233

39   30 USCA 1236

40   30 USCA 1236

41   30 USCA 1268

42   30 USCA 1272

43   42 USCA 2014, 2021 to 2021d, 2022, 2111, 2113, 2114

44   42 USCA 2021

45   42 USCA 2021a

46 Low-level Radioactive Waste Policy Act (LLRWPA). 42 USCA 2021 states that low-level radioactive waste is a "radioactive material that is not a high-level radioactive waste, spent nuclear fuel, or by-product material."

47 42 USCA 2021d

48 42 USCA 2022

Section Six: Responding to Contaminant Releases
(Chapters 22 to 24)

1 42 USCA 11001 to 11050. Spill emergency response commissions, planning districts, and planning committees must be established in every state.

2 EPCRA was enacted as a federal reaction to a disastrous international chemical spill that injured thousands. This act intends to protect surrounding communities and reduce the potential for harm from accidental chemical spills.

3 42 USCA 11002. A reportable quantity is defined and revised at the EPA's discretion.

4 42 USCA 11004

5 42 USCA 11023

6 42 USCA 11043

7 42 USCA 9601 to 9675. The first version of CERCLA was enacted in 1980. Superfund Amendments and Reauthorization Act (SARA) amendments contained further provisions. In 1992, provisions of 42 USCA 9620 were cited as the Community Environmental Response Facilitation Act. By 1996, provisions and amendments were cited as the Asset Conservation, Lender Liability, and Deposit Insurance Protection Act of 1996.

8 42 USCA 9607

9 42 USCA 9608

10 42 USCA 9617

11 CERCLIS is used as an inventory of all CERCLA sites and is used to track cleanup progress.

12 40 CFR 300. This list identifies uncontrolled hazardous waste sites and is maintained under the National Oil and Hazardous Substances Pollution Contingency Plan (NCP). The NPL guides the EPA to determine which sites warrant further investigation for public health or environmental risks. The site is evaluated for the assignment of CERCLA moneys for cleanup. In 1998, six new sites were added to the General Superfund Section (one each in Florida and Indiana, two in New Jersey and two in New York).

13 Executive Order 12580 (52 Fed. Reg. 2923, 1987)

14 40 CFR 300. National Contingency Plan means the National Oil and Hazardous Substances Pollution Contingency Plan (40 CFR part 300). The National Response Center means the national communications center located in Washington, DC, that receives and relays notice of oil discharge or releases of hazardous substances to the appropriate Federal officials.

15 62 Fed. Reg. 504422; 40 CFR 300.425

16 By 1998, there were 1,197 sites (1,046 in the General Superfund section and 151 in the Federal Facilities Section). There are 54 sites proposed and awaiting final action (46 in General Superfund and 8 in the Federal Facilities Section). 162 sites had been removed from the NPL in 1998. It contained 1,251 Final and Proposed sites.

17 By March 1998, there were 508 sites listed on the CCL.

18 40 CFR 300.400(g)

19 40 CFR 302.4. See Table 302.4 for "List of Hazardous Substances and Reportable Quantities."

20 It should be noted that petroleum additives, such as gasoline additives, are covered under CERCLA.

21 42 USCA 9601

22 42 USCA 9601

23 Recent amendments in 1996 made some changes, such as creating the "Asset Conservation, Lender Liability, and Deposit Insurance Protection Act." This act is composed of certain sections of CERCLA. The 1992 amendments (which changed provisions under 42 USCA 9620) allow the act to be cited as the "Community Environmental Response Facilitation Act."

24 42 USCA 9602; 42 USCA 9601(14)

25 42 USCA 9602

26 Similar to requirements stated in the Federal Water Pollution Control Act, 33 USCA 1251 et seq.

27 Note that registered pesticides under FIFRA and the handling and storage of such a pesticide product by an agricultural producer are not controlled by CERCLA.

28 42 USCA 9604

29 The ATSDR reports directly to the Surgeon General of the United States. This agency coordinates and cooperates with EPA and all other related agencies and departments of the federal government with regard to public health.

30 Three categories, or levels of intensity, are used: acute, subacute, and chronic health effects.

31 42 USCA 9605

32 Sullivan, 474.

33 42 USCA 9622(g)

34 15 USCA 2601 to 2692; Subchapter II: Asbestos Hazard Emergency Response, 15 USCA 2641 to 2656, was enacted in 1986.

35 15 USCA 2641(a)(b). *Asbestos* means asbestiform varieties of chrysotile (serpentine), crocidolite (riebeckite), amosite (cummingtonite-grunerite), anthophyllite, tremolie, or actinolite. An *asbestos-containing material* is one that contains more than one percent asbestos by weight.

36 15 USCA 2642(6)

Section Seven: **Nature and Natural Resources**
(Chapters 25 to 35)

1   16 USCA 1361, 1362, 1371 to 1389, 1401 to 1407, 1411 to 1418, 1421 to 1421h. The Marine Mammal Protection Act protects marine animals, creates a marine mammal commission, prohibits certain tuna harvesting, and responds to marine mammal health and stranding.

2   16 USCA 1401

3   16 USCA 1373

4   16 USCA 1411

5   16 USCA 1372

6   16 USCA 1371

7   16 USCA 1374

8   16 USCA 1386(d)

9   16 USCA 1451 to 1465

10   16 USCA 1451

11   16 USCA 1452

12   16 USCA 1452

13   16 USCA 1455(e)

14   16 USCA 1455(b)

15   16 USCA 1456(c)

16   16 USCA 1461

17   Convention on International Trade in Endangered Species of Wild Fauna and Flora, March 3, 1973.

18   16 USCA 1531 to 1534; 16 USCA 1533.

19   16 USCA 1536(h)

20   16 USCA 1536(e)

21   16 USCA 1600 to 1614

22   16 USCA 1604

23   16 USCA 1641

24   16 USCA 1612

25   16 USCA 1601(d)

26   16 USCA 1604

27   16 USCA 1681

28   16 USCA 1672

29   16 USCA 2001 to 2009; 16 USCA 2005

30   16 USCA 2005

31   16 USCA 2461 to 2466; 16 USCA 2463

32   16 USCA 2465

33   16 USCA 3951 to 3956

34   16 USCA 3951

35   16 USCA 3956

36 16 USCA 4701 to 4751

37 16 USCA 4701

38 16 USCA 4741(f)

39 16 USCA 4712

40 43 USCA 1701 to 1785

41 43 USCA 1712 and 1731

42 The Bureau of Land Management performs a review and assignation of *wilderness areas*—defined as those roadless areas of 5,000 acres or more of public lands or roadless islands.

43 43 USCA 1732

44 43 USCA 1752 to 1761

45 43 USCA 1801 to 1866

46 43 USCA 1801

47 43 USCA 1843(b)

48 43 USCA 1845

49 43 USCA 1842

50 43 USCA 1843(b)

51 43 USCA 1862(b)

52 16 USCA 1131 to 1136

53 16 USCA 1132(2)(c)

54 16 USCA 1132(3)(c)

55 16 USCA 1135

ACM	Asbestos Containing Materials (more than 1.0% asbestos)
ACFM	Actual Cubic Feet Per Minute
AEIU	Annual Emissions Inventory Update
AFR	Air Fuel Ratio
ACGIH	American Conference of Governmental Industrial Hygienists
AHCA	Agricultural Hazard Communication Act
AHERA	Asbestos Hazard Emergency Response Act of 1986, Public Law 99-519.
AMOC	Alternate Means of Control Plan
ANSI	American National Standards Institute
API	American Petroleum Institute
ARARs	Applicable or Relevant and Appropriate Requirements (ARARs)
Area Contingency Plan	Required by the Federal Water Pollution Control Act (33 U.S. Code Annotated, 1321(j)(4)).
ASME	American Society of Mechanical Engineers
AST(s)	Aboveground Storage Tanks
ASTM	American Society for Testing and Materials
BACT	Best Available Control Technology
CAIR	Comprehensive Assessment Information Rule
CAMS	Continuous Air Monitoring Stations
CBI	Confidential Business Information
CEMS	Continuous Emission Monitoring Systems
CC	Cubic Centimeters
CFR	*Code of Federal Regulations*
CMP	Coastal Management Program
CNG	Compressed Natural Gas

CO	Carbon Monoxide
COG(s)	Regional Councils of Governments
CORPS	U.S. Army Corps of Engineers
CPF	Coastal Protection Fund (established by OSPRA, 40.151)
CSI	Common Sense Initiative
CWA	Clean Water Act
DOC	U.S. Department of Commerce
DOE	U.S. Department of Energy
DOI	U.S. Department of the Interior
DOT	U.S. Department of Transportation
DRE	Destruction and Removal Efficiency
EIA	Environmental Impact Assessment
EIA	Equine Infectious Anemia
EIS	Environmental Impact Statement
ELP	Environmental Leadership Program
EPA	U.S. Environmental Protection Agency
EPN	Emission Point Number
EOR	Enhanced Oil Recovery
EPRCA	Emergency Planning and Community Right to Know Act (1986)
ERC	Emission Reduction Credits (air emissions)
ETJ	Extraterritorial Jurisdiction
FCAA	Federal Clean Air Act
Federal Fund	Oil Spill Liability Trust Fund of the Internal Revenue Code of 1986, 26 U.S. Code 9509
FIFRA	Federal Insecticide, Fungicide, and Rodenticide Act
FGR	Forced Gas Recirculation
FQPA	Food Quality Protection Act
FRP2	(DOT FRP2 Standard)
G/DSCM	Gram Per Dry Standard Cubic Meter
HCL	Hydrogen Chloride
H.R.	U.S. House of Representatives Bill Number Prefix Lettering
HRS	Hazard Ranking System

HSWA	Hazardous and Solid Waste Act
HUD	U.S. Department of Housing and Urban Development
ICC	U.S. Interstate Commerce Commission
IEI	Initial Emissions Inventory
LAER	Lowest Achievable Emissions Rate
LEPC	Local Emergency Planning Committee
LP	Liquid Petroleum
LPG	Liquid Petroleum Gas
MACT	Maximum Achievable Control Technology
MCAN	Microbial Commercial Activity Notice
MCL	Maximum Contaminant Level
MCLG	Maximum Contaminant Level Goal
MMBTU	British Thermal Unit
MOA	Memorandum of Agreement between agencies
MOU	Memorandum of Understanding between agencies
MSA	Metropolitan Statistical Area
MSDS	Material Safety Data Sheets
MSWLF	Municipal Solid Waste Landfill
MTBE	Methyl Tert-Butyl Ether
NAAQS	National Ambient Air Quality Standards
NCP	National Contingency Plan, the federal regulations for response to releases of hazardous substances, published as 40 CFR 300.
NEPPS	National Environmental Performance Partnership System
NESHAP	Federal National Emission Standards for Hazardous Air Pollutants.
NMOC	Nonmethane Organic Compounds
NORM	Naturally occurring radioactive material
NOx	Nitrogen Oxide
NSFn	National Sanitation Foundation
NSF	National Science Foundation
NSPS	New Source Performance Standards
OPA	Oil Pollution Act of 1990, 33 U.S. Code Annotated 2701 et seq.

OSPRA	Oil Spill Prevention and Response Act of 1991, Texas Natural Resources Code, Chapter 40
OSSF	Onsite Sewage Facilities
PAIR	Preliminary Assessment Information Rule
Pb	Lead
PCB(s)	Polychlorinated biphenyls
PEG	Polyethylene glycol
PEL	Permissible Exposure Limit (OSHA, 29 CFR 1926.58)
PEL	Priority Enforcement List
PEMS	Predictive Emissions Monitoring Systems
PM10	Particulate matter of less than 10 microns in diameter
PMN	Premanufacture Notice
POHC	Principal Organic Hazardous Constituent
PPM	Parts Per Million
PPMV	Parts Per Million by Volume
PPB	Parts Per Billion
PPA	Pollution Prevention Act
PRP	Potentially Responsible Party
PSD	Prevention of Significant Deterioration
RACM	Regulated Asbestos Containment Material
RACT	Reasonably Available Control Technology
RC	Reduction Credit (for air emissions)
RCRA	Resource Conservation and Recovery Act
Remediate	to clean contaminant spills so that no danger remains
Restoration Plan	Plan selected after public review and comment describing the required restoration, replacement, rehabilitation, or acquisition of equivalent natural resources
RI/FS	Remedial Investigation/Feasibility Study
ROD	Record of Decision
SARA	Superfund Amendments and Reauthorization Act
SERC	State Emergency Response Commission
S.B.	U.S. Senate Bill Number Prefix Lettering

SIC	Standard Industrial Classification Land Use System
SIP	State Implementation Plan
SLER	Soil and Liner Evaluation Report
SLQCP	Soil and Liner Quality Control Plan
SNUR	Significant New Use (chemical substance)
SOC	Synthetic Organic Chemicals
SO$_2$	Sulfur Dioxide
SOSC	State On Scene Coordinator
State Coastal Discharge Contingency Plan	Plan required by OSPRA, 40.053
Superfund	Federal Abandoned Hazardous Waste Site Program administered by EPA
SWCD	Soil and Water Conservation District
THM	Trihalomethane, one of the family of organic compounds derived from methane
TLV	Threshold Limit Values for airborne concentrations of substances
TPDES	Texas Pollution Discharge Elimination System
TTHM	Sum of the concentration in milligrams per liter of the trihalomethane compounds
TPH	Total Petroleum Hydrocarbon
TPY	Tons Per Year
TRI	Toxic Release Inventory
UIC	Underground Injection Control
USC	United States Code
USGS	United States Geological Service
UST(s)	Underground Storage Tanks
VOC	Volatile Organic Compounds
WCL	Workplace Chemical List
WQP	Water quality parameters
WTRF	Waste Tire Recycling Fund
XL	Excellence in Leadership Program

P

Government Institutes Mini-Catalog

PC #	ENVIRONMENTAL TITLES	Pub Date	Price
627	ABCs of Environmental Science	1998	$39
585	Book of Lists for Regulated Hazardous Substances, 8th Edition	1997	$79
579	Brownfields Redevelopment	1998	$79
4088	CFR Chemical Lists on CD ROM, 1997 Edition	1997	$125
4089	Chemical Data for Workplace Sampling & Analysis, Single User Disk	1997	$125
512	Clean Water Handbook, 2nd Edition	1996	$89
581	EH&S Auditing Made Easy	1997	$79
587	E H & S CFR Training Requirements, 3rd Edition	1997	$89
4082	EMMI-Envl Monitoring Methods Index for Windows-Network	1997	$537
4082	EMMI-Envl Monitoring Methods Index for Windows-Single User	1997	$179
525	Environmental Audits, 7th Edition	1996	$79
548	Environmental Engineering and Science: An Introduction	1997	$79
643	Environmental Guide to the Internet, 4rd Edition	1998	$59
560	Environmental Law Handbook, 14th Edition	1997	$79
353	Environmental Regulatory Glossary, 6th Edition	1993	$79
625	Environmental Statutes, 1998 Edition	1998	$69
4098	Environmental Statutes Book/CD-ROM, 1998 Edition	1997	$208
4994	Environmental Statutes on Disk for Windows-Network	1997	$405
4994	Environmental Statutes on Disk for Windows-Single User	1997	$139
570	Environmentalism at the Crossroads	1995	$39
536	ESAs Made Easy	1996	$59
515	Industrial Environmental Management: A Practical Approach	1996	$79
510	ISO 14000: Understanding Environmental Standards	1996	$69
551	ISO 14001: An Executive Repoert	1996	$55
588	International Environmental Auditing	1998	$149
518	Lead Regulation Handbook	1996	$79
478	Principles of EH&S Management	1995	$69
554	Property Rights: Understanding Government Takings	1997	$79
582	Recycling & Waste Mgmt Guide to the Internet	1997	$49
603	Superfund Manual, 6th Edition	1997	$115
566	TSCA Handbook, 3rd Edition	1997	$95
534	Wetland Mitigation: Mitigation Banking and Other Strategies	1997	$75

PC #	SAFETY and HEALTH TITLES	Pub Date	Price
547	Construction Safety Handbook	1996	$79
553	Cumulative Trauma Disorders	1997	$59
559	Forklift Safety	1997	$65
539	Fundamentals of Occupational Safety & Health	1996	$49
612	HAZWOPER Incident Command	1998	$59
535	Making Sense of OSHA Compliance	1997	$59
589	Managing Fatigue in Transportation, *ATA Conference*	1997	$75
558	PPE Made Easy	1998	$79
598	Project Mgmt for E H & S Professionals	1997	$59
552	Safety & Health in Agriculture, Forestry and Fisheries	1997	$125
613	Safety & Health on the Internet, 2nd Edition	1998	$49
597	Safety Is A People Business	1997	$49
463	Safety Made Easy	1995	$49
590	Your Company Safety and Health Manual	1997	$79

Government Institutes

4 Research Place, Suite 200 • Rockville, MD 20850-3226
Tel. (301) 921-2323 • FAX (301) 921-0264
Email: giinfo@govinst.com • Internet: http://www.govinst.com

Please call our customer service department at (301) 921-2323 for a free publications catalog.

CFRs now available online.
Call (301) 921-2355 for info.

GOVERNMENT INSTITUTES ORDER FORM

4 Research Place, Suite 200 • Rockville, MD 20850-3226
Tel (301) 921-2323 • Fax (301) 921-0264
Internet: http://www.govinst.com • E-mail: giinfo@govinst.com

3 EASY WAYS TO ORDER

1. Phone: **(301) 921-2323**
Have your credit card ready when you call.

2. Fax: **(301) 921-0264**
Fax this completed order form with your company purchase order or credit card information.

3. Mail: **Government Institutes**
4 Research Place, Suite 200
Rockville, MD 20850-3226 USA
Mail this completed order form with a check, company purchase order, or credit card information.

PAYMENT OPTIONS

❏ **Check** (*payable to Government Institutes in US dollars*)

❏ **Purchase Order** (*This order form must be attached to your company P.O. Note: All International orders must be prepaid.*)

❏ **Credit Card** ❏ *VISA* ❏ MasterCard ❏ AMERICAN EXPRESS

Exp.____/____

Credit Card No. _____

Signature _____

(Government Institutes' Federal I.D.# is 52-0994196)

CUSTOMER INFORMATION

Ship To: (Please attach your purchase order)

Name: _____

GI Account # (*7 digits on mailing label*): _____

Company/Institution: _____

Address: _____
(Please supply street address for UPS shipping)
_____

City: _____ State/Province: _____

Zip/Postal Code: _____ Country: _____

Tel: (____) _____

Fax: (____) _____

Email Address: _____

Bill To: (if different from ship-to address)

Name: _____

Title/Position: _____

Company/Institution: _____

Address: _____
(Please supply street address for UPS shipping)
_____

City: _____ State/Province: _____

Zip/Postal Code: _____ Country: _____

Tel: (____) _____

Fax: (____) _____

Email Address: _____

Qty.	Product Code	Title	Price

Subtotal_____
MD Residents add 5% Sales Tax_____
Shipping and Handling (see box below)_____
Total Payment Enclosed_____

❏ **New Edition No Obligation Standing Order Program**

Please enroll me in this program for the products I have ordered. Government Institutes will notify me of new editions by sending me an invoice. I understand that there is no obligation to purchase the product. This invoice is simply my reminder that a new edition has been released.

15 DAY MONEY-BACK GUARANTEE

If you're not completely satisfied with any product, return it undamaged within 15 days for a full and immediate refund on the price of the product.

Within U.S:	Outside U.S:
1-4 products: $6/product	Add $15 for each item (Airmail)
5 or more: $3/product	Add $10 for each item (Surface)

SOURCE CODE: BP01